D0012276

CHRIST IN OUR HOME

CHRIST IN OUR HOME

Devotions for
Every Day of the Year

INTRODUCTION BY RONALD KLUG

Augsburg Fortress
Minneapolis

CHRIST IN OUR HOME
Devotions for Every Day of the Year

Copyright © 2003 Augsburg Fortress. All rights reserved. Except for brief quotations in critical articles or reviews, no part of this book may be reproduced in any manner without prior written permission from the publisher. Write to: Permissions, Augsburg Fortress, Box 1209, Minneapolis, MN 55440.

Scripture quotations marked NRSV are from New Revised Standard Bible, copyright © 1989 Division of Christian Education of the National Council of the Churches of Christ in the United States of America. Used by permission.

Scripture quotations marked NIV are from The Holy Bible, New International Version. Copyright © 1973, 1978, 1984 by International Bible Society. Used by permission of Zondervan Publishing House. All rights reserved.

Editors: Mark Hinton, Scott Tunseth, James Satter
Cover image: PhotoDisc, copyright © 2003
Cover design: Marti Naughton
Interior text design: James Satter

ISBN 0-8066-4576-8

The paper used in this publication meets the minimum requirements of American National Standard for Information Sciences—Permanence of Paper for Printed Library Materials, ANSI Z329.48-1984.

Manufactured in the U.S.A.

07   06   05   04   03   1   2   3   4   5   6   7   8   9   10

Contents

Introduction

> If you continue in my word, you are truly my
> disciples," Jesus said, adding a promise: "and you
> will know the truth, and the truth will make you free.
> ❖ John 8:31-32 (NRSV)

These words of Jesus express the longings of our hearts—to
be true followers of our Lord, to know the truth about God
and ourselves and life, to be liberated from all that binds us.
Continuing in the word has always been a mark of Christian
discipleship. When we identify signs of spiritual renewal in
individuals, in the church, or in a society, that new life is often
associated with fresh attention to the word of God in the
Bible. Philip Jacob Spener, renewer of the church in
Germany, wrote: "The word of God remains the seed from
which all that is good in us must grow. If we succeed in
getting the people to seek eagerly and diligently in the book
of life for their joy, their spiritual life will be wonderfully
strengthened and they will become altogether different
people." (*Pia Desideria*, translated by Theodore G. Tappert.
Philadelphia: Fortress Press, 1964, p. 91).

To continue in the word means to live in the word, as a
fish lives in water. We have many ways of doing this: through
the worship of our congregation, in a Bible study group, in
conversation with other Christians, or by reading the Bible
and other Christian literature. We read and meditate on the
word not primarily to gain more religious *information*, but for
our *formation*, so that we will become "different people,"
more like the Jesus we follow. "Do not be conformed to this
world," wrote the apostle Paul, "but be transformed by the
renewing of your minds" (Romans 12:2, NRSV). As we read
and reflect on the word and put it into practice in our daily
lives, the Holy Spirit renews our minds and spirits.

For more than 50 years many Christians have continued in the word though daily reading of two devotional volumes, *Light for Today* and *Christ in Our Home*, which became one publication in 1990. Hundreds of writers—pastors, professors, lay people, men and women from all walks of life—have shared their thoughts and insights, creating a holy conversation among believers. When I read the devotional writings of others, I appreciate fresh insights into familiar texts and learn how faithful sisters and brothers have applied this word in their daily lives. Sometimes I'm helped by being reminded of truths I've known but which have slipped from my consciousness.

The title of this devotional anthology is significant: *Christ in Our Home*. The risen Christ longs to be a presence in our homes and workplaces and communities. This happens as we speak to one another about the things of God and follow the way of life we have learned from Jesus. When God speaks to us through the word and we respond in prayer, a relationship is nourished. The power to strengthen our relationship with God and to be transformed is in the word itself, but there are some things you can do to open yourself to receive the word into your life.

❖ Read receptively, expecting to hear a word from God. Begin with the attitude of the boy Samuel, who told God that he was ready to listen (1 Samuel 3:16).

❖ No matter what time of year you begin using this book, start with the reading for Day 1. At the back of the book are special readings for Easter, Pentecost, and Christmas.

❖ Don't read to criticize or argue with the devotional writer. If there's something you disagree with or that doesn't seem to apply to you, just let it go for the time being. Concentrate on a thought that does speak to you.

❖ If you live with a family member or friend, read the devotion aloud together and share what means the most to each of you.

❖ Try to carry one thought or image or phrase into the day ahead. It may help to copy out a thought or prayer and put it on your refrigerator, desk, or work space.

❖ Look for an opportunity to share this word with someone in a conversation, a letter, or an e-mail message—not to straighten someone out but rather to offer good news.

❖ Take a few moments to jot down the thoughts that especially speak to you through the reading. This helps focus your attention and aids in internalizing the word.

❖ If the word prompts you to take some action, do it. Jesus warned against those whose religion is only a matter of words and empty promises, telling us to "hear the word of God and obey it" (Luke 11:28).

My prayer for you, as you continue in the Word of God, is that you will experience the blessings of Jesus' promise: "You will know the truth, and the truth will make you free."

RONALD KLUG
AMERY, WISCONSIN

Day 1 ❖ Matthew 11:25-30

Strange Rest

Come to me, all you who are weary and burdened,
and I will give you rest. ❖ Matthew 11:28 (NIV)

Do you think Paul thought it restful to be a tireless wanderer
for Christ? Did any of the other apostles, for that matter?
Peter could have kept on fishing, and Matthew could have
been secure in his tax office, if they had not come to Christ.
But they all had found rest for their souls and joys that could
not be taken away.

There are things that come to rest when Christ takes over.
Old guilts that festered no longer hurt. Fears that exhausted
one's strength lose their power. Inner storms find calm. Life
on the outside may be ever so turbulent, but there is a new
peace within.

Two artists were asked to draw their concept of peace.
One threw on his canvas a mountain lake, sheltered on all
sides by boulders, the surface of its waters like a mirror. The
other drew a thundering waterfall, at its base a birch tree,
and in its branches a nest with a mother bird sweetly singing
to her young. This is called peace.

ALVIN ROGNESS

In the storms of life, O Lord, give us a place to sing.
Amen

Prayer concern: Struggling congregations

Daily Reflections_____

Shadows in the Valley

Even though I walk through the valley of the shadow of death, I will fear no evil, for you are with me; your rod and your staff, they comfort me.
❖ Psalm 23:4 (NIV)

It's natural for Christians to fear death. No matter how strongly we believe in heaven, no matter how much we look forward to being there, the only way to get there is through the passage of death.

In this way, death is like birth. No matter how much a mother wants her baby, no matter how much more freedom and room to grow the child will have after birth, the birth itself can be painful and frightening for them both.

The psalmist likens death to walking through a valley of dark shadows. We'll all have to pass through that valley in our final hours.

We won't have to walk through it alone, however. We will have an experienced guide. Christ has already been through the valley himself.

INEZ SCHWARTZKOPF

Good Shepherd, be with us now and when we have to walk through the valley to be with you eternally. Amen

Prayer concern: Those in hospices

Daily Reflections_____

_____

_____

_____

Gift of Wages?

But to one who without works trusts him who justifies the ungodly, such faith is reckoned as righteousness. ❖ Romans 4:5 (NRSV)

One morning a son placed a note on the kitchen counter. It read: "Mom owes Billy 25 cents for taking out the garbage, 10 cents for cleaning off the table, and 50 cents for being good."

At lunch the mother placed a note on her son's plate that read: "Billy owes Mother nothing for making his meals, nothing for washing his clothes, nothing for nursing him when he was sick, and nothing for being good." The tearful boy threw his arms around his mother and cried, "Keep the money, Mom. I'll do things for you because I love you."

Billy learned a lesson in grace, a lesson God is continually teaching us. We do not earn righteousness by living a good life. But when we believe in God and in the saving work of Jesus, God counts us among the righteous. Our righteousness is a gift of God's grace, given to us through faith. As for living the good life: "God, I'll do that for you because you love me and I love you."

RICHARD SIEMERS

God, we give up trying to earn your love and make ourselves righteous. We will trust in you and live your grace. Amen

Prayer concern: Thanks for answered prayers

Daily Reflections_____

_____

_____
_____

The Living Space

> The LORD declares to you that the LORD himself will establish a house for you. Your house and your kingdom will endure forever before me.
> ❖ 2 Samuel 7:11b, 16 (NIV)

To be a home owner in our society signifies that one has stepped up the economic and social ladder. One achieves a kind of primitive success when he has been able to mark out and "own" the space where he lives.

We expect God to share our values. And so it comes as a surprise in 2 Samuel that God not only rejects David's desire to build him a "house" but that he has an entirely different approach to his own "dwelling place." The Lord is at home with his people.

How appropriate that Emmanuel, God with us, lived out this theme in his life on earth. Born in a stable, Jesus once said "Foxes have holes, and birds of the air have nests; but the Son of man has nowhere to lay his head" (Matthew 8:20). This traveling teacher had supper with his friends in a borrowed upper room and was buried in another man's grave.

In this Old Testament word and in the life of Jesus, is the sure promise of a heavenly home for the people of God.

WALTER HUFFMAN

Creator of the universe, we praise you for choosing to be "at home" with your people. Amen

Prayer concern: People who are homeless

Daily Reflections_____

_____

_____

_____

Which One?

*In the same way, I tell you, there is rejoicing in
the presence of the angels of God over one sinner
who repents.* ❖ Luke 15:10 (NIV)

When Dwight D. Eisenhower was elected President of the
United States, reporters interviewed his Bible-memorizing
mother in her home in Abilene, Kansas. One reporter said,
"I'm sure you must be very proud of your son, isn't that
right?" Mother Eisenhower replied, "Which one?" She had
several boys. The world was paying tribute to her son who
was not only the famous World War II general, but who was
now being feted as America's President. Yet all her sons were
equally in her mother's love, dreams, hopes, and daily
prayers. If one were hospitalized, she was equally concerned.
If one rejoiced, she rejoiced with him. They all had her love.

God is equally concerned with each one of us. When we
are prodigal, God wants us home. When we sin, God stands
ready to forgive the repentant. God is not more forgiving to
the highly aggressive individual than to the modest and shy.
God isn't more present to someone with the high I.Q. than to
the humble seeker after his truth. God loves each one as
though he or she were the only person on earth. The cross
reminds us "it was for you."

NORMAN G. ANDERSON

*Help us, O Christ, to repent of our own sins first so we
may then pray as intercessors for others. Amen*

Prayer concern: National leaders

Daily Reflections

Praying Always

And pray in the Spirit on all occasions with all kinds
of prayers and requests. ❖ Ephesians 6:18 (NIV)

Dr. Frank Laubach gives many ideas for experiments in
prayer:

- ❖ Pray for whoever comes to memory.
- ❖ Pray when you can't sleep at night.
- ❖ Pray while taking a walk.
- ❖ Pray, using a prayer list of missionaries, pastors, of the
  sick and sorrowing, neighbors, and coworkers.
- ❖ Pray while reading a newspaper—pause and pray for
  accident victims, for world leaders.
- ❖ Pray for the Lord to give you open doors to witness.

Paul, recognizing the kind of world in which he lived, with
Satan's powers so intense, tells his friends to pray at all times
in the Spirit. And Paul also reminds the Ephesians to pray for
all Christians, "and also for me." Why not follow Paul's
example and ask many of our friends and fellow church
members to pray for us. And then, let us "give ourselves
wholly to prayer . . . and pray on every occasion in the power
of the Spirit."

CONRAD M. THOMPSON

*O Holy Spirit, give us boldness never to be afraid to
speak of Jesus Christ. Amen*

Prayer concern: Boldness in Christ

Daily Reflections_____
_____
_____
_____

One Fixed Trust

The LORD is good to all, and his compassion is
over all that he has made. ❖ Psalm 145:9 (NRSV)

More than a century ago, in the poem "The Eternal
Goodness," New England poet John Greenleaf Whittier wrote:
"To one fixed trust my spirit clings; I know that God is good!"

To have a personal faith that holds firm in the conviction
that God is good is not easy when millions of people lack food,
other millions seek haven as refugees, and individual lives are
disrupted through accident, illness, or unemployment.

Such faith requires not only knowledge of God's
compassion for people of old who cried, "How long?" It also
trust in God's wisdom.

What the psalmist states in praise of God is a matter of
faith even when it does not seem to come out by one's
present experience. That faith rests securely only when it
depends on what God continues to do for us through Jesus
Christ.

My own experience at the death of loved ones and in the
tumult of a society that seems out of control has taught me
that there is strength and comfort in the faith that God is
good.

OMAR STUENKEL

Lord, be merciful to us and help us. Amen

Prayer concern: Those who are hungry

Daily Reflections_____
_____
_____
_____

A Warning and a Promise

I put to death and I bring to life.
❖ Deuteronomy 32:39 (NIV)

Parents and teachers know that one of the most effective ways to instruct young children is by song. Many activities in the kindergarten routine are carried out with the aid of a simple rhyme or song. Music makes the process much more fun and makes lessons easier to remember.

Moses made use of this same method of instruction. Today's text is part of a song; in reality it was Moses' swan song. He was going to die and leave the Hebrews forever. They would enter the promised land without him.

To us the words "I put to death and I bring to life" sound brutal. But they fit the occasion. In them Moses expresses the totality of God's power. Conquering the land of Canaan would be no easy task. The children of Israel could never do it by their own strength. But God would be there—as he is today—to add strength to his people when the going got rough.

ARLET OSNES VOLLERS

We are your children, Lord. Help us to learn the lessons we need. Amen

Prayer concern: Someone facing a decision

Daily Reflections_____

_____

_____

_____

The Faithful One

But the Lord is faithful. ❖ 2 Thessalonians 3:3 (NIV)

It was an old vaudeville routine. A small boy stood at the top of a ladder. Underneath was a man pretending to be the boy's father. "Jump," he said. "Jump, my son. Papa will catch you." After some coaxing, the boy jumped. The "father" moved away and said, "Let that be a lesson to you. Never trust anybody."

This cynical little act expresses popular feeling today. We read about friends betraying one another, about husbands and wives cheating on their marriage vows, about children turning against their parents. "Never trust anybody," we are tempted to say.

But there is one who can always be trusted. "The Lord is faithful," Paul says. And Paul has the whole history of Israel to back him up. God made promises to Israel and kept them. He promised to send a Savior and he sent him. Paul trusts God and so can we. God may take his time. He may do things his way, not ours. But he is faithful. We can trust him.

W. A. POOVEY

Lord, may I never doubt your goodness or your love. Amen

Prayer concern: Loved ones

Daily Reflections

What Are Human Beings?

> . . . what are human beings that you are
> mindful of them, mortals that you care for
> them? Yet you have made them a little lower
> than God, and crowned them with glory and
> honor. ❖ Psalm 8:4-5 (NRSV)

Our age is not the first to ask the question: What is human? How can this strange group called humanity, and these strange individuals we call ourselves be understood?

Many answers are available. Some people suggest that humans are simply animals—talented to be sure, but animals nonetheless. Others, overwhelmed by numbers, assert that we are simply digits, insignificant dots in a great and meaningless picture. We are not even names but only numbers, not even numbers, bits of information stored on a computer.

The psalmist gives a different evaluation. Humans are the creation of a loving God; not only this but we are the crown of all creation and have been given power to mold it, to use it creatively in our own right. The universe is God's, and through God's will it is also ours to use to his glory.

We are not simply animals or numbers, we are God's creation and the lords of God's universe. What glory and what responsibility for each of us.

CHARLES S. ANDERSON

Lord, we thank you for your mercies. Teach us to use your gifts to your glory. Amen

Prayer concern: Those who feel "less than" fully human

Daily Reflections_____

_____

_____

Suffering for Others

To this you were called, because Christ suffered for you, leaving you an example, that you should follow in his steps. ❖ 1 Peter 2:21 (NIV)

❖ A mother suffers the pains of childbirth and a new life begins.

❖ A serviceman places his life at the disposal of his country and experiences dislocation and interruption of life, at best, and death, at worst.

❖ A son or daughter sacrifices many of the opportunities of life to care for a father and mother in their old age. Why do people do these things?

Perhaps for a variety of reasons. But we can sum them up by saying it is because we respond with our best when life demands sacrifice.

The greatest sacrifice was the sacrifice that Christ made. But Peter reminds us in the Bible verse for today that we can be like Christ if we are willing to suffer for others, to give of ourselves for their sakes.

No one needs to go looking for opportunities. Life offers each of us many an occasion when we can place our lives at the disposal of another and suffer for his or her sake.

SIDNEY A. RAND

O God, teach us the meaning of life through giving ourselves for the welfare of someone else. Amen

Prayer concern: Those who suffer for the faith

Daily Reflections_____

_____

_____

_____

Disciple Dorcas

In Joppa there was a disciple named Tabitha (which, when translated, is Dorcas), who was always doing good and helping the poor. ❖ Acts 9:36 (NIV)

We are apt to think mainly about the works of this good woman. These are only the fruits of more important qualities of this Christian minister. Dorcas was a disciple of Christ. Whether she saw and heard Jesus in the flesh we do not know. She certainly met his spirit-filled followers, and she was an apt pupil of those who diligently taught Christ as Savior. Those who knew Christ as Savior were diligent teachers of the Christian way. Dorcas was an apt pupil.

This disciple of Christ was filled with the Spirit. She was a friend of the friendless and the poor, especially the unloved and neglected widows. Like Christ, she went about doing good. Her ministry was the expression of her Christlikeness. Christ lived in her, in her activities and human relations.

The beautiful character and loving ministry of his disciple crossed racial barriers. She was known to the Jews as Tabitha, by the Gentiles she was named Dorcas. Christian love lifts life above racial and personal peculiarities and transforms these differences into harmonious helps.

ANONYMOUS

O God, fill the church with Christ's Spirit, that many may minister as Dorcas did. Amen

Prayer concern: Lay ministers

Daily Reflections_____

An Endless Chain

So faith comes from what is heard, and what is
heard comes through the word of Christ.
❖ Romans 10:17 (NRSV)

Faith sounds like a mysterious thing to a great many people
but it is really not mysterious at all. Wise Paul hints at what it
is and tells us plainly how to get it. Faith is believing in
Christ. If it was simply a case of believing *that* Christ was so
and so, it would be only a mental exercise and nothing more.
To mean what it should, it must be a personal attachment:
Christ adhering to me; and all of me, my heart and mind and
will and strength, touching and holding fast to Christ.

How do I get faith like that? I get it by hearing about
Christ. How can I believe in anybody of whom I have not
heard? Thank God for my faithful pastor, for patient church
school teachers in the past, for my father and mother who
have introduced me to my Lord.

The way for me to show my appreciation is by passing the
word on. Preaching—believing—preaching—believing is an
endless chain. Don't let me break it.

FRANKLIN CLARK FRY

*O God, who has made it possible for me to believe in
Jesus Christ by the words of sincere and godly people, let
my faith and love overflow into at least one other person.
Amen*

Prayer concern: World leaders

Daily Reflections_____

_____
_____
_____

Day 14 ❖ John 3:16-21

The Only Gospel

For God so loved the world that he gave his only Son,
so that everyone who believes in him may not perish
but may have eternal life. ❖ John 3:16 (NRSV)

Someone has described this famous verse as "a cluster of
continents." Its whole atmosphere is one of vastness.

❖ GOD—the biggest thought that the human mind can
entertain is the thought of God.
❖ THE WORLD—it too is large and spacious, even though
today it has become smaller.
❖ HIS ONLY BEGOTTEN SON—there is an unshared
grandeur and glory in the person of Jesus Christ.
❖ ETERNAL LIFE—something great beyond our knowing,
but it centers in Jesus Christ, who is himself the Life.
❖ Who can talk about the love of God?
❖ It is measured by what it goes out to—the world.
❖ It is measured by what it gives—his only begotten Son.
❖ It is measured by what it does—saves perishing people.
❖ No wonder Richard Baxter could say, "Thank God for that
'whosoever,' for it includes me."
❖ I, too, am embraced by the love of God.

O. K. STORAASLI

*O loving Lord, help me to realize that you love me just as
though I were the only one—and that you love all people
that way. Amen*

Prayer concern: Those who seek more discipline in
their faith and life

Daily Reflections_____

We're Number One

The revelry of the loungers shall pass away.
❖ Amos 6:7b (NRSV)

We're number one! That shout will echo in stadiums throughout the land. In most cases, it will only mean the sound of pride in a team's showing. For too many of us, it is not-so-subtle way of saying that we are better than others. We win more. We earn more. We have a fancier car or home. We have a better place in the world.

We, like Amos's listeners, have sought status in the trappings of this world. It is easy to divide the world into "we" and "they," those who have made it and those who have not.

The prophet reminds us that our worth comes not in what we have but in what God has given. In God's love, we are made one family. In that family, no one is worth more or less than another. Our status is secure: we are God's.

WILLIAM F. WALLES

Lord of hosts, kindle in us the remembrance that we have only sisters and brothers, no adversaries. Fire within us the desire to claim all people as family, even as you have claimed us in Jesus Christ. Amen

Prayer concern: Those who live in poverty

Daily Reflections_____
_____
_____
_____

Sin and Suffering

Rabbi, who sinned, this man or his parents, that
he was born blind? ❖ John 9:2 (NIV)

Have you ever heard someone say, "You must be really living
right," when things are going well? And have you ever asked
yourself, or had someone else ask, in the face of some severe
trouble of disaster, "What have I done to deserve this?"

These questions are asked, of course, because our
experience has taught us that there is sometimes a cause-
effect relationship between some of our actions and the
consequences we experience. But this text teaches us that
there isn't always a connection between the fact of trouble
and committing some sin.

Few of us will totally escape tragedy or misfortune. And
we certainly will see misfortune befall others. We would do
well not to try to explain tragedy in terms of some inevitable
connection between sin and suffering. The reason for some of
our suffering is a mystery. The possibility for living with
suffering comes from God, not from our ability to explain it.

PHILIP A. QUANBECK

*Lord our God, restrain us from eagerly looking for sin in
misfortune. Help us instead to place our trust in you.
Amen*

Prayer concern: Those battling envy and jealousy

Daily Reflections_____

_____
_____
_____

Day 17 ❖ Matthew 23:1-12

Don't Be a Show-off

They do all their deeds to be seen by others.
❖ Matthew 23:5 (NRSV)

When a toddler shows off, we think that he's cute. When a little girl recites the alphabet or a poem, we encourage her. When an athlete makes a great play, we cheer. But if the toddler or the little girl keep on showing their accomplishment, we grow tired. If the athlete tries to act like a whole team, we become irritated.

To Jesus it seemed that the Pharisees and scribes had never quite grown up. They elbowed their way to places of honor. They dressed to call attention to themselves. They were free with advice but short on the helping hand. Whatever they did, they made sure that they were seen.

The Pharisees weren't bad people. They just made sure that everyone knew how good they were. Jesus reminds us: "Whoever exalts himself will be humbled, and whoever humbles himself will be exalted."

Now what do you supposed Jesus would say to those who are proud of being humble?

HAROLD L. YOCHUM

Lord God, keep us from showing either our pride in ourselves or our pride about our humility. All we are, and have, and do should reflect you. Amen

Prayer concern: True humility

Daily Reflections_____

When God Speaks Peace

For he will speak peace to his people . . . to those who
turn to him in their hearts. ❖ Psalm 85:8b (NRSV)

Most of us remember times when we were angry with
someone else—or when they were angry with us. In such
moments it seems that anything we try to say only makes the
situation worse. It's that way in a family, among neighbors,
between nations. As long as there's anger, there's not much
hope for communication.

Things were like that between God's people and God.
They had gotten careless, sinful, and perhaps even rebellious.
God punished them. "Are you going to be angry forever?"
the psalmist asked God. And, in the verse we just read, the
psalmist has the answer.

God isn't going to stay angry. "He will speak peace to his
people . . . to those who turn to him in their hearts." In the
human family, forgiveness most often comes face-to-face. The
runaway returns—or is found by a searching parent. People
who have been ignoring one another see one another again—
and speak peaceably. And when God opens the way back to
those who turn to him, "He will seek peace." What are we
waiting for?

RUTH STENERSON

Lord, I'd like to come home. Amen

Prayer concern: Those suffering from war

Daily Reflections

New Directions

Since, then, you have been raised with Christ, set
your hearts on things above. ❖ Colossians 3:1 (NIV)

We were walking along the dusty streets of an Indian village.
We looked down most of the time as we walked to avoid the
refuse, the open sewers, the stagnant potholes. The sights
were not pleasant. But then on impulse we climbed the tower
of an ancient Hindu temple. From on top the view was
transformed. We could see lush, green rice fields, women in
colorful sarees walking along the paths, waving coconut
palms shimmering in the sunlight, and in the distance the
cool, blue ocean. By climbing up and looking out we
discovered beauty that was there all along, but hidden by our
cautious, hesitant walk with downward gaze.

Paul invites us to stand up and look out. We are to claim
ownership of the new life we share with the one who has
been lifted up from the dead by God.

Our temptation is to look down. We want to tread carefully
among the problems that clutter our days. But new horizons
emerge when we stand tall in "Christ who is our life."

JAMES A. BERQUIST

*We are beaten down and sometimes we despair. Help us,
Risen One, to look up and walk with you. Amen*

Prayer concern: Those who despair

Daily Reflections

Pointing Toward the Light

He himself was not the light, but he came to
testify to the light. ❖ John 1:8 (NRSV)

A person standing at the foot of a mountain on a dark night
looks at a star and it seems to be close to the mountain's
peak. But a person standing on the mountain-top recognizes
how infinitely higher than the mountain that star is.

John the Baptist stood on a mountaintop. Some people
thought he was the Messiah, the light they had been looking
for. But they were standing at the foot of the mountain. John
knew that he was not the light. The true light was God's
word—God in human flesh, bearing the name Jesus, fulfilling
the promise of the messiahship. The baptist, whose name
John meant "Yahweh is merciful," was just a man called to
bear witness to the mercy of God in sending the Light to
everyone on earth.

To bear witness is the mission of all of us whose lives have
been illuminated by the Light of Christ.

ROBERT R. CLARK

*We thank you, Lord, for allowing the light to shine into
the darkness of our lives. Like John the Baptist, may we
turn the attention of others from ourselves to the light of
Jesus Christ our Savior. Amen*

Prayer concern: Church missions

Daily Reflections_____

_____

_____

_____

It Is Well!

Good will come to him who is generous and lends freely, who conducts his affairs with justice.
❖ Psalm 112:5 (NIV)

Recently I heard a famous movie actor boast about how poor his family was years ago. Then he said, "Now we've forgotten how to need one another. How to borrow a cup of sugar . . ."

I had that kind of beginning, too. The neighborhood mothers constantly ran out of kitchen staples, such as sugars and flour. My mother was a constant lender, and a borrower as well.

She was generous with her time and talents, too. She watched their babies, and they watched hers on the few occasions when absence was absolutely necessary.

People don't change much. I'm sure that somewhere people still run around lending and borrowing not only flour and sugar, but also dollars. To the one who conducts his affairs with justice, doesn't the psalmist say, "It is well"?

BETTY LAWRENCE

Lord, thank you for this moment of looking back. I'm glad we have this gift of memory that allows us to see both the bad and good of the past. All we learn from looking back is that each generation has to learn the lessons over again. Forgive us and help us. Amen

Prayer concern: People in your neighborhood

Daily Reflections

He Wants Us to Be Happy

This, the first of his miraculous signs, Jesus performed in Cana of Galilee. He thus revealed his glory. ❖ John 2:11 (NIV)

There are those who seem to think that you cannot be a Christian and enjoy life. They measure Christianity by the length of a person's face as though it were wrong to smile or be happy. Nothing is further from the truth.

Jesus wants us to be happy. This we see from the first of his miracles recorded in the scriptures, Jesus was invited to a wedding. He accepted the invitation knowing that the guests would happy. He wanted to be happy with them. Even more than that when the wine failed, he worked a miracle so that no one would be disappointed. Instead of spoiling the fun, Jesus helped make the celebration a happy occasion.

God wants Christians to be happy. Being a Christian does not rob us of joy; but rather we can truly enjoy life by accepting God's blessings, knowing that they are God's gifts to us.

CLARENCE H. HINKHOUSE

We thank you, Lord Jesus Christ, that you want us to be happy. We thank you for all the good things you give us to make us happy. When we have fun together, keep us from doing anything evil so that you can be happy with us. Amen

Prayer concern: Those who celebrate

Daily Reflections_____

_____

_____

_____

A Man of Prayer

Yet his bow remained taut, and his arms were made agile by the hands of the Mighty One of Jacob. ❖ Genesis 49:24 (NRSV)

The U.S. Constitution makes no provision for the manner in which the president takes the oath of office. But when George Washington prepared to take his oath, he asked for a Bible. The president reverently kissed the page at the verse quoted above, thus starting an ongoing tradition.

This verse found remarkable confirmation in the career of Washington. His strength of character, wise decisions and competent leadership were, by his own testimony, made possible by his reliance on God. Ample testimony marks him as a man of prayer, a regular attendant at worship even during army days, and a devoted reader of God's word. It is not the "know-it-all" type that is to be trusted; but one who, admitting his own limitations, seeks help from on high. The hand of God is mightier than political machinery.

ANONYMOUS

Gracious God, as you hear me calling upon you in my prayers, so give me grace to hear you calling on me in your word. Amen

Prayer concern: That the wounds caused by bigotry might be healed

Daily Reflections_____

_____

_____

_____

Day 24 ❖ John 20:19

Sense of Fear

On the evening of that first day of the week, when
the disciples were together, with the doors
locked. ❖ John 20:19a (NIV)

Many of us have sensed the fear that crawls into our thoughts
when we hear the wailing siren that warns of a tornado in the
area. We've taken the necessary precautions. Yet, as we wait
in our hiding place, fear continues to haunt us until the "all
clear" is sounded. We're crippled by it.

So fear gripped the early disciples as they sought a place
of escape after their master had been arrested in
Gethsemane. Undoubtedly, word of his crucifixion, burial in a
borrowed tomb, and mysterious disappearance had reached
them. Yet these reports only added to their confusion. Fear
hindered them from thinking through the events and
interpreting them from the perspective given earlier by Jesus.
They chose to fend for themselves and to lock the doors,
rather than believe Jesus' words about his resurrection.

ALICE L SCHIMPF

*Dear God, give us the wisdom to understand that only by
relying on you can we meet our problems without adding
the problem of fear. Amen*

Prayer concern: Those who are abused

Daily Reflections_____

Who Covers What?

There is nothing concealed that will not be
disclosed, or hidden that will not be made known.
❖ Luke 12:2 (NIV)

We have lived in a time when many cover-ups have been
revealed and when many hidden things have been made
known. Let us be grateful for the exposures, and let us be
relentless in our search for public sins. None of us believes,
however, that everything has been revealed nor that
everything will be made known by our efforts. We know
personally that our own innermost life has not been exposed,
and that the exposure attempted by sensitivity groups is not
the answer, but may even be a new cover-up.

The only one who can know everything and who has to
know everything is God. From God we can hide nothing. Let
us therefore read the word of Jesus, not as a promise that we
shall know all there is to know about the world and our
neighbors, but as a reminder that we are known to God and
responsible to God. With God no cover-up is possible. Let
us give thanks that God loves the world—even us!

JOHANNES H. V. KNUDSEN

*Give us your aid and guidance to be open and honest in
all our ways. Help us to understand that we hide things,
even from ourselves! When we come to you in prayer,
help us to cast light upon the things hidden in the
corners—and forgive us! Amen*

Prayer concern: Indigenous people everywhere

Daily Reflections_____

_____

_____

_____

Gathering

[God] has made known to us the mystery of his will . . . as a plan . . . to gather up all things in him, things in heaven and things on earth.
❖ Ephesians 1:9-10 (NRSV)

It often appears that people don't have a plan for their lives. We run in circles doing whatever seems necessary as life happens, without ever thinking about the future. Years go by. Our families grow up and leave home. We settle into a routine. Then, all of a sudden, we are old—and death or ill health stares us in the face. These absolute realities cannot be avoided.

Even though we may not be prepared for the future, it is a comfort to know that Jesus desires to gather us into himself and into heaven forever. In John 14:2-3, we read that Jesus went to prepare a place for us so that where he is we may be also. Our Lord Jesus always has planned ahead for our eternal happiness with him.

What have we done to deserve this place that Christ has prepared for us? Absolutely nothing. It is by our faith in Christ alone that we know Jesus Christ has prepared for us an eternal home. Thanks be to God!

CAROL J. GROVER

Thank you, Lord, for sending us your Son, Jesus Christ, to die for us and give us life. Amen

Prayer concern: Those who care for the aged

Daily Reflections_____

_____

_____
_____

By Many Proofs

After his suffering, he showed himself to these
men and gave many convincing proofs that he
was alive. He appeared to them over a period of
forty days and spoke about the kingdom of God.
❖ Acts 1:3 (NIV)

It is the general assumption of scholars that Luke wrote the
Gospel named after him and also the book of Acts. His
concern was for a friend by the name of Theophilus. But
God's concern went farther. And so these two books have
become a part of the Bible.

Add to your reading for today the first four verses in Luke.
It helps you to sense Luke's friendly personal concern for
Theophilus to know that Jesus did indeed rise from the dead.
He records that Jesus "showed himself to these men and gave
many convincing proofs that he was alive."

My dictionary defines proof as "that degree of cogency,
arising from evidence, which convinces the mind of any truth
of fact and produces belief." I know of no more rewarding
exercise than to read the Easter story in the four Gospels.
Then note all the references to the resurrection in Acts and
the Epistles. The story moves from doubt to deep conviction.
"By many proofs" the disciples and the early church were held
fast in the certainty that Jesus lives.

FREDERICK A. SCHIOTZ

Father, keep us in this certainty. Amen

Prayer concern: More certain hearts

Daily Reflections

New Life!

The letter kills, but the Spirit gives life.
❖ 2 Corinthians 3:6 (NRSV)

Many people remember the film *The Ten Commandments*, starring Charlton Heston as Moses. The special effects were spectacular as Moses encountered the glory of God on Mount Sinai and brought the stone tablets to the people of Israel. The biblical accounts themselves are spectacular as well, full of fire and smoke. The Ten Commandments given by God marked a new covenant with Israel. The Commandments continue to shape our lives, protecting relationships and the gift of community.

It is all the more amazing, then, that Paul calls the Commandments "a ministry of death." The Commandments cannot and do not save us. Only Jesus Christ does that. In Jesus' dying and rising, God has crafted a new covenant. Paul calls it "the ministry of justification."

This is a new world order. Now faith is created in us as a gift, apart from works of the law. Now our care for the neighbor and the earth come not as an effort to earn God's favor, but as joyful response to God's gracious gifts.

STEPHANIE FREY

God, thank you for creating faith in me and freeing me for a life of joyful service. Amen

Prayer concern: All who are tyrannized by fear

Daily Reflections_____
_____
_____
_____

Sign of Love

Therefore the Lord himself will give you a sign.
❖ Isaiah 7:14 (NRSV)

It had been a bad week. Then I discovered that part of my earring, the part that screwed on at the back, was missing. When a half-hearted search failed, I just shrugged and tried to go to sleep. In my unhappy state, I felt I was past caring, even though it was my favorite pair of earrings. I ignored an impulse to pray, dismissing this as too trivial to trouble God about.

The next afternoon, I sat in bed reading. I got up to go to the bathroom and when I returned, there on the sheet, glistening in the sunlight, was the back to my earring! As I held it between trembling fingers, it was for me a tangible sign of God's love. I had not sought, but I had found; I had not even asked, but God had given. During the remainder of that hard week, circumstances did not change, but the memory of that tiny golden screw served as a comforting reminder of God's constant, caring presence.

In spite of his frightening predicament, and despite Isaiah's urging, Ahaz refused to ask the Lord for a sign. Nevertheless, the Lord promised him a sign—a sign named Immanuel, which means "God is with us."

TANYA FERDINANDEZ

Forgiving Lord, thank you for blessing me, even when I do not ask for or deserve your blessings. Amen

Prayer concern: Those who feel unloved

Daily Reflections

Anxiety for Tomorrow

Do not boast about tomorrow, for you do not know
what a day may bring forth. ❖ Proverbs 27:1 (NIV)

The Bible tells us not to boast about tomorrow. Tomorrow
belongs to God. God is the keeper of the world. Season
follows season just as day follows night.

Many of us think we can boast about tomorrow because
we live in a wealthy nation. Many others are afraid—they
hardly know where food and clothing will come from
tomorrow. Grocery stores complain about so much theft by
old people who life on very little money, not even enough to
buy their daily food. Stealing some small items for them is a
means of survival. Police officers do not like to punish them.
They feel sorry for the old people. So they close their eyes to
the theft, and the grocery stores lose money.

This happens too often. We ought to be ashamed that so
many aged people live in poverty. And some day those of us
who are younger will be old, too. Will we be anxious then
about tomorrow? Perhaps we will. What can be done about
this problem?

ANNE JORDHEIM

*Dear Father in heaven, help us to serve your poor, that
for your sake they may be fed and clothed. Amen*

Prayer concern: Those who are anxious

Daily Reflections_____

_____

_____

_____

Who Is Calling the Signals?

Today, if you hear his voice, do not harden your hearts. ❖ Hebrews 3:7 (NIV)

When you see a football team in the huddle between plays, they are listening to the quarterback as he gives the signals for the next play. The one who calls the plays has to be a person who thoroughly understands the game. He has to take many things into consideration. The other players have to have confidence in him and trust his judgment. His voice must be supreme over all other voices.

Huddles are a retreat from the battle for the offense to receive their instructions for the attack. However, it is the voice who gives the signals that is most important in the huddle. There has to be attention to hear clearly and correctly.

Huddles are important in the game of life as well. Huddles can take many forms. It may be a temporary withdrawing from some activity to meditate on God's word, to pray in quietness, to attend a service, or even to talk with someone. The voice that we need to hear is the voice of Christ through his word. Life becomes confusing when we try to listen to many voices in our conscience telling us what to do. Our attitude toward Christ makes a difference in our response. His voice gives strength and encouragement to obey.

KAREL M. LUNDE

Speak, O Lord; your servant hears. Amen

Prayer concern: Christians in Korea

Daily Reflections

Day 32 ❖ Acts 20:13-38

Giving Ourselves

We must help the weak, remembering the words
the Lord Jesus himself said: "It is more blessed to
give than to receive." ❖ Acts 20:35b (NIV)

Paul addressed these words to the overseers of the church at
Ephesus on his way to Jerusalem. His life was an open book
to them. He had served the Lord steadfastly in spite of trials
and sorrows. He did not hold back, even though he
was a "prisoner already in spirit" as he made his way to
Jerusalem. His arrival there would mean more imprisonment
and more persecution.

But his life was not to be wasted on words—enough of
words! His was actively bearing witness—to the lost, the
least, and the lowliest—that the relationship between us and
God has been healed.

Are we wasting our lives on words? Do we see the broken
and the weak among us? Are we adding to the world's
problems, or are we part of the solution? Paul is an example
of one who was able to help the weak in accordance with
Jesus' saying: "It is more blessed to give than to receive."

DELWIN B. SCHNEIDER

*Lord, through Paul you have given us an example of a
life that is given for others. Make us mindful of our
heritage and grateful for the privilege of giving ourselves
first to you and then to our neighbor. Amen*

Prayer concern: Those who long to hear God's word

Daily Reflections_____

God Hears Our Prayer

Give ear to my words, O LORD; give heed to my sighing. Listen to the sound of my cry, my King and my God, for to you I pray. ❖ Psalm 5:1-2 (NRSV)

I'll never forget the day our son died. He was only 18. It happened so unexpectedly. We were in shock. The pain was deep and dreadful. We didn't think we could live without him.

During the months and years that followed, I learned to pray the lament psalms, those psalms about the personal or national suffering of the Jews. Even calling the Lord's name begins to lift one out of sorrow. Such deep need opens us to throw ourselves upon God and cry out the pain in honest prayer. Lament psalms help us do this. They help us know what God can do. So we come full circle to trust God above all else and receive again God's steadfast love. We claim God's shield of protection again. So we are safe—even in deep sorrow.

E. CORINNE CHILSTROM

Lord, you only are our refuge. Save and defend us. Comfort and restore us. Give us new joy. Amen

Prayer concern: Those whose children have died

Daily Reflections

The Mystery of Faith

Beyond all question, the mystery of godliness is
great. ❖ 1 Timothy 3:16 (NIV)

In spite of all scientific and technological advances, the
universe still confronts us with many mysteries. There is
much that remains unexplained. Our Christian faith also
contains much that we simply cannot understand. With a
sense of gratitude and awe, the apostle Paul pointed to the
mystery of the Christian faith.

This mystery centers in Jesus Christ. He is the Word
made flesh; he is our righteousness, strength and hope. "He
reflects the glory of God and bears the very stamp of his
nature, upholding the universe by his word of power." He
died for our sins and rose from the dead. He forgives us our
sins and guides us by the Spirit.

Great indeed—let us confess it with believers of all
times—is the mystery of what we believe. What a sublime
faith it is! It enables us to abide serenely and securely under
the shadow of the Almighty. Our religion satisfies our soul's
deepest longing.

MARTIN E. LEHMAN

*Dear Lord, our God, gratefully we confess the awesome
mystery of our faith. We thank you that, when we are
beset by fears and a feeling of guilt, we can put our trust
in your Son, our Savior. For his sake grant us your favor
and the answer to our prayer. Amen*

Prayer concern: Scientists

Daily Reflections_____

_____

_____

_____

This Healer

Who is this fellow who told you to pick it up and
walk? ❖ John 5:12 (NIV)

The healed man did not know the healer! The invalid did
what Jesus told him to do. Then Jesus healed him. But the
curious and excited crowd of sick and well people around the
pool shut out his view of the Savior. These interfering people
were more interested in the miraculous healing than in the
miraculous master.

Note that this healed man went to the temple. For the first
time in 38 years this son of Israel entered the court from
which he had been barred by his defective body. He used his
first opportunity to go to God's house of prayer! There Jesus
sought and found him.

Jesus is still seeking sinners. Where will he find us today?
This newly healed man came to know his Savior in the house
of God.

HARRY D. HOOVER

*Grant unto us, dear Lord, that we may learn to know
you more perfectly through your gifts. May no person or
possession ever hide you from us, or interrupt our
fellowship with you, our precious Lord and Savior. Amen*

Prayer concern: Our places of worship

Daily Reflections_____

_____

_____

_____

When Ten Equals Two

Love your neighbor as yourself.
❖ Matthew 22:39b (NIV)

In mathematics, the number 10 hardly equals 2. But when Jesus finished condensing the Ten Commandments, that was his total—two: You shall love the Lord your God . . . and your neighbor as yourself.

In the original Commandments, the first three refer to our actions toward God, and the last seven to actions toward other people. Not only are we to worship God alone, and respect God's name and day, but we are also to honor our parents, and not kill, commit adultery, steal, slander, or covet.

The genius of Jesus' condensation is that he makes these commands positive. They turn out not to be restrictions on life but rather guidelines for an affirmative, appreciative response to God's love and goodness. The words of Jesus become personal. "You," he says, "love your neighbor as much as you love yourself." To do that, we have to ask God to help us see beyond our own interests.

EDGAR R. TREXLER

Dear God, help us to realize that if the world is going to see your love, it must see it through us. In Jesus' name we pray. Amen

Prayer concern: Those who teach and study science

Daily Reflections_____
_____
_____
_____

An Imperishable Reward

And if you have not been trustworthy with someone else's property, who will give you property of your own? ❖ Luke 16:12 (NIV)

My children are at the age where they are never satisfied. They always want something else. Frequently, my reply is this: "Take care of what you have, and maybe you'll get something else."

We read a similar promise in today's Bible verse. The point is an admonition for wise stewardship of the wonderful blessings we have from God. Together with the admonition is a promise of reward. Luke doesn't identify the reward. But 1 Peter 1:3-9 gives a clue. Peter says that God has an "imperishable, undefiled, and unfading" inheritance waiting in heaven for all faithful Christians.

The nature of eternal things is quite different from earthly things. But God's promise is clear: take care of what I have presently given you (perishable as it is), and one day you will possess the "imperishable."

ANONYMOUS

Merciful God, each day brings pressures and demands to use and abuse your gifts to us. Give us wisdom and strength that we may remain faithful and may gain your promised reward. Amen

Prayer concern: Christians in Taiwan

Daily Reflections_____
_____
_____
_____

God's Productive Love

Hope does not disappoint us, because God's love has
been poured into our hearts. ❖ Romans 5:5 (NRSV)

Clara, suffering from painful arthritis, came down in a
cheerful, pleasant mood to breakfast in the home of her niece
every morning.

"What is your secret?" her friend Laura asked.

"I never greet others before I read the words about love in
1 Corinthians 13," she said. She could have complained about
pain, but she let God's love fill her with cheer.

When God's love has been poured into our hearts, says
Paul, hope does not disappoint us. Love from God produces
hope and renewed attitude in the face of difficult times.

Does God's love seem far away? Read the biblical
messages of love. Say them to yourself. Telephone or write
hurting friends to say, "God loves you, especially now in your
need."

Loving others increases our own awareness of being loved
by God. We could say God's love is productive because it
seems to grow when we pass it on.

ROLAND SEBOLDT

*Thank you, God, for revealing your love to me, and for
renewing my hope in times of pain and trial. Amen*

Prayer concern: Those who are lonely

Daily Reflections_____

_____
_____

Step by Step

> The Israelites no longer had manna; they ate the crops
> of the land of Canaan that year. ❖ Joshua 5:12b (NRSV)

Infants depend on others to feed them. And for babies, trust comes easily. A baby's confident dependence melts a parent's heart. But how much pride that same parent feels when the child learns to feed and care for herself!

Through their wilderness wanderings, the people of Israel trusted that God would provide manna for them day by day. When they reached the promised land, the manna ceased. It took a big leap of faith and some hard work to reap a harvest of crops instead.

We cannot live without God's daily care. And God still provides. Some blessings appear, like manna, day by day. But as we grow in faith, God stretches our confidence. We learn to work and wait for the harvest. As you take larger steps in faith, your heavenly parent rejoices. You can move forward gladly, confident that God has gone before you to prepare all that you need.

LOWELL L. HESTERMAN

Faithful God, help us to trust in what we still cannot see. Amen

Prayer concern: Confidence in God's harvest

Daily Reflections

The Gift of Faith

"Blessed are you, Simon . . . ! For flesh and blood
has not revealed this to you, but my Father in
heaven." ❖ Matthew 16:17 (NRSV)

It seems the old song is true: the best things in life are free.
Genuine love from parent, spouse, child, or friend is not
something we earn but comes freely from the heart of the
giver. And faith is like love: it cannot be earned. Faith also
comes as a gift.

When Jesus asked Simon Peter whom he understood
Jesus to be, Simon answered confidently, "You are the
Messiah, the Son of the living God" (verse 16). This
statement depended neither on Peter's five senses nor his
acquired knowledge about Jesus. From his observations
while traveling with Jesus, Peter knew Jesus as a teacher of
parables, a healer of the sick, and a worker of miracles. Yet it
was God alone who made it possible for Peter to confess that
Jesus is the Son of God.

We live in an age when empirical proof is demanded
before something is accepted as valid, an age when what
cannot be measured often is demeaned. All the more reason
for us to affirm daily the gift of faith.

DARLENE BOWDEN MUSCHETT

*Loving God, help us to remember that faith in Christ is a
gift from you. Amen*

Prayer concern: All who search for faith

Daily Reflections_____

_____

_____

_____

Priests with Their Sins

Every high priest is selected from among men and is appointed to represent them in matters related to God, to offer gifts and sacrifices for sins. ❖ Hebrews 5:1 (NIV)

In chapter 4 of Hebrews, we read of our "great high priest who has passed through the heavens, Jesus, the Son of God." Just as the Sabbath and the wilderness journeys of the Old Testament have meaning for us, so we can also learn much from the Old Testament high priests, who because they were sinners, had to offer sacrifices for themselves as well as for the people. Our text notes that "one does not take this honor upon himself, but he is called by God, just as Aaron was."

Jesus was made our perfect Savior through patient suffering and obedience. Likewise, his word tells us we have to grow out of the milk-only stage of babyhood into maturity of solid foods. Instead of rushing through our family devotions we should discuss and "chew" on our Bible texts to really gain strength for tests of faith in all life's classrooms.

CHARLES SCHMITZ

Dear God, we thank you for the clarity and frankness of your word. Give us ears that listen and hearts that obey in all of our days and ways, in Jesus' name. Amen

Prayer concern: Pastors

Daily Reflections_____

The Cure

> But now that you have been set free from sin and
> have become slaves to God, the benefit you reap
> leads to holiness, and the result is eternal life.
> ❖ Romans 6:22 (NIV)

Everything that a person experiences leaves its mark on him
or her. Deep within, without a person's being aware of it,
there are all kinds of hidden scars, urges, and memories.
They are below the threshold of consciousness, and when
they do rise above it they become distorted. They put on a
false face and appear as something quite different from what
they really are. The only cure is to get what is hidden into the
open, in its true form and figure, so that it can be honestly
dealt with and faced for what it is.

The Christian experience of the forgiveness of sins and of
a rebirth to a new life of selflessness, love, and confidence
constitutes the basic cure. Our past is a bondage from which
we cannot rid ourselves. Freedom comes only when we face
honestly what is and know that, nevertheless, we are loved
and accepted. From the new God-relationship of submission
flow new powers of freedom.

MARTIN J. HEINEKEN

*Almighty God, unto whom all hearts are open, all desire
known, and from whom no secrets are hid, cleanse the
thoughts of our hearts by the inspiration of your Holy
Spirit. Amen*

Prayer concern: Those who work for the government

Daily Reflections

Day 43 ❖ 2 Corinthians 8:1-9

Stewardship of Riches

For you know the grace of our Lord Jesus Christ,
that though he was rich, yet for your sakes he
became poor, so that you through his poverty
might become rich. ❖ 2 Corinthians 8:9 (NIV)

The Macedonian church was alive. It heard the needs of others and wished to respond. The members gathered "according to their means"—and even "beyond their means." Out of their relative poverty, they still gave liberal gifts. But "they first gave themselves." The gifts of money and means were important, but the gift of themselves was most vital.

We live in a time of impersonalness. We are numbers, part of the crowd. We find it hard to face ourselves, to give ourselves. The Macedonians began their stewardship program with self-giving, with involvement of the person. It was not a "relief" that was shared with needy brethren; it was their interest, concern, love, and means. First, themselves!

The riches they possessed were the riches of Christ. They were his children and owned his wealth. Their poverty became nothing, since they could share from the beauty of his riches to them.

ARTHUR O. F. BAUER

Make us true stewards of thy gifts to us, our Father. Help us to give ourselves to you and to others. Amen

Prayer concern: Hearts for giving

Daily Reflections_____

_____

_____

_____

Desertion

I am astonished that you are so quickly deserting
the one who called you by the grace of Christ.
❖ Galatians 1:6 (NIV)

What greater fault can a soldier be accused of than desertion?
This is exactly what Paul says to the Christians of Galatia. In
apparently a relatively short time after their reception of the
gospel they had changed back to dependence on rules.

Was Paul justified in writing to the Galatians with such
vehemence? After all, aren't there many roads to God?

Paul's letter to the Galatians is the Christian's answer to
these questions. The gospel of Jesus involves much more
than a philosophical overtone. It witnesses to Jesus as the
only way to God.

When we are tempted to compromise the gospel to please
our friends or to get along with our coworkers, Paul's
astonishment at those who so quickly deserted the gospel
calls a halt to such desertion. To trade the gospel for a cult of
rules, however tolerant or strict, is to desert Christ.

MICHAEL E. LONG

*Help us, Lord, to proclaim the gospel of your grace.
Amen*

Prayer concern: Friends and coworkers

Daily Reflections_____

_____

_____

_____

The Impact of Easter

> . . . he began to preach in the synagogues that
> Jesus is the Son of God. ❖ Acts 9:20b (NIV)

When Saul of Tarsus was encountered by the risen Lord on the road to Damascus, his whole life was radically changed. The Pharisee became the great apostle to the Gentiles; and the man who had been notorious as a persecutor of Christians now proclaimed Jesus as the Savior! The change was so sudden and complete that, for a while, neither the friends nor the enemies of the gospel could believe it.

Such was the impact of Easter, the realization of the resurrection, on one person; and it changed the world through him. Easter allows the reality of Christ's victory to break into our values and views of life and death, our relationships and responsibilities. Are we open to the impact Easter can have on us and, through us, on the world in which we live? If we are, then we, too, will "proclaim Jesus" in how we speak and live.

JACK E. LINDQUIST

Praise to you, O God, for preserving my life in both pleasant and troubled times. Amen

Prayer concern: Those who mourn

Daily Reflections

_____

_____

_____

Day 46 ❖ Mark 1:29-34

Jesus at Home with Andrew

As soon as they left the synagogue, they went
with James and John to the home of Simon and
Andrew. ❖ Mark 1:29 (NIV)

Andrew and Simon took Jesus, James, and John home with
them after services in the synagogue. Andrew kept on
learning about Jesus. He found that Jesus' work was merciful,
mighty, curative, and creative. He was beginning to find God
in Jesus of Nazareth.

The fellowship of the synagogue worship continued in the
home in the Christ-centered group. We must never leave our
Lord at the church building. God must go home with us.
Worship has failed if it has not helped to make more real
God's presence in our home and daily life.

When Jesus entered the home, the sick were blessed.
When Jesus laid his hand upon the helpless, they arose to
become helpers of others. Miracles abound wherever Christ
is found. The family that brings Jesus into the home becomes
a blessing to the community. "All the city gathered at the
door" of Andrew's house. A Christ-centered family attracts
those who need a friend and a Savior. Christ makes his
presence known in those with whom he dwells.

ANONYMOUS

*O Lord, enter our home and make it a fit place for you to
abide. Bless all the people who live about our doorstep.
Amen*

Prayer concern: Homes centered in Christ

Daily Reflections_____

_____
_____
_____

The Builders

He is the stone you builders rejected, which has become the capstone. ❖ Acts 4:11 (NIV)

We are truly great builders. Our scientific know-how and our technological advances are amazing to behold. But among the new innovations we may have rejected or neglected the cornerstone.

The cornerstone is Jesus Christ, our Lord, who from the foundation of the world gives depth and wholeness to our lives. Today as you go forth, or reflect upon the business at hand, walk in his way. The foundation of your life is important because it is on this that you will build. If it is built on Jesus Christ, then it is on solid rock and it will endure eternally. If it is built on "sinking sand" without the foundation of Christ, then it will be as precarious and tottery as a small child's house made of toy blocks. That which you do this day will be another stone built into your life.

ROBERT A. CLARK

O Lord, the architect of our lives, grant that we as living stones may be built up into a spiritual house and an abiding temple of your glory. In your name we pray. Amen

Prayer concern: Congregations

Daily Reflections

Day 48 ❖ Psalm 33:1-17

The Weakness of Power

No king is saved by the size of his army; no warrior
escapes by his great strength. ❖ Psalm 33:16 (NIV)

Powerful rulers have come and gone. Great armies have
been defeated time and time again. That lesson was learned
centuries ago. There are enough wastelands on the earth to
bear tribute to the futility of war. Yet, each new generation is
caught up in the schemes and aggression of power politics.

Wise people know that brute strength, nuclear warheads,
armaments, and armies are not the cure-all for inhumanity.
There are other necessary ingredients. Surely justice and
charity are priority considerations. The moderating factor is
the counsel of the Lord that remains forever.

The message of the Prince of Peace recalls to our minds
the ultimate truth, "Heaven and earth will pass away, but my
words will never pass away" (Luke 21:33).

GUY BROWN

*O God, giver of life, help us to preserve the goodness and
beauty of creation. Quiet the impulsiveness of souls
imprisoned by anger, bitterness, and resentment. Grant
us the serenity of soul needful to live peaceably with all
people in these days when peace seems so remote. Amen*

Prayer concern: The meek who shall inherit the earth

Daily Reflections_____
_____
_____
_____

The Field Is the World

Blessed be the LORD, the God of Israel, who alone
does wondrous things. ❖ Psalm 72:18 (NRSV)

One of the promises that Yahweh made to Abraham was that
in him all the nations of the earth would be blessed. Is it
presumptive of the Hebrews to claim that the God who
adopted them as the "chosen people" is really the God of the
whole earth?

Note that God did not choose the Hebrews for privilege,
but for responsibility. They were not set aside from other
nations because they were favored, but because they were
challenged. Could they accept their calling humbly, as
servants, as people willing to be channels of God's message
and God's mercy to the ages?

One of the greatest challenges a nation or an individual
can face is the challenge to be humble enough to be loved
and followed.

Will you in humility let God speak through you—speak to
even the least, the lowest, the last, the lost?

GEORGE K. BOWERS

*Lord, you are great, indeed, and the wonder of your
greatness overwhelms us. But make us humble enough to
be channels of your mercy and love. Amen*

Prayer concern: Humility

Daily Reflections_____
_____
_____
_____

Day 50 ❖ Luke 6:20-26

Into the Future

Rejoice in that day and leap for joy. ❖ Luke 6:23 (NIV)

What our society calls success, Jesus calls, "Woe." What our society calls misery, Jesus calls, "Blessed."

Blessed are those who make themselves poor for the sake of others, who are willing to go hungry for the sake of others, who continue to be touched by the misery of others. Blessed are those who don't go along with the crowd, who don't try to keep up with the Joneses, who go against the accepted principles of an easygoing society. Woe to those who think only of themselves, their pleasure, their enjoyment and who are concerned only about the approval of those around them.

We belong to a strange and wonderful group of people who live by a revolutionary ethic and bring hope of a different kind of world order. We often become discouraged because the majority do not follow Jesus may even wonder if we are on the right track. Jesus gives inspiration and hope so that we can move into the future with him.

DWAIN M. OLSON

Thank you, Lord Jesus, for the hope you put in our hearts and the joy that comes from following you. In your name we live. Amen

Prayer concern: Christians in Norway

Daily Reflections

Is God at Home?

> The God who made the world and everything in it
> is the Lord of heaven and earth and does not live
> in temples built by hands. ❖ Acts 17:24 (NIV)

In this age of affluence, we are building bigger and better churches than ever before. On a choice site we erect a beautiful and functional building "to the glory of God." We are proud to show off our altar or kitchen or stained-glass windows, proud to take visitors on a tour of our church home.

But is God at home there? That depends upon the people who sit on the padded pews and walk on the carpeted floors and study under the soft lights. They may come to admire the creation of their own hands or to worship the creator of heaven and earth. The building is there to serve as an appropriate setting for worship and as a testimony to the faith of the worshipers. God doesn't need any building. It is our own need we fulfill when we build a church. Our greater need is for God to be at home in us. Then we will experience God's love and forgiveness both inside and outside "his house."

JOHN H. HAYNER

Lord, we ask your Spirit to dwell in our hearts that as we come and go from church, we may be living extensions of the church in the world. In Jesus' name we pray. Amen

Prayer concern: Those who teach Sunday school

Daily Reflections_____

_____

_____

_____

Open the Window

Now when Daniel learned that the decree had been published, he went home to his upstairs room where the windows opened toward Jerusalem. ❖ Daniel 6:10 (NIV)

Daniel had an upper room for prayer. He went there three times a day to pray to God, even after King Darius made a law against such petitions. Daniel shut the door, but he kept the windows of his prayer room open. God in heaven was able to see and to deliver his servant, even from the lions' den.

There were windows in that upper room in Jerusalem where the believers assembled after Jesus' ascension. The door was shut. They were in quiet place, praying to the Father who sees in secret. Thus their window was opened toward heaven. At the moment of his martyr death Stephen said, "Behold, I see the heavens opened, and the Son of God standing at the right hand of God." The "windows of heaven" were opened for this hero of faith.

When we pray we should shut the door to keep out distractions. Yet it is just as important to open the window. We are to look up and commune with the one who in mercy stoops down to hear and answer our prayers.

MILTON H. SCHRAM

Our hearts are open to you, O God. Fill them with your peace. Amen

Prayer concern: Our places of worship

Daily Reflections_____

_____

_____

_____

Pity Even on the Planets

Jesus wept. ❖ John 11:35 (NIV)

In Graham Greene's novel *The Heart of the Matter*, Major Scobie has charge of bringing a group of victims of a crash at sea into a hospital in the harbor city. As he leaves the hospital with all of its pain, he looks up at the stars and the lighted windows of the building and says that if one would see only those lights in the window he would think everything was all right inside. But if one really knew the pain and suffering that was going on in there, if one really understood what is called the heart of the matter, he would have pity even on the planets.

Jesus brings this understanding, wisdom, and love into our world. When he saw Mary and the mourners weeping at the tomb of his friend, Lazarus, Jesus "was deeply moved in spirit and troubled . . ." (John 11:33). He showed divine sympathy, empathy, and compassion with us and for us.

HAROLD H. ZIETLOW

Keep us evermore in your compassionate pity, merciful God. Show us your miracles of new and everlasting life. We thank you for hearing our prayers, and we ask you to manifest your glory in our lives. Amen

Prayer concern: All who mourn

Daily Reflections_____

_____
_____
_____

The Cross, Our Focus

[Jesus] rebuked Peter . . . "Get behind me,
Satan!" ❖ Mark 8:33 (NRSV)

A pastor in Sweden was surprised on a Sunday to see the king
sitting in one of the pews. He was so excited by the royal
visitor that he set aside his planned sermon and began to
extol the greatness of the king. A few days later, a package
and letter was delivered to the pastor from the king. The
package contained a cross, and in the letter the king had
written: "Hang this cross opposite the pulpit so that all who
stand there will know their proper subject."

How easy to be swayed by things of glory and power. But
note the prominent place of the cross in today's text. Peter
had answered rightly the question about who Jesus was: "You
are the Messiah." But when Jesus said that he would suffer
and die on the cross, Peter could not accept this. So Jesus
had to rebuke him.

Like that pastor in Sweden and like Peter, we too need to
be rebuked if we glory in anything but Christ's cross: the
cross Jesus has chosen to carry for us, and the one he asks
us to carry following him.

FREDERICK SCHUMACHER

Lord, help us to glory in our cross. Amen

Prayer concern: Clergy

Daily Reflections_____

_____

_____

_____

Freedom Indeed

So if the Son sets you free, you will be free indeed.
❖ John 8:36 (NIV)

Much oratory and propaganda are employed today to convince people that freedom is achieved by force and violence. When the tragic events are over, the freedom won is both restricted and artificial. Christ taught us that only when the Son makes us free are we "free indeed." Even the dispossessed and politically enslaved are truly free if they are Christ's. If not, they are really slaves even in the most self-sufficient "free society."

Let it be our prayer, that all nations may attain that freedom.

OSCAR A. BENSON

Source of all blessings, make us thankful for the freedoms we enjoy and for your servants who helped establish them. Teach us to seek always the "liberty of the children of God," which frees from every bondage, in the Redeemer's name. Amen

Prayer concern: Christians in Russia

Daily Reflections

Feeding the Hungry

They ate and were filled. ❖ Mark 8:8 (NRSV)

The miracles of feeding the 4,000 takes on new meaning for our day. A study of the account in Mark will show the similarities.

The number: "The multitude being very great." To the disciples four thousand was a great number! Today, the multitude of hungry people is indeed very great. Not merely 4,000 but even more than 4,000 times 4,000.

The condition: Having nothing to eat. The world is hungry. Babies are crying for food. Children's stomachs are distended, their limbs are spindly. Disease seizes the undernourished bodies. Death by starvation today is a common occurrence.

The concern: Who cares but Jesus? "I have compassion on the multitude." No one else does. A current magazine carries a full-page picture of a child lying dead on the pavement, a victim of starvation, and the people walking on unconcerned!

The solution: "He took bread and gave it to his discipline to set before them." Christ will feed the hungry through us.

ANONYMOUS

Lord of the living harvest, as you fed the multitude of old through your disciples, use us today to share our daily bread with the hungry, through Christ our Lord. Amen

Prayer concern: Those who work in agriculture

Daily Reflections_____

How Are We Ready?

You also must be ready, because the Son of Man
will come at an hour when you do not expect him.
❖ Luke 12:40 (NIV)

The ancient slogan reads: "BE ready; you cannot get ready!"
The five virgins were caught unprepared. No one knows
when his or her hour comes or when the hour comes for this
our world.

Let it be established that we must be ready. The question
is this: How are we to be ready? The answers are many. Some
voices stress that we must make a one-time, decisive, willful,
and verbal commitment to God. Others emphasize the daily
renewal of mind and spirit.

Is the readiness one of human achievement, however?
Has God not readied us by his act in Jesus Christ? Has he not
given us the privilege of participating in this readiness
through our baptism? Is readiness not the trust that our
baptismal life is real? If readiness means instant alertness,
I should despair. If it means baptismal grace, I shall hope.

JOHANNES H. U. KNUDSEN

*O God of our covenant in Jesus Christ, give us grace to
live in the covenant, so that our lives are ever yours.
Help us also to trust, so that whatever may come to us,
we can rest secure in that covenant, forever and ever!
Amen*

Prayer concern: That we are always ready

Daily Reflections_____

From a Fence ...

"What shall I do, Lord?" I asked. ❖ Acts 22:10a (NIV)

A young man serving in the Peace Corps received news one day that the father of one of his friends had died. Many were the visits he had made to this man's farm as a young boy. A flood of happy memories were loosed by the sad news.

That evening he sat down and wrote a letter to the bereaved family, recalling some of the incidents of earlier days. Among them, this one: "I shall never forget the day when I sat on the fence watching the men driving a herd of cattle into a corral. Some of them were being obstinate, and the herd was about to turn and break for the open field, when your father called out to me, 'Can't you see we need your help? Get off the fence and give us a hand!' It was a lesson I hope I shall never forget!"

The kingdom of God has never included fence-sitters. It belongs to the person who not only says, "What shall I do, Lord?" but also, "Here am I, send me!"

A. EJNAR FARSTRUP

Lord, overcome my hesitancies and my rationalizations for not heeding your call with joy and abandon! Amen

Prayer concern: Those who struggle with greed

Daily Reflections_____

_____

_____

_____

Magnificat

My spirit rejoices in God my Savior. ❖ Luke 1:47 (NIV)

Mary was probably quite young, with little education, humble, and devoted to the God of her ancestors when one day she was told that she would be the mother of the Messiah.

Try to put yourself in Mary's place. What do you think your reaction would have been? Inwardly excited but outwardly calm? Thinking, "As you will, Lord" or "This is a wild dream, am impossible fantasy"? Would you dismiss the thought and forget it?

Perhaps this is an impossible exercise, trying to stand in Mary's shoes. One thing is certain: Mary's reaction was a truly lovely thing.

Later, her lyrical outpouring of feelings (Luke says it was in Elizabeth's house) lifts us directly into her exalted frame of mind. Read her song in the text. Now can you put yourself in her place?

I can—almost. In special ways God has looked graciously on me, too. He has done great things for me, keeping for me his ancient promise to Abraham. I have known his strength, and his grace is my greatest blessing.

GERTRUDE VOGELEY

With all my heart I praise and thank you, Lord. Amen

Prayer concern: Christians in Sweden

Daily Reflections

How to Get What You Want

> You want something but don't get it. You kill and
> covet, but you cannot have what you want. You
> quarrel and fight. You do not have, because you
> do not ask God. ❖ James 4:2 (NIV)

According to a popular expression, "If you want something
enough, you will do anything to get it." Is that true? James
says it is. If you really want something, you may even kill
someone to get it. A youth kills his mother to get money out
of her apron pocket to buy a bicycle. A general assassinates
his king that he may succeed to the throne. A nation wanting
more access-to-the-sea, goes to war to get it.

That is a fact of life, but what is the solution? James says
there is no need to kill and fight to get what you want. The
answer for your desires is prayer. Ask God and he will
provide. God may not fulfill all your desires, but God will
supply all your needs.

Should you desire what you desire? If it is an appropriate
and legitimate desire, prayer will fulfill it. It is time to ask
yourself the basic question, "What do I want out of life?"

JOHN R. BROKHOFF

*Dear God, before I try to get what I want by foul means,
help me to desire only those things that you will through
prayer. For your Son's sake. Amen*

Prayer concern: Those who struggle with desire

Daily Reflections_____
_____
_____
_____

Day 61 ❖ Psalm 25:15-16

Eyes in One Direction

My eyes are ever on the LORD, for only he will release
my feet from the snare. ❖ Psalm 25:15 (NIV)

Some sights draw our eyes like magnets. With appreciation
we say, "I can't take my eyes off of it." Maybe it's lovely
Mount Shasta reaching into billowy clouds, a magnificent
painting, or that youngster romping around the living room
floor.

When the psalmist refers to eyes, he is speaking of more
than visual images. For him, the eye is a symbol of our
deepest being. So eyes in a direction indicate the direction of
our hopes, longings, and loyalties. The psalmist makes it very
clear that his eyes are adjusted to one direction—to his Lord.

Eyes, however, have a way of being diverted. The driver of
a car "just took his eyes off the road for an instant," and ran
into the ditch.

When our eyes are diverted, God calls us back. He plucks
us out of the mire of our follies. Knowing this, we strive
diligently to keep our eyes toward the Lord.

LAWRENCE M. REESE

*O God, whose eyes are ever on us, direct our eyes to you.
If we falter, call us back. Should we be preoccupied, alert
us to the source of our destiny. In the name of Christ we
pray. Amen*

Prayer concern: Those who feel their faith faltering

Daily Reflections_____

One in Christ

There is neither Jew nor Greek, slave nor free, male nor female, for you are all one in Christ Jesus. ❖ Galatians 3:28 (NIV)

God created all people and in that act made them one. Having one creator, we were meant to be one family. And that is not all. One redeemer has saved us. Jesus did not look at our skins, first, or our nationality, or our sex. We all looked the same to him. Beneath our surface differences he saw our captivity, our fears, our loneliness, and our need. The things that bound us together in our sin and helplessness were much stronger than any minor variations that separated us. It is still truer now since we have been rescued and forgiven.

What does it mean to be one in Christ Jesus? It means that as we come closer to him we also come closer to every human being who approaches him from any direction. In his presence, in his church, we must gladly link arms and hearts with all. If we rebuff a single one, we lose him too, for he will not let my brother go.

FRANKLIN CLARK FRY

Blind me, O Lord, to the little differences among people that have looked so big to me. Wash out of my mouth all disdainful names that I have called my brother or sister. Cut down all pride that makes me feel superior to any one whom you have redeemed. Amen

Prayer concern: Equality and justice

Daily Reflections_____

To Whom Do You Belong?

Give to Caesar what is Caesar's, and to God what is God's. ❖ Matthew 22:21 (NIV)

My books belong to me; they bear my name and were purchased by me. My car belongs to me for the same reasons. Look around your house and see how many things can be said to be yours.

Our Lord was once questioned by some opponents who wished to trap him. They asked if one should pay taxes. They were sure that no matter how he answered, they could cause trouble. If he said, "Yes," then it would seem to other Jews that he was a traitor who supported the Roman soldiers; if he said, "No," then he could be reported to the same Romans as a revolutionary. But our Lord turned the question around and taught them a lesson about ownership.

The coin they showed him had on it the mark, the image of Caesar, the Roman ruler, similar to the way our coins are marked by former leaders in our nation.

What is it that belongs to God? We do. For we have the image of God from creation and in addition he has redeemed or purchased us in our Lord Christ. For these two reasons then we are his, created in his image and redemption. We bear the stamp of our maker and are his.

CHARLES S. ANDERSON

O Lord, you made us for yourself and our hearts are restless until they find their rest in you. Amen

Prayer concern: Church leaders

Daily Reflections

A Deeper Peace

. . . for the Most High himself will establish it.
❖ Psalm 87:5b (NRSV)

"Surely," we think, "if I could just get that job, everything
would be fine. Then I could do all of the things I have been
looking forward to doing." Or some of us might be saying to
ourselves, "When I get my degree, then I can establish my
life and get going." We might also be feeling this way if we
are looking for a new residence and are getting ready to
move—that once we have moved and are settled in, then we
can establish ourselves and our lives.

But God reaches into our lives and establishes us in a
peace that does not depend on outward appearances! We may
be in the midst of change or turmoil, and we may not know
what will happen next in our lives; but when God establishes
us, we can rest our hearts in his peace, knowing that God is
leading us on and that all will be well.

JANICE TOBIE

*Creator God, help us to turn to you and to trust that,
when you establish our hearts, we will have the peace
that does not need to know what will happen next, but
can be at rest in you at all times and in all circumstances. In Jesus' name. Amen*

Prayer concern: Those experiencing life transitions

Daily Reflections

Born Anew

A city on a hill cannot be hidden.
❖ Matthew 5:14b (NIV)

At the time of this writing, Ruth is almost 91 years young. She is stooped and laboriously uses her walker. Her mind, however, is alert, as one soon discovers. Ruth has been a Christian all her life and intends to stay that way.

Wednesdays are filled to the brim. 9:30 A.M.—Bible study; 10:30 A.M.—help in the library until senior-citizen luncheon, and then it's time for more responsibilities in the afternoon.

On Saturday mornings Ruth has store hour—Christ Store Hour, that is—for the children in her apartment building. She would love to stand high on a hill and shout, "Save the children for Christ now, or you will lose them." The love of her live has been children.

Ruth has been a teacher, a librarian, a wife, and a mother. She has tasted life to the fullest, she says, because she has always been freshly "born again." Each morning of her life she is born anew to Christ!

BETTY LAWRENCE

Father, thank you for the Ruths of this world, for there are many. Help us all to give of ourselves in whatever small ways we can. We can't attain perfection, because we are sinful creatures; but, if we put our feet on the right track, you will help us. Amen

Prayer concern: Teachers and school board members

Daily Reflections

Hidden Glory

Zion hears and rejoices and the villages of Judah
are glad because of your judgments, O Lord.
❖ Psalm 97:8 (NIV)

We do not know the day or the hour, but a time is coming
when the heavens will proclaim the righteousness of God and
all people will behold God's glory. For those who see with the
eyes of faith, that day has already come—we recognize God's
majesty in the dingy manger. The wise men knew the
meaning of the star, even though few other people even
looked up at the sky on that holy night.

God did not come into the world the way people expected
him to arrive. Yet seeing the glory of God in this humility
leads us to rejoice. He may not order our lives the way we
expect him to—or the way we would like him to. Yet with the
eyes of faith we may see him at work in our lives in small,
unpredictable ways: in a small word of encouragement or
reproof; in a tedious or a satisfying task; in a large
disappointment or in a small success.

EDWARD W. UTHE

*We thank you, O Lord God, that you have granted to us
the eyes of faith; that you have enabled us to behold your
glory in your Son, Jesus Christ. Open your eyes that we
may see your work in our lives today; through the same
Jesus Christ, our Lord. Amen*

Prayer concern: Those who bear witness to Christ

Daily Reflections

A Lesson from Hardship

Consider him who endured such opposition from sinful men, so that you will not grow weary and lose heart. ❖ Hebrews 12:3 (NIV)

Most parents work hard to provide for their children a life as good as or better that they life they have had. Our parents or grandparents may have left a homeland across the ocean because they saw the possibilities for a better life in North America, both for themselves and for their children.

There's nothing wrong with wanting life to be "good" or in working hard to make it that way. But life does include suffering, pain, and hardship. Few, if any, of us escape this common lot of humanity.

The Bible is concerned with human suffering; the Bible pictures for us what God has done and continues to do about suffering because of his concern for us.

But in our lesson for today we are reminded that sometimes Christian people suffer because they are believers. If that happens they are to see that such an experience can be for good. It can draw a believer closer to God. That makes any hardship an experience of grace.

SIDNEY A. RAND

Lord God, teach us to learn from life the lessons which you are seeking to teach us. Amen

Prayer concern: Children in need

Daily Reflections_____
_____
_____
_____

Silence Isn't Golden

Announce this with shouts of joy and
proclaim it. Send it out to the ends of the
earth. ❖ Isaiah 48:20b (NIV)

Good news can't be kept! When something good happens to us, we've just got to tell someone about it. Here the prophet's aim is that the people called Israel should become a nation proclaiming the wonders and the miracles of their God to all the world. What was that wonder and that miracle? That they had been captive and that God had brought them to freedom. In grateful response, one must then proclaim God's grace.

Because of Easter, we also have news of a miracle to proclaim. If the prophet could call for mission zeal about what God had done for Israel, imagine how much more must we proclaim with mission zeal what God has done for us! God has delivered us from sin, death, and the devil! God has given us the forgiveness of sins and eternal life! Have you told anyone lately about this gift of yours?

DONALD H. HEIST

God of grace, who does wondrous things: grant us grace that we may never keep silent about those things that you have done for us. Give us courage, strength, power, and boldness to proclaim the miracle of life in Jesus' name. Amen

Prayer concern: Those who proclaim Christ

Daily Reflections_____

Day 69 ❖ Luke 4:23-30

Jesus the Powerful

But he walked right through the crowd and went
on his way. ❖ Luke 4:30 (NIV)

With this clear, short verse, Luke demonstrates to people of
all ages the power and majesty of our Lord Jesus Christ.
Jesus was attacked by his own townsmen. He did not meet
their attack with anger or physical power. Rather, he simply
passed through the midst of them and went his way.

Even though the people hated him no one dared to
interfere with his leaving. Either they sensed his divinity or
they were restrained by his divine power. His hour had not
yet come.

In Jesus Christ we find power. This is the power in which
our faith must be grounded. As Martin Luther put it, it is in
Christ that we find the power to overcome "the devil and all
his works and all his ways." Through Jesus we witness the
power of the cross and the power of the empty tomb. It is
through the suffering and death of Jesus Christ that we find
the power and assurance of eternal life. In Jesus we find the
power to do our daily tasks. And it is through daily prayer and
worship that we renew our faith in the power of Jesus.

JAMES KALLAS

Dear Lord Jesus, give us power to do your will. Amen

Prayer concern: Those in need of hope and assurance

Daily Reflections

Consider Jesus

Therefore, brothers and sisters, holy partners
in a heavenly calling, consider that Jesus . . .
was faithful to the one who appointed him.
❖ Hebrews 3:1-2 (NRSV)

Make no mistake, the writer of Hebrews knew what be believed! And he was sure that what he believer is all we need today. Christianity, he says, is everything. Accept Christ; and willingly love and obey him. What else important is there? God in Christ suffered and died for our sins *then*. But we can enjoy the *present* miracle of his forgiving love.

Yes, we are invited to share in a heavenly call. God seeks us. God wants us to accept his love in Christ. God calls us through his word, through Christian people, through his activity in history and in nature. "God is love . . . he gave his Son." That's God's part. But we should believe, and give ourselves to him. That's our part. Then follows the greatest miracle of all: God's Spirit lives in us; forgiving, strengthening, cleansing, giving purpose, and guiding.

"Therefore, . . . consider that Jesus." Of course! Who else?

JAMES L. KEYSER

Lord Jesus Christ, we want to consider you, and give you first place in our lives. But so many things crowd you out. Forgive us for not wanting you enough to put you first and thus allow you to crowd them out. Amen

Prayer concern: Widows and widowers

Daily Reflections_____

The Right Words

The LORD God has given me the tongue of a teacher, that I may know how to sustain the weary with a word. ❖ Isaiah 50:4 (NRSV)

Some people say that talk is cheap. Others consider a person's word just as a binding as his or her signature on a legal document. Sometimes the right words can be hard to find, especially when we long to comfort a friend.

Today's Bible reading gives us encouragement as we search for the right words. Listening first to God is the key. Morning by morning we seek God—and God, in turn, opens our ears and teaches us. What a wonder! The God who created the universe and everything in it waits for a special time of closeness and communion with each of us every day.

When we take time to listen to God through the scriptures and prayer, we hear the right words—the words of comfort or challenge or encouragement we need for that day. And we also discover the right words to share with others. These words are not pious platitudes or easy answers to life's struggles; they are truths that remain constant regardless of what life hands us. God loves you. Jesus died for you. You are forgiven. You are safe in the palm of his hand.

JANICE KERPER BRAUER

Jesus, thank you for telling me the words I need to hear. Amen

Prayer concern: Those who need encouragement

Daily Reflections_____

One Flesh

"The two will become one flesh." So they are no longer two, but one. ❖ Mark 10:8 (NIV)

In Jesus' day, marriage was a patriarchal institution. Women left their homes and families to continue men's family lines and to preserve their property. It is in this context that Jesus acknowledges the necessity of divorce. Jesus said that Moses commanded divorce when men had a "hardness of heart" and exerted power over women.

Jesus tells us that this is not what God intended in creation. "From the beginning God made them male and female" (Genesis 1:27). "For this reason a man shall leave his father and mother and be joined to his wife" (Genesis 2:24). In marriage, men are to leave old ways of life behind them and are to create a new life together in God.

God created marriage to be a blessing for both men and women. Marriage is a relationship in which God's love might be reflected.

JANET M. CORPUS

Dear Lord, we are so used to the way in which we have remade your world that it is sometimes hard to believe and trust in your plan, which is so different from our own. Teach us your way and give us the courage to follow together in love. Amen

Prayer concern: Couples that are experiencing troubled marriages

Daily Reflections_____

_____

_____

_____

Honor

These people honor me with their lips, but their
hearts are far from me. ❖ Matthew 15:8 (NIV)

Honor is a jewel with facets of "beauty," "majesty,"
"preciousness" and "weighty-ness." The actual word that
Jesus used as honor would be the implication of weighty in
contrast to light or insignificant. When we give honor, we
place great weight on people we respect because of their
character or achievements. Our Lord was frequently crowned
with verbal honors of beauty, majesty, preciousness, or
weighty-ness, but in some of them he detected a mere lip
service. Honorable words call for honorable actions. It is not
difficult to live these professions of faith and respect. Words
can scarcely have meaning when denied by life. The prophets
Amos and Isaiah demeaned assemblies and holy days that
were a compensation for dishonest living and more in-
difference.

GEORGE P. BERNARD

*Let the words of my mouth and the meditation of my
heart be acceptable in your sight, O Lord, my rock and
my redeemer. Amen*

Prayer concern: Those contemplating marriage

Daily Reflections_____

Christian Unity

For it is with your heart that you believe and are justified, and it is with your mouth that you confess and are saved. ❖ Romans 10:10 (NIV)

No man lives to himself, says the New Testament. It is just as impossible for churches to live to themselves, and wrong of them to try. No Christian communion that clings to Christ can want to tear loose from the company of all other believers in him, and build a high wall around itself. Christian isolationism is not only a contradiction of terms, it is a danger signal.

Having the gospel involves an obligation to share the gospel. One thing is sure, the Holy Spirit did not give us this treasure of the church simply for us to hug it to ourselves and hoard it. We are to publish it with out mouths, compare our beliefs with others without fear, and submit everything to the final test of God's word. Churches, like Christians, are not to hide the light of truth under a bushel basket but instead put it on a candlestick in the midst of the house.

FRANKLIN CLARK FRY

O Christ, who prayed to your Father that those whom he had given to you might be one, make us ever to be one in love, increasingly one in faith, and ultimately one with all our fellow Christians even in outward appearance before the world. Amen

Prayer concern: Christian unity

Daily Reflections_____

_____

_____

_____

Day 75 ❖ Mark 13:5-13

The Gospel First

The good news must first be proclaimed to all
nations. ❖ Mark 13:10 (NRSV)

If you asked your friends and neighbors what is the most
important task facing us today, what do you think most of
them would say? Would any of them say that the preaching of
the gospel to all people should be at the top of the list?

Even Christians seem these days to have accepted the
evaluation placed on life by newscasters and other self-
designated authorities. Perhaps this is the reason for Jesus'
repeated stressing of the *firstness* of Christian evaluations.
See first the kingdom of God and God's righteousness. This
is top priority for the Christian. Therefore, we need to re-
examine all of our personal priority lists and see whether we
are putting first things first, or last.

Jesus here is describing the trials and sufferings that his
followers will see. At the same time, he is giving them a clear
statement of their responsibility under stress. The gospel
must be preached.

TERRANCE Y. MULLINS

*Dear Lord, set in my heart your word of burning truth to
lead me out of blindness to your light. Amen*

Prayer concern: Those you meet today

Daily Reflections_____
_____
_____
_____

Christian Giving

> But when you give to the needy, do not let your
> left hand know what your right hand is doing.
> ❖ Matthew 6:3 (NIV)

When some people give generously to others, they expect to receive much gratitude as a reward. If they do not get it, they feel cheated.

A Christian, however, should not give for the sake of any reward. We give because our neighbor needs something and we have it to give. That's the end of the matter, as far as Christians are concerned. We hope that our neighbors will be grateful, and will show it some day by giving to some other neighbors who is in need. But true love doesn't keep any books. We forgive the sins of others against us because God has forgiven our sins. We give to our neighbors because God gives to us.

Sometimes people who are the most generous are also the most painful. They seem to be trying to prove what good people they are. That spoils everything. There is always some risk in service to others. It may not produce any results. But we take that chance, because God takes such a change in giving to us.

G. ELSON RUFF

*Lord, you so loved the world that you gave your only.
Teach us to respond to your love by loving our neighbor.
Amen*

Prayer concern: Economic justice

Daily Reflections_____

_____

_____

_____

Day 77 ❖ John 14:15-19

God Is Love

I will not leave you as orphans; I will come to you.
❖ John 14:18 (NIV)

Prometheus was the tragic Greek hero found guilty of stealing fire from the gods and bringing it to earth. He was swiftly punished by these angry, revengeful deities.

The deities of Greek mythology were not like our God. In Greek mythology, many people had to steal things they wanted, or discover some way of wheedling what they desired from their reluctant gods.

We speak of "stealing" a few minutes of peace and happiness. Sometimes we feel that we must wrestle good things from our God. Occasionally we even dare to think we can get things from God conniving. But it's not this way really. God may give us crosses to bear. Jesus tells us we will have tribulation. But he also tells us that God is kind and loving, generous and good. God will not forsake us. God is always ready with his words of infinite tenderness.

ROBERT BLAIR RUBLE

Almighty, everlasting God, help us to have always a devout will toward you, and to serve your Majesty with a pure heart; through your Son, Jesus Christ our Lord. Amen

Prayer concern: Those who are feeling sorry for themselves

Daily Reflections_____

Back on the Right Track

For the Son of Man came to seek out and to save the lost. ❖ Luke 19:10 (NRSV)

Saints are simply "found" sinners. Zacchaeus had been lost for a long time. Cut off from his own people, he had strayed further and further from the true God. Zacchaeus had begun to think that God didn't care about him at all.

The crowd was convinced of it. Surely God's Anointed would someday come on a "search-and-destroy" mission, finding the sinners and eliminating them. Tax collectors ought to be number one on the list!

Jesus was more interested in restoration than destruction. He saw Zacchaeus as "a sheep of his own fold, a lamb of his own flock, a sinner to be redeemed."

God's love in Jesus Christ is the path to lead any sinner home.

DAVID W. CLARK

Redeemer, thank you for bringing us home again. May we learn to share your zeal for saving the lost, by which we have already benefited. Help us follow Zacchaeus's example. Amen

Prayer concern: Those struggling with their faith

Daily Reflections

Fear

My times are in your hand. ❖ Psalm 31:15 (NRSV)

Cancer! The dreaded diagnosis came to my husband for the second time in two years, meaning surgery this time, with extensive treatment to follow. He would not work for months. Since I have a disability, he is our chief breadwinner. As with countless others who receive the same diagnosis, I reacted with fear: "How will we make it this time, Lord?"

When fear nags, tempting me to doubt that my faith is valid, it helps to recall great people of the Bible who shared the same emotion. Moses and Elijah, for example, were afraid when God spoke to them. Mary too was frightened when the angel Gabriel spoke to her.

Even Jesus, God incarnate, prayed, "If you are willing, remove this cup," when agonizing in Gethsemane" (Luke 22:42). The human Christ dreaded what he faced, so he understands when we are afraid. It helps, too, that the psalmist reminds us that our times surely are in God's hands.

ISABELLE GILTANEN SMITH

Thank you, Lord, for understanding our fear and for your promise to be always with us. Thank you for life in Jesus. Amen

Prayer concern: Those with cancer

Daily Reflections_____

_____

_____

Who Really Is a Sinner?

He replied, "Whether he is a sinner or not, I don't
know. One thing I do know. I was blind but now
I see!" ❖ John 9:25 (NIV)

Some people thought Jesus was a sinner. They were certain
that he was not from God because he did not keep the
Sabbath. They said that Jesus disobeyed God's law, so
therefore Jesus was not on God's side.

But the man who had received his sight from Jesus had
quite a different perspective. When asked what he had to say
about Jesus, this man said he thought Jesus was a prophet.
(verse 25). And his answer came from his experience. "When
he is a sinner or not, I don't know. One thing I do know. I was
blind but now I see!"

The incident suggests two things. First, that it is possible
for us to try to define too precisely just who the real sinners
are. We are warned about this danger. Second, that Jesus
constantly escapes the descriptions we have made. Our
expectation of the way God works does not limit the way God
works.

PHILIP A. QUANBECK

*Lord our God, keep us open and awake to the character
of your presence. Help us not to limit your presence to
our expectations. Amen*

Prayer concern: Being judgmental

Daily Reflections_____
_____
_____
_____

Give God the Glory

Immediately, because Herod did not give praise to
God, an angel of the Lord struck him down, and he
was eaten by worms and died. ❖ Acts 12:23 (NIV)

Herod Agrippa, ruler of Palestine, sought to win favor by
persecuting the early Christians. He killed James, the brother
of John, with the sword. He arrested Peter and cast him into
prison, but the angel of the Lord delivered the apostle.

Proud, ambitious and self-seeking, Herod was angered by
this divine intervention. He went to his palace in Caesarea
where, resplendent in his royal robes, he addressed the
people. Here the angel of the Lord smote him. He was the
victim of his own life of luxury and self-indulgence.

God is ever on the side of right. God still protects his own.
When we achieve success, when we come out of disaster
unscathed, when health and happiness are our portion, let us
humbly and gratefully give God the glory. Our lives are in
God's hand.

JOHN F. HARKINS

*Eternal God, you created us, sustained us, and redeemed
us that we might grow into your likeness. Forgive us
when we selfishly seek to fulfill our own worldly desires
and make us humble, obedient servants of yours, through
Jesus Christ, our Lord. Amen*

Prayer concern: Christians in Jordan

Daily Reflections_____

_____

_____

_____

Philip: Faith Is God's Gift

We have found the one Moses wrote about in the Law, and about whom the prophets also wrote—Jesus of Nazareth, the son of Joseph. ❖ John 1:45 (NIV)

There's a great temptation for Christians to claim the discovery of their faith as their own. "I Found It!" proclaims a bumper sticker popular with some Christians. They delight in relating the day they made the decision to follow Jesus as Lord.

Telling others about our faith is logical consequence of our faith. Yet we must be careful not to create the wrong impression.

Jesus first found Philip. Then Philip told Nathanael. We are found by the Lord first. He makes his decision for us. "I believe that I cannot by my own reason or strength believe . . ." writes Martin Luther in *The Small Catechism*.

Faith is not our discovery. It is God's gift to us, so that we might know him and share the miracle of his love with others.

BARRY L. RALPH

God our Father, keep us from boasting about our faith. Help us to acknowledge it as your gift to us. Fill our hearts with such gratitude for your gift of faith that we cannot help but tell others that your Son is our Savior, Jesus Christ our Lord. Amen

Prayer concern: Elementary students

Daily Reflections_____

_____

_____

_____

Grace Sufficient

So we rebuilt the wall till all of it reached half its height, for the people worked with all their heart.
❖ Nehemiah 4:6 (NIV)

What a dismal sight greeted the Israelites as they returned from captivity. The walls of Jerusalem were a mass of rubble; Solomon's temple had been destroyed. But under Nehemiah, they set to work to restore things. Immediately their enemies got busy to prevent the walls from being built. However, by prayer, organization, and zeal, they were able to continue. As the Bible account tells us, "the people worked with all their heart."

Much in life depends on our will to do certain things. This fact of history is also an allegory of a great spiritual truth. When we would be good or do good, Satan is always ready to thwart our plans, as he tried in the wilderness to thwart Christ's plans. If we really want to grow in grace, we need to pray, ever being on the alert against temptation, with a mind made up to fight it. In prayer, we shall find the grace of God will be sufficient to give us victory.

HENRY W. SNYDER

O God, give us the needed faith, and by your grace grant that we may win the victory. Amen

Prayer concern: Those who build in Christ's name

Daily Reflections_____
_____
_____
_____

By the Power of the Spirit

I am sending you out like sheep into the midst of wolves; so be wise as serpents and innocent as doves. ❖ Matthew 10:16 (NRSV)

In the book of Genesis the serpent is the most malevolent and, in its own crafty way, the wisest of wild creatures. In the Gospels, the dove is the symbol of innocence and peace, and of the Holy Spirit. Throughout the Bible, the sheep illustrate our utter dependence on God.

Jesus invites us to trust him as sheep trust their shepherd in a world filled with ruthless people. Jesus bid us use for right purposes the wisdom that serpents poison and dishonest stewards abuse. We are not to bite back or fight poison with poison, because that way of preserving our religion would make us as snaky as the thing we fight. As wise and fearless stewards of our resources for meeting the world's opposition, we are to pray for, feed, and forgive our enemies, never hurting but always healing. For this task we have the power of the Spirit of Jesus.

RAYMOND T. STAMM

God, help us to bear the troubles and testings which lie before us that we may be true followers of your Spirit. Give us patience and perseverance lest we grow weary and fainthearted. Let us ever remember how Jesus endured the cross for us. Amen

Prayer concern: Our enemies

Daily Reflections

A Supernatural Love

I tell you: Love your enemies and pray for those
who persecute you. ❖ Matthew 5:44 (NIV)

I don't think I have any enemies as such, yet I could name
people who cause me hurt, discomfort, or strife:

- ❖ The one who makes me feel like an adolescent.
- ❖ The one who knows what words cut deepest.
- ❖ The one who got "my" promotion.
- ❖ The one who puts me down in front of others.
- ❖ The one who always fails to recognize me.
- ❖ The one who purposely misunderstands me.
- ❖ The one who "stole" my best friend.
- ❖ The one who laughs at my misfortunes.
- ❖ The one who gossips about me.
- ❖ The one who takes advantage of my trust.
- ❖ The one who causes the loss of a loved one.

All these are to be recipients of my love and my prayers.
I'm to work actively for their good. It sounds impossible, yet
it is what the Lord commands. I know that since God
commands it, God will empower me to do it. I wouldn't be
surprised if the Lord gave me joy in the process!

EILEEN POLLINGER

*Lord, teach me to love my enemies and show me how to
pray for those who persecute me. Amen*

Prayer concern: Christians in Indonesia

Daily Reflections_____

_____

_____

_____

What a Wonderful God!

From you comes my praise in the great congregation. ❖ Psalm 22:25a (NRSV)

We have a lot of trees in our backyard, and they have attracted quite a "congregation" of birds. Early in the morning, they fill the air with the sweet melody of their voices. The various kinds of birds offer different melodies. But it is God who puts the song into each, and from each the melody is an offering of praise to God. It's their way of saying, "Look what a wonderful God we have!"

The psalmist, too, offered a song of praise. He confessed that it came from God. "From you comes my praise." It was God who had reached down and delivered him from the despair expressed in the earlier verses, and then it was God who had put a song of praise in his mouth.

Let's take a lesson. If we confess to God our abject need for his help, he can turn on the full extent of his power for us. And what's more, he will enable us to say, "Look what a wonderful God we have!"

PAUL T. DAUNENFELDT

O wonderful Lord and God, I have so many things for which to praise you, but I confess I don't always know how to go about it. Open my lips, so that I can tell everyone what a wonderful God you are! Amen

Prayer concern: The word *praise*

Daily Reflections_____

_____

_____

_____

As Water Wears Away Granite

I will do what you have asked. I will give you a wise and discerning heart, so that there will never have been anyone like you, nor will there ever be. ❖ 1 Kings 3:12 (NIV)

In his book *Adventure of Ideas*, Alfred North Whitehead presented us with a history of all the creative ideas which have influenced human culture. He concluded that the most powerful and triumphant idea that won over all others in Western civilization was that of the love taught by Jesus Christ. The love of the gentle Galilean won over the barbarous countenance like water which wears away granite over a period of centuries.

At its best the church has always encouraged education. The roots of the church's emphasis on education go back to the time of the Old Testament. The psalmist wrote that the fear of the Lord was the beginning of wisdom. Once a child was trained in the ways of the Lord he would not depart from them. Solomon prayed for wisdom so that he could be a leader who would lead his people into that which was good for them. (1 Kings 3:10-14).

HAROLD H. ZIETLOW

Almighty God, give to us and our children the wisdom to guide our lives in work which will be helpful to others and honor your name. Preserve among us and our descendants the saving truth of your love. Amen

Prayer concern: Philosophers and theologians

Daily Reflections_____
_____
_____
_____

What Is Love?

Whoever does not love does not know God,
because God is love. ❖ 1 John 4:8 (NIV)

This familiar word *love* can mean many things. A man says, "I just love apple pie," and uses the same word when describing his feelings toward his dog, his family, his job, and God. The Greeks had a good system when they used four different words to describe the various aspects of love. But in English we are bound to one word, and if we are to know what that one word means, we have to take our cue from God.

God's love is not dew on the roses but rather it is a bloody sweat. It is the lasting and winning power that was focused clearly on the cross. It is the cornerstone of faith. In Paul's famous "love" chapter, 1 Corinthians 13, you can learn about the nature of God's love by substituting the word *Christ* for the word *love*. Try it. Christ is patient, kind. So are faith and hope—but the greatest of these is Christ.

EDGAR R. TREXLER

Love divine, all loves excelling, joy of heaven to earth come down. Fix in us your humble dwelling, all your faithful mercies crown. Jesus, you are all compassion, pure unbounded love you are; visit us with your salvation, enter every trembling heart. Amen

Prayer concern: Those persecuted for Christ's sake

Daily Reflections_____

Two Modes of Life

The mind of sinful man is death, but the mind controlled by the Spirit is life and peace.
❖ Romans 8:6 (NIV)

There are people who doubt that the Christian faith really makes any distinctive differences in our society. They see little difference between the believer and the unbeliever. Far from brushing such criticism aside, we need to be willing to reappraise our mode of life. Do we celebrate the fact that God, in Christ, has sent us free, even from death, by actually relating faith and life to what Christianity proclaims?

How do we make our important decisions? Paul sees two diametrically opposed ways of life. One way centers around the interests of self; the other way is God-oriented and Spirit-guided. God confronts us with an either-or. Despite the fact that Paul says that following the impulses of nature results in death, we are tempted to play the game of life both ways.

ERNEST D. NIELSEN

Almighty God, we thank you for Christ Jesus who took upon himself our human nature. Help us in every way to set our minds on the Spirit. May we care for others in the right way. Set our priorities straight. Give us the joyous experience of seeing our task carried out. Amen

Prayer concern: The Spirit's guidance

Daily Reflections

Loans

Therefore I have lent him to the LORD; as long as he lives, he is given to the LORD. ❖ 1 Samuel 1:28 (NRSV)

Our lives are shaped in many ways by others—not only by our heroes, but also by those individuals who, day by day, show us love, kindness, and care.

Hannah certainly had an impact upon her son, Samuel. She had been childless, and had prayed to God that if she could have a child, she would dedicate that child to him. God was faithful to her petitions and she, in turn, was faithful to him. Without question, Hannah had instilled in Samuel a deep realization of God's presence, and had helped prepare him for future leadership of his people.

Hannah lent to God what God had lent her. Everything we are and have is a gift of God, lent to us for our use. Let us use our talents and gifts faithfully in God's service.

A. DONALD MAIN

Gracious God, we have been blessed in so many ways by Your lovingkindnesses. You have filled our lives with good things. Teach us to be better stewards of your gifts. Amen

Prayer concern: Teachers

Daily Reflections_____

_____

_____

_____

Wise and Honest Stewards

Whoever can be trusted with very little can also be trusted with much, and whoever is dishonest with very little will also be dishonest with much.
❖ Luke 16:10 (NIV)

A teacher told his class in plane geometry that he was willing to stay at the foot of the ladder to help others climb higher. A wise steward showed his classes how to live without bitterness and resentment in a world where few people have work that is altogether to their liking.

Because of competition aggravated by chronic un-employment, millions of people have little prospect of ever getting a better job. As a village carpenter, Jesus shows how to take the sting out of this exasperation by being faithful "with very little." By doing our work in such a way as to produce the fruit of his Spirit—"love, joy, peace, patience, kindness, goodness, faithfulness, gentleness, self-control"— we shall be wise stewards of "the true riches" which will be ours forever.

RAYMOND T. STAMM

Forgive us, Lord, for past failures to do our work in a way that will make it easier for our colleagues to believe in you. Show us the joy of creative living as we look not only to our own interests but also to the interests of others. Amen

Prayer concern: Christians in South Africa

Daily Reflections_____
_____
_____
_____

Lonely

Then he said to them, "My soul is overwhelmed with sorrow to the point of death. Stay here and keep watch with me." ❖ Matthew 26:38 (NIV)

Being lonely is not the same as being alone. We can be alone without feeling lonely; and we can feel lonely in a big, noisy crowd. When we are lonely, we feel sad and depressed, and our health often suffers. And this happens to any of us at any age. We feel misunderstood and we wonder what is wrong with us.

Nothing. God made us that way. We want love and acceptance, friendship and companionship. We want conversation and shared activities. The older we get, the more we miss friends no longer with us.

It helps to remember that Jesus felt the pain of loneliness. In Gethsemane he begged three favorite disciples to join him in prayer. And they slept!

When you are lonely, Jesus understands. He can be with you to comfort and reassure you, to share your concern. Pray, read favorite Bible passages, hymns, and devotional material. He will be with you.

HAROLD L. YOCHUM

Lord, help us find relief from loneliness; and help us comfort those who are lonely. Amen

Prayer concern: Those who are lonely

Daily Reflections_____

_____

_____

_____

The Lost Art of Praise

Ascribe to the LORD glory and strength.
❖ Psalm 96:7b (NIV)

In so many ways, offering praise to God seems to have become a lost art, even as worship has seemed to become a very human-centered experience. All too often worship is considered in a casual way. It is viewed in terms of "what you get out of it." Did it meet your needs? Was it too long? Were the hymns appealing? Was Jane Jones sitting next to that new boy again?

The tragedy of all this lies not in the recognition of the human elements of worship. They are there and always will be. It lies rather in missing the vital, exhilarating experience of praising the one true God who has revealed himself in Christ Jesus. He is the God who created the universe. He is the same God who speaks to us through the worship of his church. And while his love of us does not depend on our praising him, we can grow in his love only as we do.

DWIGHT A. HUSEMEN

Lord, may we declare our praise of you, your glory, your strength, and your power over heaven and earth. May our hymns of joy ring out through all creation as our worship finds it center and heart in you. Amen

Prayer concern: People who are homebound

Daily Reflections_____

_____

_____

_____

Day 94 ❖ Mark 10:46-52

Jesus Takes Time

> He began to shout . . . "Jesus, Son of David, have mercy on me!" Many sternly ordered him to be quiet. ❖ Mark 10:47-48 (NRSV)

There had been visitors in church that rainy Sunday morning. Folks smiled at them as they were leaving at the close of the service. But as the family prepared to drive away, they backed off the edge of the blacktop into some very soft mud. The car's rear wheels were buried. The husband got out and pushed. Mud sprayed everywhere, including on his suit. Other church members hurried to their cars. They had on their good clothes and had places to go for Sunday dinner. Stopping to help just did not fit in with their schedules. After several had passed by, one man stayed to help.

We do not like interruptions. The disciples did not either. They were on their way to Jerusalem where Jesus would be gloriously hailed with palm branches. But blind and poor Bartimaeus calls to stop them. He needs Jesus' help. The disciples tell him to be quiet. But Jesus, who cares more for the pain of others than for glory and honor, stops to heal him.

JEANETTE STRANDJORD

Thank you, God, for taking time for each of us. Help us to care for others in this same spirit of love. Amen

Prayer concern: People who are impatient

Daily Reflections_____
_____
_____
_____

A Helping Hand

Taking him by the right hand, he helped him up, and instantly the man's feet and ankles became strong. ❖ Acts 3:7 (NIV)

We can do many things with our hands. We can help up someone who has fallen or save a child from danger. If our hands are strong and callused as Peter's were, we can pull in a net filled with struggling fish.

Peter's hands came into contact with the divine hand of Jesus. One night Peter wanted to walk on the water and join the Lord, but in the weakness of his faith he began to sink. Immediately Jesus took him by the right hand and lifted him to safety.

When Peter saw this helpless man at the gate of the temple, he remembered the touch of Jesus' hand. So he took the man by the hand and, in the name of the Lord, raised him up a cured man who could walk and even leap for joy.

Our hands are very important. We can keep them clean. We can fold them in prayer. We can train them to become more skillful and obedient. We can use them daily in acts of Christian love. Through world missions we can even stretch our hands across the seas and reach others who may become fellow members in the kingdom of our Lord.

MILTON SCHRAM

For your sake, Lord, we assist and comfort others. Amen

Prayer concern: World missions

Daily Reflections

_____
_____
_____

Day 96 ❖ John 8:31-39

Truth

If you hold to my teaching, you are really my
disciples. Then you will know the truth, and the
truth will set you free. ❖ John 8:31-32 (NIV)

On many college campuses we see these words chiseled in
the stone over the entrance to one of the major buildings:
"The truth shall make you free." The word *truth* can have
different meanings for different people.

In education the pursuit of truth usually follows the
scientific method. In the sense that Jesus used the word, it
refers to the reality of God in the lives of people. When we
recognize our dependence upon God and accept God's grace
then we know this truth. The reality of God as the ultimate
truth is not incongruous with scientific truth.

We marvel at the great advances in science, with new
discoveries and new truths. Yet the ultimate truth of life
remains—the truth of our destiny that is meaningless apart
from God and the gospel of his Son, Jesus Christ. This truth
must be a part of our lives as Christians if we are to solve the
great problems of living in a world exploding in population
where people are in ever closer association because of
marvelous new means of communications and transportation.

ELWIN D. FARWELL

*Lord, guide us to bring about a better understanding
among people and nations. Amen*

Prayer concern: College faculties and administrators

Daily Reflections_____

_____

_____

Rules or Renewal?

Do not call anything impure that God has made
clean. ❖ Acts 10:15b (NIV)

In a sense, all Christians fall into one of two categories: those
who think Christ came to reinforce whatever religious rules
and proprieties they hold dear, and those who know he came
to renew all of life and overcome our divisive notions of
"clean" and "unclean," holy and profane, sacred and secular.

In today's text, we see Peter move from the first category
to the second: "Do not call anything impure that God has
made clean" is a message both to him and to us. Through
Christ, God has cleansed and renewed everything to be used
by us for our good and God's glory. In the Christian life, *all* of
life is renewed and fresh and full of divine possibilities. On
this new day, let us live as Christ's renewed people, affirming
the whole world as God's!

JACK. E. LINDQUIST

*O Christ, you are the Lord of all creation, of every aspect
of human life. May we never call common what you
have cleansed, but enjoy all things in service to you and
to the world you love. Amen*

Prayer concern: Young people

Daily Reflections

Go and Tell

Jesus replied, "Go back and report to John what
you hear and see." ❖ Matthew 11:4 (NIV)

Jesus testified that John the Baptist was great. John was
genuinely great. He was a man of God, and God's prophet.
But while John was great, he insisted emphatically that the
GREATER ONE was coming.

John did not point to himself; he pointed to the OTHER
ONE. When John saw Jesus coming, he pointed to him and
said, "Behold, the Lamb of God, who takes away the sin of
the world."

God revealed the great truth to John in a special way.
When John had baptized Jesus, the Father's voice was heard
from heaven saying, "This is my beloved Son, with whom I
am well pleased." John in turn said of Jesus, "And I have seen
and borne witness that this is the Son of God." John said that
HE IS THE ONE.

When John, though innocent, was lingering in prison his
faith evidently needed strengthening. John sent two disciples
of his to Jesus to ask, "Are you he who is to come?" The
evidence to which Jesus pointed reassured John.

EDGAR P. EBERT

*Convince us ever by your Word and Holy Spirit, dear
Father, that Jesus is the promised one. Amen*

Prayer concern: Those who long for rest

Daily Reflections_____

Above the Snake Line

> When he saw the crowds, he had compassion on
> them, because they were harassed and helpless, like
> sheep without a shepherd. ❖ Matthew 9:36 (NIV)

To drift aimlessly without purpose and without guidance is to
be in constant danger. Long ago some colonists were settling
in New England. They found a beautiful valley and were
about to build their homes there, when suddenly they
discovered that the ground was infested with poisonous
snakes. They dared not live there, that they knew! As they
plodded upward toward the plateau, they noted that the
snakes were fewer and fewer, until finally they reached a level
where the snakes were gone altogether. There they built
their homes, cleared the ground, and planted their crops.
They settled "above the snake line."

The Good Shepherd leads us through the pitfalls, beyond
the poison of warped values, to the still waters and the green
meadows. He knows the dangers we face. He helps us to
build our lives "above the snake line."

ALVIN ROGNESS

*Make us will, O Lord, to have you lead us, even when we
are lured by the false voice, that entice us away from you.
Amen*

Prayer concern: Christians in Nigeria

Daily Reflections_____

God's Endless Search

God looks . . . to see if there are any who understand, any who seek God. ❖ Psalm 53:2 (NIV)

God is constantly looking for those who seek him. God is
engaged in a constant search for those who love him.

But this psalmist is greatly discouraged. God feels that
many play the role of the fool who says, "There is no God."
The psalmist's pessimism, however, goes too far: "There is
none that does good, no, not one."

Such was the mood of Elijah in his cave when he was
being persecuted by King Ahab. In the depth of his despair,
Elijah felt that, "I, even I only, am left." But as it turned out,
there were 7,000 people in Israel who had not bowed their
knees to Baal! (1 Kings 19).

God is never without witnesses. There are always some
who try to trace God's footsteps in the paths of time and
history. Still others seek to discern God's purposes in the
journey of their lives. And there are still others who are
concerned about the way they can express God's will in their
relationship to their neighbor.

ALTON M. MOTTER

*Lord, we are truly thankful for those who seek to live out
their understanding of your will. Help us to understand
more clearly your will for our lives. And, above all, give
us the courage to do it. Amen*

Prayer concern: Those who bear witness

Daily Reflections_____

_____

_____

_____

Where Is the Lord?

The Israelites quarreled and tested the LORD, saying, "Is the LORD among us or not?" ❖ Exodus 17:7 (NRSV)

Where *was* God when that happened? How can God allow this to happen? You've heard these questions before, especially when people face great tragedy and unexpected violence. God's chosen people asked a similar question when they faced scorching thirst in the desert wilderness: Did God bring us out of Egypt just for us to die of thirst? Their leader, Moses, was beside himself with fear: "They are almost ready to come and stone me," he tells the Lord (verse 4).

Notice how God responds to the complaining—not with punishment but rather by using Moses to work a miracle. Water flows from a rock, and complaining turns into rejoicing.

In the midst of pain, tragedy, and uncertainty, we often are tempted to blame God and to curse our situation. Expressing grief or anger can be healthy and a necessary part of recovery, but it can get out of hand, especially if it blinds us to God's promise to be with us in the midst of tragedy. "Is God among us or not?" Because of Jesus the answer is always a resounding and comforting "Yes."

VICTORIA KIBLER

Dear God, thank you for being there when we need you. Comfort us in times of trouble. Amen

Prayer concern: Those enduring difficult times

Daily Reflections_____

_____

_____

_____

God's Symphony

The eyes of all look to you. ❖ Psalm 145:15 (NIV)

Watch a symphony orchestra. The musicians may be busy tuning up, talking to one another, or waiting quietly. But when the conductor steps on the podium and raps for attention, everyone looks up. Indeed the leader will not begin until he or she has the attention of all the players. Good music requires attention.

"The eyes of all look to you." That's a beautiful description of how we are to live in our relationship to God—eyes forward, intent on our conductor, our leader. It's easy to get distracted, easy to let our attention wander to petty and unimportant things. Too often Christians spend time with details and bicker over minor matters.

But if you would play in God's symphony, the order is simple and strict: Eyes to God; hands posed to follow his will. We are to seek first the kingdom of God and his righteousness. And the result will be beautiful music.

W. A. POOVEY

Lord, keep my eyes from the things of the world that distract me. Amen

Prayer concern: Musicians

Daily Reflections_____

_____

_____

Jacob Hung On

So Jacob called the place Peniel, saying, "It is
because I saw God face to face, and yet my life
was spared." ❖ Genesis 32:30 (NIV)

Religious imagination is necessary to understand this verse.
You don't *see* the face of God as though through a photo-
graphic lens or at the far end of a telescope. What kind of a
God would God be if he could be located "out there?"

But Jacob saw God, not through the retina of the eye but
through the eye of the soul. The meeting was person to
person, though they did not see "eye to eye." There was a
struggle. The struggle was over what Jacob wanted for
himself and what God wanted of Jacob. It was a clash of
interests. But in all the wrestling, Jacob hung on because he
could not bear to be separated from God. In the struggle,
Jacob lost and found a name. He lost his own selfish interests
("Jacob"); he won his purpose in life ("Israel").

LAWRENCE D. FOLKEMER

*Heavenly Father, fire our faith with imagination that we
may truly learn to walk not by sight but by insight. Help
us to see you as Jacob saw you. Grant us the wisdom to
know that the things that are unseen are the things
eternally real. Amen*

Prayer concern: Those who struggle in faith

Daily Reflections_____

_____

_____

_____

Quiet Obedience

They all joined together constantly in prayer, along with the women and Mary the mother of Jesus, and with his brothers. ❖ Acts 1:14 (NIV)

The ascension was now history. The eleven disciples returned to Jerusalem and the Upper Room where they were staying. There they became a group at prayer. Mary, the mother of Jesus, other unnamed women, and Jesus' brothers became a part of the prayer group.

In the four Gospels we have no record of a prayer meeting like this one. But Jesus had asked them to return to the city (Luke 24:49) and to remain there "until you have been clothed with power from on high." The return to the city and to the Upper Room for prayer was an act of obedience to their Lord.

None of the prayers offered on this occasion have been preserved for the church. There probably was a minimum of petitioning. This was an occasion for praise and thanksgiving. It was a time for rejoicing in the goodness of God who had blessed them so richly through the life, death, and resurrection of Jesus Christ. In such moments the Spirit confers the love and unity that are marks of the body of Christ.

FREDERICK A. SCHIOTZ

O God, pour into our lives the love and unity you desire. Amen

Prayer concern: A spirit of joy and thanksgiving

Daily Reflections

Not Limited

Such great crowds gathered around him that he got
into a boat and sat there. ❖ Matthew 13:2 (NRSV)

A family visited our worship service one Sunday. No one
knew who they were. They spoke and dressed differently
than we did. Rumor had it that they moved to the area from
another part of the country. None of us went up to talk to
them after the service because we were uncomfortable with
strangers. The family never came back.

Sometimes we are far from the open congregation of
Jesus. Imagine its great, diverse crowd! It was filled with
short people and tall, thin people and fat. People came from
all walks of life. No one was turned away. All had the good
news preached to them.

The good news is not to be limited to a select few. Faith in
Jesus Christ is not restricted to those who talk and dress as
we do. The good news of Jesus Christ does not know any
barrier; it encompasses all people.

KEVIN E. RUFFCORN

*Lord, so often we limit the spread of your gospel because
we share it only with people like ourselves. Help us to
be accepting and loving to all people. Amen*

Prayer concern: New people we meet

Daily Reflections

Babel Becomes Pentecost

But each man has his own gift from God; one has this
gift, another has that. ❖ 1 Corinthians 7:7b (NIV)

The miracle of the human being is in the unique individuality
of each person. Every thumbprint is different. Each signature
says something never heard before. Despite our feelings of
"oneness" in our family or in some congenial group, there is
still that priceless individuality. History is filled with the
tragedies of those who overlooked this fact. Whenever we
have forced people of one group into the mold of another,
we've produced hatred and misery that could have been
avoided.

The amazing faith of the Christian is that God's presence
is in all of this individuality and that God's love is shining
through all of these differences. Remembering this changes
our attitude as we confront people of tastes and talents unlike
our own. Understand this, and life becomes colorful. Babel
becomes Pentecost.

RALPH W. LOEW

*O God, whose greatness gives meaning to our littleness,
whose love conquers our fears, and whose presence saves
us from the idolatry of ourselves; teach us how to restore
broken relationships. Forgive us, Lord, as we forgive,
through Christ our Lord. Amen*

Prayer concern: Help us to recognize the miracle of
each individual

Daily Reflections

Who Can Fathom?

Thus says God, the LORD, who created the heavens
and stretched them out, who spread out the earth
and what comes from it. ❖ Isaiah 42:5 (NRSV)

At creation, the Lord "stretched" out the heavens. That's a
mild way of putting it. God created a gargantuan universe!
The star Alpha Centauri, the one nearest to our sun, is more
than 24 trillion miles away. Some astronomers theorize that
the outer edges of the universe (with a probable radius of
13,000 million light years) could be expanding at the rate of
nine-tenths of the speed of light—approximately 5 trillion
miles per year!

The psalmist was right in asking the Lord. "What is man
that you are mindful of him? (Psalm 8:4). Who can fathom
God's creation? Our overwhelming universe causes some to
see humanity as puny specks. But for Christians, humanity
has been loved into significance. Planet Earth was chosen as
home for the covenant-bringer, the light maker, the blind-
healer, and the prison-opener—our Lord Jesus Christ!

WILLIAM A. DECKER

*Lord, what can we do but bow before such a great God as
you! In Jesus' name. Amen*

Prayer concern: Astronauts

Daily Reflections_____

_____
_____
_____

Repent or Perish

But unless you repent, you too will all perish.
❖ Luke 13:3b (NIV)

Unless you repent, you will perish! Is this a threat? Does Jesus say, "Unless you think and act as I tell you, you will suffer fatal punishment?"

Hardly! The Christian life does not come through as a threat; it comes as an invitation. If the threat is ruled out, must we conclude that Jesus is speaking about the realities of living?

The ancient word that we translate "to repent" in our language means "to turn or to change." Repentance in the biblical usage means to turn *from* something and *to* something. We must turn from the way that leads to death, and turn to the way that leads to life.

Jesus said, "I am the Way." We are baptized into him as the way. We cannot always be sure of the ways we travel and the way we turn, but we can turn, again and again, to the covenant of our baptism.

JOHANNES H. V. KNUDSEN

O God, we have come to you once and for all in our baptism, and you have taken us in. You who are the way, the truth, and the life for us, help us to live in the spirit of your love! Help us to turn from evil and toward good. Guide us to eternal life with you! Amen

Prayer concern: People who have suffered a recent loss

Daily Reflections_____

_____
_____
_____

It Makes a Difference

And Jesus said to them, "Follow me and I will
make you fish for people." ❖ Mark 1:17 (NRSV)

Moments of decision sometimes come as a surprise. Two
pairs of brothers were busy with their daily work as
fisherman when the moment came for them. Probably there
were questions already in their minds—questions about this
extraordinary man who had touched their lives, questions
that could lead to complete change for each of them.

Their fishing business was established. They'd planned
always to be commercial fishermen. Could they afford to
change their way of life—even if Jesus said they would still be
fishermen, though in a different way?

In the end, their "yes" to Jesus caused them to move
outward from that small corner of Galilee. It made them the
very beginning of an international movement that hasn't
stopped—preaching the gospel of God in Christ.

The difference in life may be less dramatic for us. But in
one way or another, to say "yes" to Jesus does make a
difference.

GERTRUDE MEES

*Lord, my "yes" to you needs renewal from time to time
because I forget what it means. Help me to accept with
joy the difference it makes. Amen*

Prayer concern: Commercial fishers

Daily Reflections_____

_____

_____

_____

It's Special

When the Counselor comes, whom I will send to you from the Father, the Spirit of truth who goes out from the Father, he will testify about me.
❖ John 15:26 (NIV)

An old man showed me his stamp collection. They were all stamps that he had received on letters over many years. He pointed out a stamp and said, "This is my special stamp."

I asked him what made the stamp unusual. He told me that the stamp had come on a letter from a son. When World War II broke out, his son was a missionary in Asia. Finally a letter came with the news that his son was safe and would soon be home. Of all the special-delivery stamps in the collection, this one was special.

Jesus gave the disciples some good news. They were worried about Jesus' words that he was going to leave them. But Jesus promised to send the Holy Spirit to be his witness.

The good news came to the disciples on Pentecost. The Spirit of God brought more than 3,000 people into the group of believers. The church was begun.

JAMES E. LESCHENSKY

Send us your Spirit, Almighty God, that we may be guided as we share the good news of Jesus. Amen

Prayer concern: Christians in Great Britain

Daily Reflections_____

_____

_____

_____

Increased Strength

On the day I called, you answered me, you increased
my strength of soul. ❖ Psalm 138:3 (NRSV)

"Give me strength," we cry when we need help to live through
a crushing blow. "Just for today," the recovering alcoholic
prays to avoid a drink. "One more breath," we implore at the
end of a task.

Can we meet life's burdens and overloads with our own
power? Are we self-sufficient enough? Alone, we cannot face
and carry life's tasks. We may be addicted to chemicals, to
pride, to work, to power, or to idolizing ourselves.

We may even need to stand on the brink of despair to
realize that we cannot make it on our own. Then we admit
we are helpless, surrender to God, and cry for help. "You
answered me," says the psalmist. We receive God's increased
strength.

Now is the time to admit our weakness, to call on God for
renewed strength for today's needs.

ROLAND SEBOLDT

*O God, I surrender myself to you and pray for your Spirit
to guide me and give me strength. Amen*

Prayer concern: Control of drug abuse

Daily Reflections_____

Knowledge or Love

Knowledge puffs up, but love builds up.
❖ 1 Corinthians 8:1b (NRSV)

A little knowledge may be a dangerous thing. Paul certainly seems to think so in relation to a number of the members of the church at Corinth. Because they knew that the eating of food offered to idols was an empty act and had no worthwhile religious significance, they felt they could eat the food with impunity.

There was a sense of superiority felt by those who had knowledge. Paul reminds us that the only worthwhile knowledge is knowledge that recognizes God as the source of life.

Human knowledge is often utilized to enhance one's position in relation to others. It frequently provides one with a sense of superiority that is really based on being able to put someone else down.

Contrary to this is love. Love is essential to build up life. Founded upon God, it provides us with the opportunity to appreciate the worth of all others with whom life is shared. Love enables us to accept one another as members of God's family.

E. FREDERICK HOLST

Dear Lord, help us to fill our lives with your love so that, in wisdom, we may share your gift. Amen

Prayer concern: Those who need building up

Daily Reflections_____

_____

_____

_____

Live Good

Jesus . . . went around doing good and healing . . .
because God was with him. ❖ Acts 10:38 (NIV)

She was a humble woman, of foreign birth. Her husband a janitor. Her four children were grown. Their home was a small. Modest flat. Yet all Chicago was paying her tribute as Chicago's "Mother of the Year."

What had she done to merit such acclaim? Just helped her neighbors, gone in and out among the homes, moved here and there among the people, along the grimy streets of Chicago's noisy, polyglot West Side.

What was the secret? "You gotta live till you die. So you live good." That was her simple, sustaining philosophy. And it had its roots in the church across the street, its source and inspiration in God the Father and Christ the Son.

ANONYMOUS

O Lord, may we always remember that to whom much is given, much is required. May we help others at home and abroad to know and love and trust and serve you. Amen

Prayer concern: Reconciliation in families and churches

Daily Reflections_____

_____
_____
_____

The Divine Choreographer

So it was not you who sent me here, but God; he
has made me a father to Pharaoh, and lord of all
his house and ruler over all the land of Egypt.
❖ Genesis 45:8 (NRSV)

I have lived one-third of my life equally in each of three
states. Rewinding my history reflectively, I see God's
fingerprints all over it. I recognize my life as an "if I hadn't
been there, then I wouldn't be here now" sort of thing.

Joseph knew it was *God*-incidence and not *co*-incidence
that got him to Egypt and established him there. Jealous
brothers, the fury of a woman rejected, dreams, and a
drought all served God's plan. Joseph understood that God
is ultimately in control.

We have a lot of weddings at our church, and at rehearsals
people often ask me to pray for good wedding weather. I tell
them I am in sales, not management. God is in management.
As Shakespeare's Hamlet tells Horatio, "There's a divinity that
shapes our ends, rough-hew them how we will." Horatio
replies, "That is most certain."

A little boy underlined this sense of providence when he
prayed this simple prayer, "God, take care of yourself,
because if anything happens to you, we're in big trouble."

PHILLIP H. BARNHART

Lord, thank you for always being on the job. Amen

Prayer concern: Vision and clear-minded faith

Daily Reflections_____

_____

_____

_____

Born to Serve

Walk in newness of life. ❖ Romans 6:4 (NRSV)

The story is told of Sir William Wilberforce, who as a young member of the British Parliament had a decisive encounter with God. For a time he thought to surrender his seat in Parliament and go into "religious" work. His friend, William Pitt, dissuaded him and convinced him to give his life in a fight against the cancer of the empire—legalized slave traffic.

Years later, parliament met one night to abolish the traffic once and for all. It was reported that the principal speaker that night ended his remarks with these words: "I am thinking tonight of two heads and two pillows. One is the head of Napoleon, tossing feverishly on a pillow on the island of Helena, after having left a trail of blood from Jena to Waterloo. One is a man who tonight will see the consummation of his life's work. If I were to choose, I would not choose the pillow of Napoleon. I would choose the head that will rest tonight, after our vote is taken, on the pillow of Wilberforce."

ALVIN ROGNESS

Lead us in the paths of service to the downtrodden and the needy, O Lord, so that we will praise you. Amen

Prayer concern: Those who work for justice

Daily Reflections

Good Out of Evil

Then he prays to God, and is accepted by him, he
comes into his presence with joy, and God repays
him for his righteousness. ❖ Job 33:26 (NRSV)

The sun never looks brighter than after a storm, and joy is
never greater than after sorrow. So there is a compensation
for suffering, as suggested in a line by William Shakespeare,
"Sweet are the uses of adversity."

One of the few statements by Elihu and Job's three friends
that we can accept was their insistence that God can bring
good out of evil for those who trust and obey. In this chapter,
Elihu points out to Job that after a man has suffered afflictions
he prays to God and then experiences joy. He tells others what
God has done for him and sings God's praises before them.

Has this every happened in your life? After illness of
operation, have you felt a surge of joy because God has
brought you though this experience, and life has fuller
meaning to you? Has your faith been strengthened by such a
testing of it, by such a demonstration of God's mercy?

And then what? Did you also testify to others how good
God has been to you? Did you sing God's praise so that
others might hear, believe, and glorify God?

HAROLD L. YOCHUM

*Teach us, O Lord, that even out of the evil we experience
may come good for ourselves and others. Then open your
lips that our mouths may show forth our praise. Amen*

Prayer concern: Those who share Christ's love

Daily Reflections_____

_____

_____

We Are All Special

> We have gifts that differ according to the grace
> given to us. ❖ Romans 12:6 (NRSV)

If only . . . ! If only I could speak like that, if only I could teach, if I could be more helpful, if I could just do something special.

Why do we insist on putting ourselves down? How many times have we thought of the wonderful people we could be if only . . . ? To reject what we are is like telling God, "You goofed!" We are saying that we aren't satisfied with God's undeserved kindness.

A gift becomes a gift when it is received. When we accept our abilities and offer ourselves to God, we become part of God's plan. God has a purpose for making us just as we are— not duplicates, but interlocking pieces. We are to complement each other and together create a complete reflection of God.

Aren't you glad we're all different? No one is insignificant, because each is part of God's image. It's not what we do, but for whom we are doing it.

LINDA TIKKANEN

Lord, help me accept myself as I am. I am your creation, and that makes me very special. Help me now to use my abilities to your glory. Amen

Prayer concern: Better stewardship of our talents

Daily Reflections

True to Christ

Genuine, yet regarded as impostors.
❖ 2 Corinthians 6:8b (NIV)

"I am not bound to win, but I am bound to be true. I am not bound to succeed, but I am bound to live up to what light I have." These words of Abraham Lincoln are an echo of the words of Paul in the Bible passage for today. The apostle did not measure truth by consequences, or success by popularity. His only concern was to be true to his mission, to be a faithful witness of Jesus Christ. What if some people were stuck so fast in their old ideas that they closed their minds to the gospel and made fun of it? It was up to Paul to keep witnessing. The results were up to God.

Our witness to Christ is not determined by earthly fears. We may be treated as impostors, but actually it is success and failure, as the world defines them, that are the "twin impostors." The Lord has the last word. Win or lose, we must be true to Christ.

TAITO A. KAUTONEN

Through good and bad, Lord, we are still guided by your faithful word. Amen

Prayer concern: Those who feel lost and confused

Daily Reflections_____

_____

_____

_____

Words to Build On

Heaven and earth will pass away, but my words
will never pass away. ❖ Luke 21:33 (NIV)

To many people, this seems to be a time of constant change.
It seems that religion is changing; it seems that values are
changing. As if we were caught in an earthquake, the ground
appears to be continually shifting under our feet.

Jesus has said that although everything else changes, or
even passes away, his word will not. Does this refer to the
written word? I think not. Jesus was saying that there will
always be some to speak his word. He was also saying that he
said—the truth that he taught—will always be with us.

It is on those words—that truth—that we can build, ever
asking his help to understand, ever interpreting in love.

LINDA WEIMEISTER

*Lord Jesus, bless us with a faith that will sustain us in
these changing times. Lead us to read your words, and
help us to understand. Help us not to fear change, but to
welcome the changes that are in the direction of love,
compassion, understanding, and truth. Amen*

Prayer concern: Those experiencing change

Daily Reflections

A Promise

Do not let your hearts be troubled, and do not let them be afraid. ❖ John 14:27b (NRSV)

When I asked a group of preschoolers where God was, many of them responded, "He's in church." How many of us adults also tend to acknowledge God's presence only when we are in church or participating in congregational activities? How often do we forget his presence as we worry about problems, and struggle through our everyday routines?

As Christ was preparing for his final days on earth, he made a promise to his disciples. He promised to send a helper, the Holy Spirit, who would be with them always.

That promise is for us, too. God is with us all the time and in all places; not only on Sundays, in church, but on Mondays as well—at school, at work, at home, at play. God is with us and we need not be afraid.

SUSAN R. DIEHL

Lord, make your presence known to me. Help me to call on you as I struggle, as I worry about the problems of everyday living. Thank you for your promise to be with me always. Amen

Prayer concern: Everyone you meet today

Daily Reflections_____

Day 121 ❖ John 20:21-23

Moment of Assurance

And with that he breathed on them and said,
"Receive the Holy Spirit." ❖ John 20:22 (NIV)

Being caught in the act like the "cat swallowing a canary" is a
universal experience. Children get caught eating a forbidden
cookie. Older folks get involved in the telling of a lie. The
slick try cheating; the slow "forget." Whatever the offense, a
sense of guilt accuses us when we stand in the presence of
the person offended.

Such guilt shook the disciples when Jesus appeared to
them. In his presence, their cowardly acts were seen in
perspective. Yet Jesus did not condemn them. Instead, he
forgave them. Instead of punishment, he bestowed on them
the gift of the Holy Spirit. After his resurrection appearances,
the weak men who had crawled into a closed room to escape
death became changed people. The weak became strong!
With the help of the Holy Spirit, they assured others of God's
deliverance. At this time, they truly began to reflect the
confession earlier stated by Peter, "You are the Christ, the
Son of the living God" (Matthew 16:13-16).

ALICE L. SCHIMPF

*Help us to remember that you forgive when the world
condemns. Bestow on us the power of the Holy Spirit so
we can assure others of your gift. Amen*

Prayer concern: Forgiving hearts

Daily Reflections_____

Our Friend

Do not cast me from your presence or take your
Holy Spirit from me. ❖ Psalm 51:11 (NIV)

President Abraham Lincoln was beset by requests for
government jobs, personal favors, and pardons. Hundreds of
requests were accompanied by stacks of letters of support
from influential friends.

A convicted army deserter wrote for a pardon. The crude
note had no attachments, so Lincoln asked his secretary,
"Has this man no friends?"

"No, Mr. President," came the reply.

"Then I will be his friend," Lincoln said, as he signed the
pardon.

We too were without a friend before God, the judge of our
souls. But out of the desire to forgive, God sent Jesus to be
our friend. Through Jesus we enter the very presence of
God. We need not rely on ceremony, sacrifice, or any other
advocate, only on our friend Jesus.

CHARLES A. LEHMAN

*Dear God, thank you for sending us your Son, Jesus, as
our advocate and friend. Amen*

Prayer concern: Your friends

Daily Reflections_____

_____

_____

_____

Elijah and the Lord

The Israelites have rejected your covenant . . .
I am the only one left, and now they are trying to
kill me, too. ❖ 1 Kings 19:14 (NIV)

Felix Mendelssohn wrote the oratorio Elijah—a beautiful musical creation based on the Old Testament. Mendelssohn's family became Christian, and he married a Lutheran pastor's daughter. He understood the meaning of both the Old and New Testament. In a bass aria, using the words of today's text, Elijah tells the Lord God exactly how he felt.

Elijah wished to die. He could no longer face the world's troubles. He could no longer carry out the wishes of the Lord. He felt hopeless, defeated and useless. It would be much easier to give up than to try to keep on living. But God had other plans for Elijah.

What plans does God have for us? We do not know. Should we complain, tell him what we want to do? No, whatever his will might be, it is best for us. All of us feel a little like Elijah once in a while. We might even think it is better to give up than keep on with life. But the Lord will help us take the risk of unknown paths!

ANNE JORDHEIM

Dear God, please help us to walk in faith down yet unknown paths. We trust in you. Amen

Prayer concern: Church musicians

Daily Reflections

It's Just Too Much!

When you pass through the waters, I will be with you; and through the rivers, they shall not overwhelm you; when you walk through fire you shall not be burned, and the flame shall not consume you. ❖ Isaiah 43:2 (NRSV)

"What next?" Sandra asked me. "First my dad was diagnosed with cancer, then Rich lost his job. We have no insurance, and Jenny needs to go to the doctor. Mom is worried sick about Dad, and I hardly have the strength to be as supportive as I want to be. What else can happen to us?"

At times, life is overwhelming. It can feel like we have no resources for coping with the disasters that come our way. The huge burdens that land on us can make even the most minor stress feel like the straw that broke the camel's back.

To the people of Israel, who had suffered exile and humiliation, the world seemed to be an overwhelming and unfriendly place. In this time of desperation, Isaiah brought words of comfort and promise—of restoration and steadfast love. That same promise holds true for us today.

DONNA HACKER SMITH

Let me feel your powerful presence with me today, loving God. Amen

Prayer concern: Those who feel overwhelmed

Daily Reflections_____

_____

_____

_____

Of Logs and Sawdust

Do not judge, or you too will be judged.
❖ Matthew 7:1 (NIV)

Where Jesus lived, glass wasn't often used for buildings. So Jesus wouldn't say, "People who live in glass houses should never throw stones." He used another illustration—that people who have a big log in their eye should be careful not to point at people who have sawdust in their eye.

I think we know what he meant. I love to think that Jesus' listeners must have laughed as they heard it. Imagine a doctor with a plank sticking out of his eye trying to cure someone with a speck of dust in his eye.

Jesus warns us that it is so very easy to be judgmental. The loving thing is to encourage and strengthen people. Martin Luther said it well in the meaning of the Eighth Commandment: "Defend him [the neighbor], speak well of him, and explain his actions in the kindest way."

Why not determine that for today you will be complimentary instead of critical? You might discover a new dimension of life by showing people that you really care about them. And it could be that you will find that they care about you.

OLE WINTER

Lord, help us to see in others the needs they have rather than the wrongs they do. Amen

Prayer concern: Christians in Canada

Daily Reflections_____
_____
_____
_____

Breaking the Sound Barrier

He asked for a writing tablet, and to everyone's astonishment he wrote, "His name is John." Immediately his mouth was opened and his tongue was loosed, and he began to speak, praising God. ❖ Luke 1:63-64 (NIV)

There is a time to keep silent about God. Zechariah had been in such a time. When the angel came to him at the altar and told him that his prayer was answered, he would have a son, Zechariah doubted. You can't blame him. You too would probably have doubted it.

But God means business. When he tells us a secret, he expects us to believe it. If we can't believe it, we should shut up about it until we can. Sometimes God helps us to keep our mouths shut. At least he did Zechariah. When we can't believe the mysteries of God, we should keep quiet until we can.

There is a time to speak about God. That is when we do know that he keeps his promises. When this time came to Zechariah, he spoke. His mouth was opened and his tongue was loosed, and he spoke. When one speaks believing, the Holy Spirit may give the gift of prophesy. He did to Zechariah. Having seen what God did do, he was given to see what God would do in his son John. Believing is seeing. And that's the time to speak.

JAMES H. HANSON

Holy Spirit, give us faith that sees and believes. Amen

Prayer concern: Courage to speak of our faith

Daily Reflections_____
_____
_____
_____

No Longer a Slave

So you are no longer a slave but a child,
and if a child then also an heir, through
God. ❖ Galatians 4:7 (NRSV)

For some people, freedom from bondage is too much. Freedom calls for responsibility, and some will seek to avoid that. After the breakup of the Berlin Wall many East Germans rushed into the western sectors. But after a few months, some returned to East Germany, unable to accept their new conditions of more freedom.

Perhaps we should consider carefully the freedom that God offers us in his Son, Jesus Christ. After all, if we are to live in the Father's house as adopted sons and daughters then the tasks of the kingdom become ours. Would it not be easier and a lot cozier to focus only on our own needs? As sons and daughters, do we have a responsibility to others, even those we don't like?

We certainly do, and it's not always easy. "Me first" is a brutal bondage. It leads to arrogance, to undeserved pride, to prejudice, to contempt. Only God can break down the walls we put up, and through faith in God we see the bondage of those walls. As heirs and children we inherit a marvelous freedom, freedom to really live, freedom to really love, freedom to hope, the freedom to eternal life.

JOHN COFFEY JR.

God, remove the shackles that blind us. Amen

Prayer concern: Those who think, "Me first"

Daily Reflections

_____

_____

_____

Boring Chores?

Whatever you do, work at it with all your
heart, as working for the Lord, not for men.
❖ Colossians 3:23 (NIV)

The young man scouring the greasy pots and pans in the
army kitchen was a brilliant scholar. Before entering the
army, Leonard had earned his master's degree at a noted
university and graduated with high honors.

An army buddy who knew of Leonard's achievements
came by the kitchen. At the sight of Leonard scrubbing
greasy pots, the friend shook his head and exclaimed, "What
a shame! A man with your ability and training—and you have
to scrub dishes."

Leonard, however, went on with the scrubbing. "Well," he
said, "right now this is my assignment, and it's more
satisfying to scrub well and think of better things than to slop
through the job, despising it."

What job, what place in life, does not have its boring chore
or tiresome task? Even people who hold glamorous jobs have
responsibilities that may nag and irritate. How much happier
we are when we just get on with the boring chore, praying,
"This, too, I do in your name, my Lord and Savior."

ANONYMOUS

*Dear Lord, thank you for being with us no matter how
lowly the work we do. Your presence brings blessing to
every task. Amen*

Prayer concern: Migrant workers

Daily Reflections

Go in Peace, Serve the Lord

> So Ananias went and entered the house. He laid his hands on Saul and said, "Brother Saul, the Lord Jesus, who appeared to you on your way here, has sent me so that you may regain your sight and be filled with the Holy Spirit." ❖ Acts 9:17 (NRSV)

Ananias, filled with the promise and hope of Christ, is now sent to bring God's peace to one who had been breathing threats and murder. Saul, full of passionate fury, is now to be touched and blessed.

Into what unexpected places does the Spirit of God, loose on the earth, lead us to bring the gospel promise? Where or to whom are we sent today? Is there an aching heart, a fearful and anxious soul, or a raging spirit that is in need of our prayerful support, an embrace, a blessing, a word of comfort, or a word of challenge?

When we leave our places of worship on Sunday with the hint of bread and wine in our mouths and the word still clinging to our ears, it is the Monday through Saturday of our lives that are addressed when we hear the last word: "Go in peace and serve the Lord."

ERIK STRAND

O God, give us courage and vision to see the places where you would send us to share the light of the resurrection. Amen

Prayer concern: People in need of vision and hope

Daily Reflections
_____

_____

_____

_____

A Gift of Love

For whoever wants to save his life will lose it.
❖ Mark 8:35a (NIV)

The birth of a child is one of the most marvelous events one can witness. Focused in that instant of emergence into the world, of new breath and first sight, are all our thoughts and musings, our hopes and feelings of awe at the thing called "life." Who can forget the reverence and joy one feels for life when a child is born—a son or daughter, grandchild or godchild?

How precious is life, how miraculous! We fall in love with life, our own and others'. Is it any wonder that we cherish it and cringe at the thought of giving it up?

Life is a mystery to us, even to scientists who study DNA. We understand so little of what life is. How then can we save our life when we don't even know what it is? Life comes to us as a gift. Who but the giver, the creator of life, can save it? Christ, who lives eternally, gave his life to save ours. We are lost if we turn away from the source of ourselves; but we are saved if we believe in and live for the love that made us.

LINDA OLSEN PEEBLES

Blessed creator of the universe, thank you for the gift of life and for the love you showed us in the life and death of Jesus Christ. Help us to live according to your way, strengthened in your Son. Amen

Prayer concern: New parents

Daily Reflections_____
_____
_____
_____

Day 131 ❖ Jeremiah 1:4-10

True Confidence

"Do not be afraid of them, for I am with you
and will rescue you," declares the LORD.
❖ Jeremiah 1:8 (NIV)

Imagine an 18-year-old addressing a session of the General
Assembly of the United Nations—preaching a sermon on
repentance and faith! This is roughly the modern-day
equivalent of what Jeremiah was commissioned to do. No
wonder he held back, offering an excuse as Moses had done
in a similar situation. But then came the ringing assurance of
the Lord's presence with him.

Isn't this the way it always is? When a challenge seems too
great, God raises us to meet it with resources that he
provides. The challenge is not cut down to our size; we are
raised to meet it. When asked to make an evangelism or
stewardship call or to teach a Sunday school class, we may
quake inwardly. Afraid of personal failure, we hold back. If we
trust God and accept God's promise to be with us, he will put
words in our mouths and give boldness to our profession of
faith. Our confidence will be restored, enabling us to get the
job done.

JOHN H. HAYNER

*O Lord, don't let us excuse ourselves from some impor-
tant task before asking your help. For Jesus' sake. Amen*

Prayer concern: People who have helped us

Daily Reflections_____

_____
_____
_____

Not a Sometimes-God

Let us know, let us press on to know the LORD;
his appearing is as sure as the dawn; he will come
to us like the showers, like the spring rains that
water the earth. ❖ Hosea 6:3 (NRSV)

When the weather gets dry, we all notice. The grass turns
brown and crops take a beating. We've seen dry spells before.
In the end, it always rains. It's the waiting, the damage
control, that we worry about.

In this passage, God's people have grown proud. Like dew
in the morning, their praises disappear by noon. A dry spell
allows them to hear the voice of God again, and they wait for
the spring rains to run warm. Water into dust. Clay to be
formed once again in God's image.

God is not a sometimes-God. As sure as the dawn, as
predictable as spring rain, God continues to call us from our
dusty existence back to the garden to be refreshed.

BARBARA DEGROTE SORENSEN

*Gracious God, thank you for the many signs of your
faithfulness. Amen*

Prayer concern: People and nations endangered by
drought

Daily Reflections_____

_____
_____
_____

Obey God Moment by Moment

> No . . . because while you are pulling the
> weeds, you may root up the wheat with them.
> Let both grow together until the harvest.
> ❖ Matthew 13:29b-30a (NIV)

You may have heard a story like this: A task is assigned with specific instructions on how to do it, but the person has an "easier, better way" to do it and ignores the directions. After the inevitable disaster comes the equally inevitable reply: "I only tried to help."

Impatient for a son, Sarai and Abram tried to "help" God by bringing in Hagar. Moses tried to help God by striking the rock to bring water. Rebekah and Jacob tried to help God through deception. They all thought that they could help God, and the results were tragic.

Like the servant in the parable, we sometimes are tempted to "help" God by doing things our way; but God wants our obedience, not our sacrifices. If the servant had used his method, some valuable wheat would have been lost. It's always better to do something God's way. That is another important part of Christian growth.

DANA PHIPPS

Lord, help me to echo the words of Jesus when he said, "Not my will, but thine be done," and to obey you more and more, day by day, moment by moment. Amen

Prayer concern: Those who are stubborn

Daily Reflections

Day 134 ❖ Psalm 121

Looking Toward the Heights

I lift up my eyes to the hills—where does my help come from? ❖ Psalm 121:1 (NIV)

The family had put in a beautiful new lawn. But toward the end of the summer spots appeared here and there to their dismay. "Look at the lawn across the street," said the wife. "It looks like a green carpet." A few days later she walked down the other side of the street. The other lawn had more larger spots than their own, and their own from that distance had the appearance of green velvet.

Sometimes we get so close to our own problems that they overwhelm us. To get the right perspective, we should view our problems from a distance. We must take the long look, looking toward the heights, if we would see life in its right proportions.

ANONYMOUS

Gracious God, our hearts are filled with gratitude for all your matchless blessings, though we have deserved nothing. May we show our gratitude in lives of helpful service. For Jesus' sake. Amen

Prayer concern: Keeping things in perspective

Daily Reflections_____
_____
_____
_____

The Bounties of Nature

You care for the land and water it; you enrich it abundantly. The streams of God are filled with water to provide the people with grain, for so you have ordained it. ❖ Psalm 65:9 (NIV)

Anyone who has ever lived on a farm knows how directly dependent we are on God for our sustenance. This is something that city dwellers, who live once-removed from nature, often forget.

The bread we eat came from the grocery store on the corner. It was delivered there by a baker. But the flour he used came from a mill in Minnesota. And the wheat that was milled into the flour grew on a farm in Montana. And, had God not provided rain and the sun in the right amounts, there would have been no wheat—no flour—no bread.

You might try tracing back the food you ate for dinner. There may be many, many intermediate steps—but sooner or later you come back to God. Without God's goodness, you would have gone hungry. The bounties of nature exist by God's will.

ANONYMOUS

O God, you satisfy the desire of every living thing. Make us thankful for your goodness to us; through Christ, our Lord. Amen

Prayer concern: Farmers and ranchers

Daily Reflections_____

_____

_____

_____

Day 136 ❖ Psalm 69:1-12

Encouraging Others

May those who hope in you not be disgraced
because of me. ❖ Psalm 69:6 (NIV)

Almost everyone is held in high regard by someone else.
Children look to their parents; friends admire friends;
students their teachers; church members their pastors.

It's an awesome responsibility to be a role model or
positive example for someone. We are all human. We all have
failings. But as followers of Christ, we have no option but to
assume the responsibility for encouraging others by the way
we live. If they become disappointed they probably won't lose
faith in God. But sometimes it's hard for them to hang on in
their disillusionment.

When her friend died, Mary said, "It was much easier to
be good when Jane was here." What a tribute it is for
someone to feel that because of us it's easier to love, to hope,
to be cheerful, and to have courage.

The world has taken on new courage with the coming of
Jesus. He has not only shown us the way to the good life but
has promised to help us on the way.

ALVIN ROGNESS

Thanks, Lord, for giving us hope. Amen

Prayer concern: Christian day schools

Daily Reflections_____
_____
_____
_____

Keeping Up with Christ

So then, God has granted even the Gentiles repentance unto life. ❖ Acts 11:18b (NIV)

No doubt about it, Peter was "called on the carpet" back to Jerusalem after associating with—and even baptizing—the Gentiles at Caesarea. "Why did you do that?" demanded those who still saw Christ as a Savior "for Jews only." "Who was I that I could withstand God?" answered Peter. The Gentiles had believed; they had received the same Spirit. Who was Peter (and, indeed, who are we?) to try to contain Christ within whatever is revered as "tradition"?

What the early church had to learn, and what we must relearn today, is that Christ has plans of his own that are bigger than our plans for him, and that the essence of discipleship is to keep up with him as he moves out into the world and on toward his kingdom, his future for the whole human race. We don't need to "get back" to God or the Bible, because God is not behind us in the past. We need to catch up and keep up with our Lord, because he is always way ahead!

JACK E. LINDQUIST

Jesus Christ, Lord of the future, forgive our resentment when you break out of the old boxes of our religious thinking; and help us to keep moving with you toward your kingdom. Amen

Prayer concern: Those who work in hospitals

Daily Reflections_____
_____
_____
_____

One to One

Therefore encourage one another and build
each other up, just as in fact you are doing.
❖ 1 Thessalonians 5:11 (NIV)

Two boys who were close friends were confirmed in the same class. One of them stopped coming to the services at once. The other, under parental pressure, continued in church regularly. Unhappy without his friend, the latter kept urging his classmate to start coming. One Sunday he returned. From that day on he was among the most faithful of church members. A friend's encouragement had enlisted a youth permanently for a happy Christian life.

What Paul said in the second part of our verse reads, "Build each other up." Individuals building each other up spiritually, what kingdom potential! Imagine husband and wife, parent and child, brother and brother, sister and sister, yes, friend and friend, mutually concerned. What a group of builders, not of outward edifices but of dedicated personalities!

OSCAR A. BENSON

Lord, you have asked us to make intercessions for all people. Prompt us to be especially tender in our concern for those we love best. Grant us to be mutually helpful also by frank witnessing, through Christ our Lord. Amen

Prayer concern: Christians in Egypt

Daily Reflections_____
_____
_____
_____

Be Not Anxious

They are not afraid of evil tidings; their hearts are
... secure in the LORD. ❖ Psalm 112:7 (NRSV)

While serving in the armed forces, I encountered a situation
that challenged me to draw upon the resources of my faith.
With hundreds of replacements, I was being transported on a
troopship at night through waters that had been seeded with
mines. As we left the shore my anxiety increased. I offered a
silent prayer, and repeated Psalm 23. Before too long I sensed
God's peace settling over me. I didn't get much sleep that
night. I still had concerns. But I did not panic, as I was
reassured that I was in his care.

As the years go by, we are all confronted with reasons to
fear evil tidings. It is a part of life. Through it all, those who
learn to entrust their lives into the Lord's hands find that he
gives a peace that helps one to cope and to conquer.

MARSHAL H. GANTE

*Loving Father, we release ourselves into your hands
today, that we might have your peace that passes
understanding. Amen*

Prayer concern: Members of the armed forces

Daily Reflections

Living the Word

The manager said to himself, "What shall I
do now? My master is taking away my job."
❖ Luke 16:3 (NIV)

We honor God by returning the best of ourselves to him.
Faithful Christians are stewards (managers) not only of
money but also of time and talents. Each of us possesses
unique abilities. As reborn people in Christ we all have
common gifts, too. Faith, hope, and love, in some measure,
are present in every Christian.

We are stewards both of our common and of our special
gifts. Using them faithfully brings its reward.

Like the steward in this story we must use money
wisely—according to our goals. Money need not be despised;
it's to be used in good, godly, and charitable ways.

We rob God when we fail to manage our gifts properly.
They are not to be used just for ourselves, but for the
common good also. Therefore Christian stewards prayerfully
seek godly purposes for using their gifts.

PATRICIA A. PUNT

*Lord, help me not to overlook one of your greatest gifts
. . . time. Amen*

Prayer concern: School administrators

Daily Reflections_____

_____

_____

_____

Day 141 ❖ Psalm 120:1-7

From Lying Lips, Deliver Me

> I call on the LORD in my distress, and he answers me. Save me, O LORD, from lying lips and from deceitful tongues. ❖ Psalm 120:1-2 (NIV)

Don't get caught in your own mouth-trap! A lying tongue brings harm, grief, and sorrow. But why do we lie? Sometimes we are afraid to face the consequences of truth and try to protect ourselves from its hurt. But truth is more healing than hurting. At other times we lie to gain personal advantage. But by putting another falsely in a bad light, we give the impression that we are elevated and good by comparison. However, you can't whitewash yourself by blackening others. Although we gain temporary advantage our position is insecure. Truth will come out; our deceit will be exposed. A wise person said, "Bread gained by deceit is sweet, but afterward his mouth will be filled with gravel."

We cannot afford to let a day go by without a prayer that we be delivered from the lying barbs of others and the desire to use them ourselves.

VERLE C. SCHUMACHER

Make us conscious, O Lord, of danger in idle words and malicious talk. Lead us by your Spirit to speak of others as we would want others to speak to us. Knowing that they must be patient with us, make us patient with others. Amen

Prayer concern: Those who speak the truth

Daily Reflections_____
_____
_____
_____

One above All

The one who comes from above is above all.
❖ John 3:31 (NRSV)

Moses was a great man and a mighty leader. He was not afraid to stand before Pharaoh, nor did he fear Pharaoh's chariots. He led his people out of Egypt and through a desert. He carried God's law from Mount Sinai. His memory shall be without end. But he that came from heaven is greater than Moses.

The prophets were mighty people. They raised their voices against wicked kings. They denounced corrupt politics, dishonesty in business, lust and selfishness among men and women, and evil wherever they found it. They were moral giants. But, behold, one greater than them all is here.

Solomon shall be remembered for his wisdom as long as the sun and moon endure. But behold, one greater than Solomon is here.

A greater one has come to love us, forgive us, help us, and save us. Can we believe in him? Those who find it possible shall see life.

WILLIAM R. SEAMAN

O Lord, we beseech you, increase our faith and kindle in us the light of your Holy Spirit; through Jesus Christ, your Son, our Lord. Amen

Prayer concern: Church leaders

Daily Reflections_____

_____

_____

_____

Holy Day

He read from it facing the square before the
Water Gate from early morning until midday.
❖ Nehemiah 8:3 (NRSV)

As a child, growing up in Madagascar and raised by my
grandparents in the rural area of Fianarantsoa, Sundays were
always holy. The preparations for each Sunday began the day
before, on Saturday. We walked to the river to do the laundry,
and we thoroughly cleaned the entire house. Saturday
evening my grandma cooked and made all the preparations
for the big Sunday family dinner. We all went to bed early.

At first light on Sunday, Grandma would wake me up to
prepare for church. By 7:00 A.M. we were walking through
dense forests on narrow dirt paths and climbing steep
hillsides, being careful not to stain our Sunday clothes. Two
hours later, we met other church members who came from
afar just in time for worship. At noon, we received the
benediction—time to go home, having been fed with God's
word, looking forward to feeding on Grandma's cooking.

The days and times to gather and to worship our God are
holy days indeed. How do you prepare and welcome those
holy moments in your life?

LALAHERY ANDRIAMIHAJA

*Our Father in heaven, impress in our hearts your desire
that we spend quality time with you. Amen*

Prayer concern: Those who have a difficult time getting
to church

Daily Reflections

Day 144 ❖ Isaiah 63:7-9

Selfless Suffering

In all their affliction he was afflicted.
❖ Isaiah 63:9 (NRSV)

I was age 7 and my brother was 9 when we moved. School was not far away, but I was afraid to go by myself so my brother and I walked together. One day, arriving at school, my brother said, "I'm not feeling well. I'm going home." After school, my mother walked me home where I found my brother in bed, very sick. He had been sick when he woke up, but knowing I was afraid to walk by myself, he had not said anything. After all, it was his job to walk his little sister to school. It never occurred to him that my mother would take me. My fear was his only concern.

Isaiah tells us that God's love is so great that God sent his Son to walk with us in our fear, to share in our suffering, and even to die for us. I remember my brother's selfless act with great tenderness. I remember God's selfless suffering and death with humble thankfulness and praise.

LINDA W. FRADO

O Lord, you are always by our side, sharing our pains and our fears. Through your example, help us to walk with each other and to share our love with those who are afraid and suffering. Amen

Prayer concern: Police officers and fire fighters

Daily Reflections_____

_____

_____

_____

Day 145 ❖ Psalm 84:10

An Important Choice

Better is one day in your courts than a thousand
elsewhere; I would rather be a doorkeeper in the
house of my God than dwell in the tents of the
wicked. ❖ Psalm 84:10 (NIV)

In this world of complexity and increased temptation, we are
often faced with difficult choices involving right and wrong,
good and evil.

The psalmist in today's Bible reading suggests an
important, ultimate choice that each of us must make. Will
we be content to cleave to the kind of life God desires of us,
even if it means sacrifices? Can we free our lives of immoral
business practices that may add to our material richness, of
cruel assaults spoken to our neighbor that may strengthen
our egos, or of boasts of our own accomplishments that grant
us a feeling of temporary superiority?

A life devoted to God may not be easy. Christ's life was not
easy, but he who patterns his life after the perfect example
set by our Savior will reap far greater rewards than will those
who selfishly dwell in wickedness.

BETH R. LUDWIG

*God, grant us the strength and courage to live up to your
expectations of us. In Christ's name. Amen*

Prayer concern: Role models

Daily Reflections

An Untroubled Heart

Do not let your hearts be troubled. Trust in God;
trust also in me. ❖ John 14:1 (NIV)

What is troubling you today? Concern over your finances, health, children, marriage, friends, or job? Emotional unrest? Sudden tragedy?

None of us can escape life's trials and tribulations. As a Bible teacher once said, "We were never meant to live this life apart from God. Sooner or later it will break us. God wants us to come to the point where we say, 'It's too much. I can't handle it without you.'"

When we surrender control of our burdens to God, then, as Paul says in 2 Corinthians 4:7, even though we're afflicted (with stress), we won't be crushed; perplexed (with mental anxiety), we won't be driven to despair; persecuted (in relationship problems), we won't be forsaken; struck down (with illness), we won't be destroyed.

Whatever is troubling us, our heavenly Father wants us to bring our concerns to him. Only if we are bigger than God, can our problems, our needs, or our heartaches be too much for God.

ROSEANNE BLISS

Thank you, Lord, for being there to turn to when life's burdens seem too much to bear. Amen

Prayer concern: Christians in Thailand

Daily Reflections

The Free Gift

For you know that it was not with perishable things
such as silver or gold that you were redeemed
from the empty way of life handed down to you
from your forefathers, but with the precious blood
of Christ. ❖ 1 Peter 1:18-19a (NIV)

One of the difficult things for Christians to realize is that there
is no inherent merit or worthiness in us—none. Even Paul,
possibly the greatest of Christ's disciples, said, "For what I
want to do I do not do, but what I hate I do . . . For I know that
nothing good lives in me" (Romans 7:15, 18). We are human
and sinners, one and all, just as our ancestors were.

How wonderful it is, then, when we accept and
acknowledge the sacrifice that Christ made for us in the
shedding of his precious blood! We know that salvation
cannot be purchased with silver or gold, or with any efforts
or works of our own. It is a free gift, made available only
through the mercy and grace of God. All we need to do is
accept it. "I do believe; help me overcome my unbelief"
(Mark 9:24).

JAMES J. FRANKENFIELD

*Lord, open our hearts and minds to the understanding
that salvation is a free gift. Through your Holy Spirit
may we be led to accept it, and offer you our lives in
gratitude and praise daily for it. In Jesus' we pray. Amen*

Prayer concern: Christians in Australia

Daily Reflections

The Soft Answer

With this in mind, we constantly pray for you.
❖ 2 Thessalonians 1:11 (NIV)

An old fable tells how the wind and the sun tried to make a man take off his coat. The wind blew as hard as it could, but the man only pulled his coat tighter. Then the sun gently poured on its heat and the man soon removed his coat. The gentle approach was the better one.

The point of the fable is that the soft answer of love is more effective than a display of power and harshness. Paul knew that. He could scold, as he did the Galatians, but he often used the gentle approach. "We constantly pray for you." Those were his words to the Christians at Thessalonica.

We can learn from the fable and from Paul. Sometimes we are moved to scold and criticize, and angry words may be necessary. But the soft answer, the warmth of the sun, the message of love and concern is generally more effective. Praying that others will do right must go hand in hand with scolding them for doing wrong. Showing love may seem weak, but it does God's work.

W. A. POOVEY

Father, help me to remember others in prayer and to speak words of love to them. Amen

Prayer concern: Christians in Nepal

Daily Reflections_____

_____

_____

We Are Forgiven!

He will again have compassion upon us, he will tread
our iniquities under foot. ❖ Micah 7:19a (NIV)

Think back to when you were a little child. How many times
were you given rules that you broke—not just once, but over
and over again? To parents it might even have seemed that
you were willfully disobedient. Children are far from being
perfect—even in the sight of indulgent grandparents.

For some of our misdeeds we were punished. That's one
way we learn. But such punishment was not extended to the
point of rejection. We learned to know forgiveness and love.
And many a childish sin was overlooked.

So it is with God. He too has given us rules for our lives.
Like children, we test the limits to which we can go. So we
learn how wrongdoing and punishment go together.

In far greater measure than out earthly parents, God
forgives us. God sent his own Son, Jesus, as God's pledge of
forgiveness.

GARLAND E. GOTOSKI

*Dearest Jesus, we thank you that you have come to be
our King and our mediator with God. Amen*

Prayer concern: Children who are neglected and abused

Daily Reflections

A Win-Win Situation

For to me, living is Christ and dying is gain.
❖ Philippians 1:21 (NRSV)

The world is not inclined to settle for win-win situations. We often prefer win-lose outcomes: we want a winner, no ties— always a winner and a loser. In all avenues of life we are intrigued with keeping score.

I suppose there is nothing wrong with that. After all, what is a Super Bowl, a World Series, or a U.S. Open without a winner. Properly taken, a bit of competition adds zest to our lives, as long as we are out to test ourselves and not to humiliate others.

But the apostle Paul indicates that we who follow Christ in faith are always in a win-win situation. We win when we live, we win when we die. There are no losers in the kingdom of God, for the victory of Christ on the cross is our victory over the sin that plaques us and the death that awaits us. Because Jesus lives, we too shall live. That is the marvelous promise of God that brings so much hope and certainty to us.

Our faith in Christ will not assure us World Series rings or Olympic gold metals. But when Christ captures us and stamps the cross and the resurrection on us, we are then declared winners. In both life and death, we cannot lose.

JOHN W. COFFEY

Almighty God, usher us into that eternal win-win condition. Amen

Prayer concern: Those in despair

Daily Reflections_____

Memories

I will forgive their iniquity, and remember their sin no more. ❖ Jeremiah 31:34c (NRSV)

Sometimes, long after we've forgiven incidents or pain, memories linger or come back to haunt us. It troubles us when this happens.

We know from our Lord's Prayer that we ought to forgive others as God has forgiven us. But when the memories return, we are confronted by our sin. God's forgiveness is so unlike our own. Our God declares that forgiveness in Christ is forever. It is forever united with the power to forget. God's word is not limited by human memory. God remembers our sin no more.

We cannot honestly say we have forgiven our debtors unless we have forgiven them in Christ. With Christ all things are possible. So I give Christ my memories and slow-mending wounds, trusting that he has forgiven before I have forgotten.

JOACHIM PROBST

Eternal God, for Jesus' sake, stir up in our hearts the memory of your forgiving forgetfulness. We call upon your name in times of temptation, when our flesh will not forget what your Spirit seeks to erase. Come, Holy Spirit, and teach us. Amen

Prayer concern: Those suffering with Alzheimer's disease

Daily Reflections_____

_____
_____
_____

God's Love

Little children . . . ❖ John 13:33 (NRSV)

If they are fortunate, children begin life in an atmosphere of love and security. Their family protects them for a time from some of the harsher realities of the world. Eventually, however, childhood ends, and parents and their children must separate.

The disciples were in a similar situation when Jesus, addressing them as his "children," told them that he would soon be leaving them. The time had come for the disciples to enter lives of new responsibility without the security that Jesus' physical presence had provided. As children should know that they still have their parents' love even after they have begun an independent life, the disciples knew that they went with God's love as they began the task of spreading God's word. In this way, we all are fortunate children; all through our lives, God's love is with us.

BRUCE BROMAN

Lord, our memories of childhood often seem very carefree in comparison to the complexities of life as an adult. Please give us strength and faith to live your word each day. Amen

Prayer concern: Parents

Daily Reflections_____

_____

_____

_____

Day to Refocus

Observe the sabbath day and keep it holy,
as the LORD your God commanded you.
❖ Deuteronomy 5:12 (NRSV)

After a hard week of too much paperwork on the job, and too many interruptions at home, the weekend beckons like an oasis of calm.

Even the thought of crawling out of the comfort of bed on Sunday morning is enough to bring forth a groan.

As busy as our daily lives are, God asks us to take one day a week to focus on worship.

For the Israelites this meant stopping and setting up camp for thousands of people. Talk about hassle! For them worship was the focus not just of their week, but of their very lives.

Yet the command to worship was and is not a punishment for either the Hebrews, nor us. A day of worship is instead meant as a time of mental, physical, and spiritual renewal. It is time out to refocus priorities, and ready ourselves for the week ahead.

CAROLYN SCHEIDIES

Thank you, Lord, for giving us a day of rest. Help me use this time to renew both mind and spirit. Amen

Prayer concern: All who plan and lead worship

Daily Reflections_____
_____
_____
_____

Noticing What God Has Made

I remember the days of long ago; I meditate on all
your works and consider what your hands have
done. ❖ Psalm 143:5 (NIV)

For many years our family has spent at least one week of
vacation each year at the lake and one week in the mountains.
I have always enjoyed the splendor of God' creation in both
places. But I've often failed to notice the beauty in the
everyday things at home.

One morning last winter, I marveled at the sparkle of the
sunlight on frost-laden rosebushes after a snowfall. I hurried
into the house to get my camera for a picture to record this
scene. Then it struck me that God makes lovely things even
at home in western Texas!

Then I began to remember rosy sunsets and vast
stretches of star-embroidered skies on clear nights. There
have always been lovely things here. I just need to
acknowledge them and to express my thanks to the creator.

MARGENE BRYANT

Creator, thank you for the wonders of this world around
us. Give us the ability to preserve the beauty of your
handiwork so that future generations may also enjoy it.
Amen

Prayer concern: Painters and sculptors

Daily Reflections

Do We Know the Lord?

The LORD will make himself known to the
Egyptians. ❖ Isaiah 19:21 (NRSV)

A certain man went to heaven and at the gateway the Lord
asked him some questions. "Did you observe any of my
wondrous works on earth?" "No," said the man, "I was too
busy answering the telephone."

Is this characteristic you? We are too busy with trivia,
running here and there, working hard at nothing. Just
answering the phone, or taking part in worthless prattle and
small talk. God wants to be known to the "Egyptians"—those
who are not yet believers. He works through the many
faithful of his church.

There was a time that Egypt and many other nations
worshiped the true God. Isaiah prophesied this. They
worshiped the true God of the Jews in about the seventh
century B.C and later in the early centuries of Christianity.

The Lord paved the way. The followers of God were the
instruments. They still are!

ROLAND SEBOLDT

*Lord, help us in our daily labors and in our recreation
that we remain mindful of you. Help us so that our
decisions may be pleasing in your sight. Amen*

Prayer concern: Christians in the Middle East

Daily Reflections_____

Looking Back

But Lot's wife looked back. ❖ Genesis 19:26 (NIV)

There is a way of living in the past that is unhealthy. Longing for "the good ol' days" is evidence of spiritual senility, a spiritual hardening of the arteries. In the case of Lot's wife that hardening is graphically illustrated.

There has been no "golden age." Certainly the Sodom of Lot's day was anything but a model. Yet there is a great temptation to begin living in the past. A person's habits become dear to them, even in a mean and perverse community. Family ties run deep, even when the relatives have glaring faults. Most people manage a measure of security that becomes very dear, even in an insecure society. His wife could not keep from looking back. Remember how Israel in the wilderness uncertainly began to look longingly at the awful, but certain, old days in Egypt?

Nostalgia for the past is understandable. If it becomes a hindrance to positive forward action it is destructive. It will harden its adherents into an unmoving block of salt.

DAVID PREUSS

Lord, protect us from being so enamored by the past that we fail to move ahead. Amen

Prayer concern: Openness to the future

Daily Reflections_____

_____

_____

The No-Yes-Yes-No Man

Jonah obeyed the word of the LORD and went to
Nineveh. ❖ Jonah 3:3a (NIV)

Read only this part of an unlikely story from long ago and far
away, and you have a certain picture of Jonah: an obedient,
God-fearing man who very much wants to do God's will. A
fine example for all. But the whole picture of the man is
something else.

In chapter 1 of Jonah, we hear him saying, "Not me, God,"
and running the other way. In chapter 2 he is yelping, "Get
me out of here, God, and I'll do just what you want." In
chapter 3 we see him doing just that—and a difficult job it is.
In chapter 4 we find him pouting, resentful that God would so
readily save a city full of wicked people just because they
turned back to him for mercy.

Chapter 4 also brings another emotional swing. Jonah is
grateful to God for the miracle of a shade plant to protect him
from the blazing sun where he sits pouting. Then once more
he is bitterly critical when the plant dies.

A "no-yes-yes-no" kind of man. "Yes" when the going is
good; "no" when it doesn't please him. Not too different from
me, I guess.

GERTRUDE MEES

*Lord, when I'm like Jonah, forgive—and be to me the
God of steadfastness and encouragement. Amen*

Prayer concern: Those living under tyranny

Daily Reflections

_____

_____

_____

The Painful Shortfall

I press on toward the goal to win the prize for
which God has called me heavenward in Christ
Jesus. ❖ Philippians 3:14 (NIV)

I hate running worse than anyone I know. That is why I was
so utterly surprised when I rounded that final turn at a high-
school track meet and found that I stood a good chance of
placing in the quarter-mile. I willed speed into my tiring leg
muscles as they filled with lactic acid, the substances that
makes a runner's legs feel thick and slow.

Just before crossing the white line, I threw myself ahead
of yet another runner and collapsed on the old-fashioned
cinder track. "Second place," I thought.

Unfortunately the other runners didn't stop until they
crossed the second white line, the true finish line. I came in
last place!

My mistake? I had taken my eyes off the goal and had
quite literally fallen short.

DAVID A. SORENSON

Lord, keep my eyes always on you. Amen

Prayer concern: Youth counselors

Daily Reflections_____

_____

_____

_____

Atonement

In this way he will make atonement for the Most
Holy Place. ❖ Leviticus 16:16a (NIV)

The book of Leviticus is a book of laws—ceremonial, moral,
and purifying. These laws were to be known and obeyed.
Violation of them was sin.

Once a year on the Day of Atonement the high priest
entered the holy of holies to make an atonement for the sins
of the people. That day he sprinkled the blood of the slain
goat on the mercy seat. The sins of the people made
everything unclean—not only themselves, but also the
tabernacle, the altar, and the holy of holies.

Atonement was made by the shedding of blood, for
without shedding of blood there was no remission of sins. As
Christians we do not keep the Day of Atonement. On Good
Friday, Jesus gave his life for us. The holy of holies is now
available to all. Christ is the high priest whose blood was shed
for our sins.

RODERICK N. SENFT

*God, we thank you for the sacrifice of Jesus whose blood
was shed for our sins. We thank you that we have been
forgiven and pray that you will make us worthy of what
Christ has done for us. We pray in his name. Amen*

Prayer concern: Those who feel trapped in isolation

Daily Reflections

Reversing Our Goals

If it is possible, as far as it depends on you, live at
peace with everyone. ❖ Romans 12:18 (NIV)

We demand our rights! No one is going to shove us around!
If they want a fight, we'll give it to them!

That's how most of us feel most of the time. We're not
going to let anyone put anything over on us. It's humiliating
to be a loser. We have to prove that we're as good as anyone
else.

Paul tells us we're all wrong. Do whatever you can, he
says, to get along with people who are obstinate, unpleasant,
selfish, insulting. Don't even try to get even. Forgive and
forget. Do not be overcome by evil, but overcome evil with
good.

If we asked him why, Paul would probably answer with a
verse from another of his letters: "Love does not insist on its
own way; it is not irritable or resentful; . . . Love bears all
things, believes all things, hopes all things, endures all
things."

EDWARD W. UTHE

*Help us, O God, to substitute a desire to serve humbly for
our desire to be respected and admired. Help us to
substitute an interest in the well-being of others for our
own pride. Help us to bear, to believe, to hope, and to
endure all things. We ask it in the name of Jesus Christ,
our Lord. Amen*

Prayer concern: Those who feel afraid

Daily Reflections

Christ Alone

But now, by dying to what once bound us, we
have been released from the law so that we serve
in the new way of the Spirit, and not in the old
way of the written code. ❖ Romans 7:6 (NIV)

Faith in Christ is the gift of the Holy Spirit. By the Spirit we
are made members of the body of Christ. As members of
Christ, we must also follow Christ. "If we live by the Spirit,
let us also walk by the Spirit" (Galatians 5:25).

Alas, many Christians have a false notion of the Christian
life. They believe that they ought to live by the law. But this is
not according to the New Testament. Paul says we are dead
to the law because we are free from the law. Not even in the
Christian life is the law able to bring forth works pleasing to
God, for no one is able to do good by being told to do so. Yet
this is all that the law can do; to demand the good life. Hence
the law always kills, driving people to despair. Only through
faith in Christ is the new life a reality, for the Spirit of Christ
sets us free from the law of sin and death.

OTTO W. HEICK

Holy Spirit, strong and mighty,
Thou who makest all things new,
Make thy work within me perfect,
Help me by thy word so true. Amen

Prayer concern: Athletes

Daily Reflections_____

_____

_____

_____

The Greater War

For what I do is not the good I want to do; no, the
evil I do not want to do. ❖ Romans 7:19 (NIV)

A war rages in the human heart and will. Good is arrayed
against evil, selfishness against unselfishness, honesty
against deceit, pride against humility. Every human being
who is honest with himself will join in the cry of Paul:
"Wretched man that I am! Who will deliver me from this body
of death?"

We would much rather rise above our own security and
make the generous choice. But we sink back into our fears.
We make brave resolutions to stop some wretched habit.
But we slip again. We plan in marble. But we build in crumbly
clay.

Each of us is a military target for the cosmic powers doing
battle for our souls. God is pitted against Satan; the new man
in Christ battles the Old Adam.

"Who will deliver me?" cried Paul. There is a deliverer:
Christ Jesus who conquered evil and lets victory be ours.
The war that rages within us has already been won. Through
Christ we are victors!

ALVIN ROGNESS

*Thanks be to God, who gives us the victory, through
Christ our Lord. Amen*

Prayer concern: Discipline in our faith

Daily Reflections_____

_____

_____

_____

Mastering Life

Those who hope in the LORD will renew their strength. They will soar on wings like eagles; they will run and not grow weary, they will walk and not be faint. ❖ Isaiah 40:31 (NIV)

A crisis may come to you at a time of illness, or death in the family, or in the midst of your work. Moments will be sprung upon you without warning during which you will feel that the future depends on the decision of an instant. Great tasks will confront you unexpectedly that will demand the gathering together of all your resources. There is only one way to be ready for such times as these and that is to live near Christ. Then nothing will seem to be impossible for you. However rough and however severe the struggle, you will be able to keep going. You will be master of the crisis. But in order to do this you must start from Christ—setting out on your journey from the foot of the cross. You must walk as Christ walked so that he might sustain you amid your trials. You must walk toward Christ for he endured the Cross is waiting for you.

WILLIAM GORDEN JOYCE

Lord Jesus, you have redeemed us, fill us with a pure and perfect love that we may do your will. Whether we live or die let us be yours alone and forever. Help us or we perish! Amen

Prayer concern: Those who work for peace

Daily Reflections

The Cost of Discipleship

If the world hates you, keep in mind that it hated me first. ❖ John 15:18 (NIV)

How hard it is to be a true follower of our Lord! So easy to pretend the way, to mimic the motions, to echo the words. So hard to be fully committed to him who is the way, the truth, and the life. But if, by his help, we succeed and truly follow, what then? Rewards and popularity here and now? Hardly. The "world" is allergic to the goodness of Christ.

How long has it been since you felt rejected by others because you intend to be true to Jesus Christ? Maybe you know well the hot scorn or the cold contempt with which people try to hurt those whom they cannot manage. At work or at play, within the family or all alone, each of us must sooner or later learn what it costs to confess and to live up to the name we bear by Christ's love.

"Penintently, patiently, even thankfully . . . in suffering the church discovers the freedom it has only in Christ." Cut off, scattered, persecuted, he nevertheless unites us; he never leaves us.

E. THEODORE BACHMANN

O Christ, cost what it may to follow you, lead on—today and in coming days. Be our strength, and show us how to answer hatred and love, in you most precious name. Amen

Prayer concern: Those people who are persecuted for their faith

Daily Reflections_____

_____

_____

_____

Don't Give Up

Because of the increase of wickedness, the love
of most will grow cold. ❖ Matthew 24:12 (NIV)

Do we follow the crowd? Is Christ's way the way of
conformity and similarity? We all remember The apostle
Paul's advice in Romans characterizes the Christian life as
one of transformation rather than conformity. We do not
determine our pattern of living according to public opinion,
social popularity, or even personal danger. We follow Christ.

And yet, the temptation comes to all of us to slow down, to
easy up, to be less a disciple of Christ and more a duplicate
of our contemporaries. At a time when many are giving only
lip service to the church of Jesus Christ, it isn't easy to give
"life service."

Jesus tells of an increase of evil and a decrease of devotion
in the days before his return. There are those who will desert
him when the going gets tough. Whatever tomorrow brings,
however great the odds, let us pledge our lives to him.

H. CARL ROESSLER

*We need your presence in our daily lives, O God our
Father, to see us through our temptation to falter in
faithfulness. You alone are the source of the kind of
strength we need. When all are forsaking your Son, may
we still be found faithful. Amen*

Prayer concern: Those experiencing peer pressure

Daily Reflections

The Visitation

But with righteousness he shall judge the poor.
❖ Isaiah 11:4 (NRSV)

The store suddenly fell quiet. A family of strangers had entered. Their clothes were tattered, their faces dirty, and the smell of sweat surrounded them. They had come to purchase a few necessities with their meager resources, but the clerks ignored them and other customers shied away from them. They were poor, and the people around them judged them harshly because of their condition.

When the Lord comes, the poor shall be judged with righteousness. The Lord is able to judge from this new perspective because the Lord has become one of us. The Lord does not see us as separated by money, social position, job, or talents. The Lord sees us as people who need to be loved, and as sinners who need to be forgiven.

As we strive to bring in the kingdom of God, may we see people as the Lord sees them.

ANONYMOUS

Lord, help us to see the world through your eyes of love. Amen

Prayer concern: People living in poverty

Daily Reflections_____

The Remedy for Anger

But I tell you that anyone who is angry with
his brother will be subject to judgment.
❖ Matthew 5:22 (NIV)

Once I was defending my belief in forgiveness through a God
of grace to two missionaries who professed "another gospel."
They could not understand how someone who had committed
murder could get to heaven with "lesser sinners." I have
always regretted I did not think to share today's passage with
them, for it aptly shows that sin is not only an act we commit
but is part of our inborn nature. (Who hasn't been angry?)

It is difficult to perceive that something as common as
anger can be as vile as murder, but we must believe it, for
Jesus said it is so.

I have a pet anger that Satan tries to stir up in me from
time to time. When it resurfaces, there are two things I can
do: I can nurse it, or I can yield it to Jesus. Foolishly I may try
to do the former for a while, but I always find I have no peace
until I relinquish it to the only one who is equipped to handle
it for me.

NANCY LEE SASSER

*Lord Jesus, still my anger and help me to forgive others.
Amen*

Prayer concern: A relative

Daily Reflections

Beloved Teacher

Guard me as the apple of your eye; hide me in the
shadow of your wings. ❖ Psalm 17:8 (NRSV)

In ancient Israel, to be "the apple of the eye" was to be a
pupil. Rabbis and teachers cherished their students and
considered it a privilege to teach them. Likewise, students
were honored to be chosen and loved their instructors dearly.
Thankfully, today many teachers still cherish their students
and many students respect and value their teachers.

Take a moment to remember and give thanks for a special
teacher in your life and for a special young person whom you
many have taught in Sunday school or taught simply by
standing in line at the grocery store and striking up a caring
conversation.

The prayer of the psalmist, "guard me . . . hide me," is
about teaching and learning one's faith. As children of God,
we are students who seek learning, counsel, and direction
from our Lord. Like the psalmist, we too pray that we will
always feel the love of our beloved teacher. The psalmist also
speaks about the need for protection and deliverance during
times of trial. A teacher does much more than impart
knowledge; a teacher provides for a student's safety. God
provides us with such a sanctuary whenever we need it.

JAMES LYNCH

Jesus, guard and hide us as we grow in faith. Amen

Prayer concern: Teachers and students

Daily Reflections_____
_____
_____
_____

Passing on the Faith

I am reminded of your sincere faith, a faith that
lived first in your grandmother Lois and your
mother Eunice and now, I am sure, lives in you.
❖ 2 Timothy 1:5 (NRSV)

Is faith taught or caught? It is probably both. A child who
grows up in a home where family members model faithful
Christian living cannot help but catch the sense of wonder
and awe at the great power and tender mercies of God.

On the other hand, a 1990 study of Christian education by
the Search Institute showed that the number one influence
on a person's faith maturity is conversation about God with
one's mother. Paul recognized this in Timothy, whose mother
and grandmother were both women of faith. What a rich
heritage Timothy must have had, sitting at the feet of these
women. When such teaching goes on in the home, the child
will grow into a faithful Christian who is able to share God's
love with the world.

We can foster faith nurture in the home. God will grow that
faith so that our children will become mature Christians who
will both know and proclaim God's word with power and love.

CAROL A. BURK

*God of power, help us to form a circle of God's love
around all our children. Give us courage to proclaim
your good news to all generations. Amen*

Prayer concern: Christians in Kenya

Daily Reflections

Meaning Beyond Words

*. . . because our gospel came to you not
simply with words, but also with power, with
the Holy Spirit and with deep conviction.*
❖ 1 Thessalonians 1:5a (NIV)

When we are listening to someone, we pick up subtle cues
from inflections of voice, facial expressions, and bodily
language that convey meanings along with the words we
hear. And familiarity with another's way of life adds a further
dimension to how we interpret what he says.

It is for this reason that any distinction between word and
deed is artificial when we are communicating the good news—
the gospel. How good this news may be to those who hear it
depends to a great extent upon how good the news is to those
of us who tell it. Our certainty as to its truth, our openness to
its power, our sensitivity to the nuances of the Spirit among
us—these come across when we speak of God's love.

The variety represented in our individual experiences in
Christ lends a richness and diversity to the message through
which others hear and believe. Each of us is a unique
communicator for Christ.

GERALD E. CURRENS

*We thank you, Lord, for those who led us to faith and for
the opportunity to tell others what we believe. Amen*

Prayer concern: Christians in Mexico

Daily Reflections_____

_____

_____

_____

Day 171 ❖ Ephesians 1:3-14

The Names We Inherit

In Christ we have also obtained an inheritance.
❖ Ephesians 1:11 (NRSV)

A friend of mine used to say that the only thing he knew about raising teenagers was that when the going got rough, he would remind them of their inheritance. I smiled when I heard him say that, thinking that perhaps a bribe or threat of cutting off funds might work with my teenager, too.

"Oh, no," he said, "this has nothing to do with money. Whenever my teens get into a potentially difficult situation, I tell them to remember the names they inherited. First they have a family name that belongs to them, their brothers and sisters, and their parents, as well as to their grandparents and forebearers. But even more important than that, they have the name Christian, with its deep spiritual connections that extend globally and reach far into the past. I simply tell them to remember their inheritance, to remember who they are, and then act accordingly."

NORMA JEAN MATZKE

For our inheritance, for our names as your children, may we be grateful, O God. Amen

Prayer concern: Adolescents and young adults

Daily Reflections_____

Peculiar Peace

Again Jesus said, "Peace be with you! As
the Father has sent me, I am sending you."
❖ John 20:21 (NIV)

Ambassadors of peace is one way of describing Christ's true
apostles. But what peace does he intend extending through
his "sent ones"? He distinguished it from the world's "peace"
(Matthew 10:34). He confounds his followers by describing
their mission as that of sheep among wolves (Matthew
10:16)—hardly a peaceful picture. He insists on the priority of
his claims over those of the family (Luke 14:26), hardly a
peaceful picture.

More than giving us a sense of security in an upsetting
situation, Jesus gives his peace as the knowledge that in the
reality of the resurrection, the awful abyss separating human
beings from their creator has been overcome. Death is not
a dead end. The death of Christ and his consequent
resurrection give us a handrail into history, grounds for
grasping an ultimate anchoring, and a message to carry:
"Peace be with you."

ROGER F. COOPER

*Lord Jesus, I am often afraid to accept your blessing of
peace. Help my unbelieving. Amen*

Prayer concern: Those who long for peace

Daily Reflections_____

_____

_____

_____

The Mark the Angels Will Honor

> This is how it will be at the end of the age. The angels will come and separate the wicked from the righteous and throw them into the fiery furnace, where there will be weeping and gnashing of teeth. ❖ Matthew 13:49-50 (NIV)

When we think of the role of angels in God's world, we first think of them as God's messengers. In modern times, angels are seen in the role of guardians—protectors from danger and harm.

In Matthew 13, Jesus speaks twice of another assignment. At the close of the age, angels will be called to "separate the wicked from the righteous and throw them into the fiery furnace."

Although we seem to be reluctant to speak about judgment and furnaces of fire today, Jesus was not. Jesus, the Alpha and the Omega, the beginning and the end of time, had a clear view of both. His very mission in life was to destroy the power of death. These parables, though warning of the evil, give assurance to believers. Will the angels recognize us at the end of the age? Yes! We bear the sign of the cross on our brows and in our lives.

LOWELL C. HESTERMAN

Thank you, dear Savior, that we can look forward to the end of the age with hope and assurance. Amen

Prayer concern: People who fear the end of the age

Daily Reflections_____

_____
_____
_____

Stress and Strength

Not only so, but we also rejoice . . .because we
know that suffering produces perseverance.
❖ Romans 5:3 (NIV)

I once read that a bridge is stronger when it has weight on it.
We all know that metal ore must go through great heat to be
purified and strengthened. And even fibers, such as wool or
cotton, must be pulled and twisted in the spinning process to
make threads that are strong and usable. Stress and
strengthening go together.

People need strengthening too. It isn't when things are
easy for us that we grow strong. Just as our muscles must be
exercised to make our bodies strong, so must our spirits be
exercised to make our faith strong.

Spiritual exercise often comes in the form of suffering.
Suffering is not an easy exercise, but no worthwhile effort
ever is. However, those who love our Lord Jesus and trust
him to be with them can rejoice even in suffering, knowing
that they are growing in faith and endurance.

BARBARA WILLS

*Dearest Lord, thank you for being with us at all times.
Help us to learn endurance from our times of suffering
so that we may grow in faith. Amen*

Prayer concern: The newly confirmed

Daily Reflections_____

Sacred Cows

They have cast for themselves an image of a calf,
and have worshiped it. ❖ Exodus 32:8 (NRSV)

"Keep the sermon short," a parishioner jokes with the pastor. "The Bears are playing today."

Many of us have our own "sacred cows," and they often get in the way of genuine worship and thanksgiving to God. The question we have to ask is whether the situation of the Israelites worshiping at Sinai a golden calf they molded was as unique as it may sound.

Today we, too, very often mold our own gold calves—sports, food, jobs, status, studies, leisure activities—and worship them. They may be important, but are we neglecting the one who gave them to us as gifts to enjoy?

Christ came to show us our golden calves. And Christ died for the sake of our sins, those golden calves to which we often turn instead of God. With Christ in our lives, we are able to identify the one who deserves real worship and praise, the one who is central to our lives.

EMILY DEMUTH ISHIDA

Lord, thank you for all the good things you have give us. Help us to keep them in proper perspective, not usurping your place and our lives. Amen

Prayer concern: Entertainers

Daily Reflections

Christian Service

Don't I have the right to do what I want with my own money? Or are you envious because I am generous? ❖ Matthew 20:15 (NIV)

The Christian serves God out of pure delight because the grace (undeserved mercy) God has bestowed on us through his Son, Jesus Christ.

God is saying to us: "If you want to work with me, don't start bargaining; don't start saying you are worth so much, or that you put in so much time for me, and, therefore, you deserve so much in heaven; for the kingdom of God doesn't rate on so much per hour.

I want people who are willing to follow me to the ends of the earth—to visit those who are sick mentally and physically, to clothe the naked physically and spiritually, to visit the imprisoned, and to give food and water to the hungry and thirsty—to do my will simply because they love me. Give me people who work their hearts out and expect nothing— and they will receive all the glories of the kingdom."

It's a good thing for us that the rewards of the kingdom are not decided by human beings, but by the love and mercy of our heavenly Father.

KENNETH R. ANDERSON

Lord Jesus Christ, help us to give witness to your grace and mercy to others. Keep us, by your Spirit, thankful in your service. Amen

Prayer concern: Those who serve with joy

Daily Reflections_____

Accepting the Unacceptable

"For this son of mine was dead and is alive again; he was lost and is found." So they began to celebrate. ❖ Luke 15:24 (NIV)

"Will you go to church with the children and me today?" a wife asked her husband.

"You know what they will all think of me. They don't want me there," he said.

Her eyes filled with tears. Her husband had been unfaithful to her. All of the people in the community and the small congregation knew about it.

He began to buy drinks for those in the bar who would then be his friends as long as his money lasted. Soon alcoholism began to destroy his health.

He had arrived in the far country of hardships that the prodigal son had experienced. The prodigal son confessed, "Father, I have sinned against heaven and against you. I am no longer worthy to be called your son."

"But the father said to his servants, 'Quick! Bring the best robe and put it on him. Put a ring on his finger and sandals on his feet. Bring the fattened calf and kill it. Let's have a feast and celebrate'" (Luke 15:21-23).

HAROLD H. ZIETLOW

O God, our loving Father, help us to accept for ourselves and make known to others your acceptance of unworthy sinners such as us. Amen

Prayer concern: Those in the legal profession

Daily Reflections

The Indwelling Word

No, the word is very near you; it is in your
mouth and in your heart so you may obey it.
❖ Deuteronomy 30:14 (NIV)

Christ, the living Word, makes his abode in our hearts. The
Spirit quickens us to faith in him. The Spirit widens our view
and deepens our concern for the world. The Spirit rules us,
empowers us, directs us.

This living Word is always with us. He dwells within us.
Our bodies become the "Temples of the Lord"—the place of
God. Our hearts become a throne for the King. He has
chosen to dwell in our very "midst"—to be "at home" in us.

So God's word is very near us. Our lips and lives reflect
him. He controls our hearts—motive, purpose, dedication. By
his Spirit, the word of the living Word, Christ, can be done,
and is done, through us. Behold, how blessed are the
commandments of our God! The power of the living Word
guides us each day.

ARTHUR O. F. BAUER

*Almighty God, you have revealed yourself in the living
Word, Jesus Christ. Dwell within our hearts this day and
always. Overwhelm us with your love and mercy that we
may truly commit ourselves to you. We pray in Christ's
name. Amen*

Prayer concern: Those in prison

Daily Reflections_____

_____
_____
_____

Questions from the Heart

The righteous live by their faith.
❖ Habakkuk 2:4b (NRSV)

This is the only book in the Bible that opens with three questions addressed to the Lord: How long shall I cry for help, and you will not listen? Or cry to you 'Violence!' and you will not save? Why do you make me see wrongdoing and look at trouble?" Wicked people were winning the battle of God's justice. Destruction and exile were certain. Where was God in all of this?

Do you awaken in the night with questions on your mind? And do you keep asking the same questions during the day? Why doesn't God respond to the questions you have? If you ask this question from the bottom of your heart, you have good company,

Habakkuk, one of God's prophets, asked those same questions. The Lord did answer the prophet (2:2). The heart of God's answer is in 2:4, "The righteous live by their faith." This favorite phrase also is found in Romans 1:17 and Galatians 3:11. So be of good courage. Stand firm in the power and the grace of God when your faith is fragile, or when the summer of your life turns to winter.

ROY SATRE

Dear listening God, I know that you hear my questions. Remind me to listen to your answers. Amen

Prayer concern: People who struggle with their faith

Daily Reflections_____

Plant a Tree!

*. . . not to be quickly shaken in mind or alarmed,
either by spirit or by word or by letter, as though
from us, to the effect that the day of the Lord is
already here.* ❖ 2 Thessalonians 2:2 (NRSV)

When will the world end and the judgment day foretold in the
Bible arrive? People of faith have wondered this for years.
The prospect of that day fills some dread and fear, others
with joy, and still others with a fatalistic resignation.

In his first letter to the Thessalonians, Paul conveyed with
a sense of urgency the teaching that Christ would return
soon. The young church as Thessalonica responded much as
we modern Christians do to preaching about judgment day.
Paul apparently found it necessary to amend his message to
the Thessalonians, and in this second epistle reminds them
that the time of Christ's return will be a surprise. He advises
them to pursue normal and orderly lives until that day.

Martin Luther is widely quoted as saying that if he knew
the world was to end tomorrow, he would plant a tree. We,
like Luther, and like the Thessalonians, are to live in positive
hope until our Lord's anticipated return. We need not be
paralyzed by dread or fear.

DONNA HACKER SMITH

*Help me to look for your return with hope, not fear, Lord
Christ. Amen*

Prayer concern: People who live in fear

Daily Reflections

Tsk, Tsk

This man welcomes sinners and eats with them.
❖ Luke 15:2 (NIV)

We all know the full implication of such simple arrangements of letters as "tsk, tsk." The scribes and Pharisees were muttering similar first century sentiments, finding fault with Jesus. They whispered in scorn that he dared to eat with sinners. With a tone of condescension in their voices the religious leaders wanted to set themselves apart from what they considered to be such appalling action.

Does their attitude have a familiar ring? Perhaps. Too often we try to build ourselves up by disparaging others. Our lapses don't seem so bad if we look at the sins of others. We say, "At least I've never stooped to what they are doing."

The religious elite sneered that this man, Jesus, actually fellowshipped with undesirables. But what is the church if not a gathering place for sinners? Thank God that Jesus does receive sinners! We are all part of that club, and Jesus invites us all to the fellowship of faith! We all stand equal at the foot of the cross.

BARBARA BIRKELAND

Forgiving Lord, silence our muttering and murmuring as we enter your open arms. Amen

Prayer concern: People who have been hurt by the pornography industry

Daily Reflections_____

_____

_____

_____

Alone

Then, because so many people were coming and
going that they did not even have a chance to eat,
he said to them, "Come with me by yourselves to a
quiet place and get some rest." ❖ Mark 6:31 (NIV)

Whether we are age 8 or 80, there are times when we
desperately want to be alone. We need to go alone so we can
think, remember, daydream, plan, and pray. We need to "get
it all together," so to speak. Like a weary player after a hard
game, we need to rest our battered nerves.

That's the way God made us. Even Jesus and his followers
had to get away from the crowds at times. Sometimes Jesus
left everyone to go into the hills to pray alone. In this, Jesus
becomes an example for us.

So don't feel ashamed if you have to tell friends and family
that you want and need to be alone. And don't feel hurt if
your dear child or parent wants to be left alone. This is not
rejection or a sign of mental illness. It is natural, normal, and
right. In a complex world, such moments alone may be a way
to survive.

HAROLD L. YOCHUM

Lord, help us use well those times when we can be alone.
Help us understand the needs of our dear ones to be
alone at times. Amen

Prayer concern: Those who need a rest from their
burdens

Daily Reflections_____
_____
_____
_____

A Short Course in Godliness

And what does the LORD require of you? To act justly and to love mercy and to walk humbly with your God. ❖ Micah 6:8 (NIV)

"You can't just talk the talk; you have to walk the walk." That is not a verbatim translation, but it carries the freight of what Micah was saying. God has three expectations of those who claim to be part of God's family: do justice, love kindness, and walk humbly with God. Here are three short phrases that reflect God's nature.

Do justice. Micah says that there is too much talk and not enough action. Justice begins in each person's heart. God desires that we treat people with compassion that goes above and beyond the letter of the law.

Love kindness. Sometimes charity is done with a sense of expectation or obligation. We do things that are received kindly, but our hearts have no delighted in the sharing. We are urged to go beyond the rules of etiquette—to express kindness with such lavishness that our hearts cannot help but be aglow with love.

Walk humbly with your God. We owe everything to God. In no sense can we claim God's special favor because of our faithfulness. We can only stand in awe and gratitude that God gave everything for us, even his Son, to be our Savior.

JOHN M. BRAATEN

Holy God, let us reflect your goodness in all we do. Amen

Prayer concern: Those who seek to do justice

Daily Reflections_____
_____
_____
_____

Lord of My Life

But in your hearts set apart Christ as Lord.
❖ 1 Peter 3:15 (NIV)

Every year someone sponsors a movement to put Christ back into Christmas. Such an effort is a good one, but there are times when it would seem more necessary to put Christ back into Christianity.

The Christian religion is summed up in the person of Jesus Christ. Christianity is not just being kind to your neighbors, or doing the best you can, or living according to the Golden Rule or being in favor of the democratic way of life. These things are not the central theme.

Christianity means making Christ the Lord of your life. It means putting your whole faith in what God did for people in Christ on the cross. The smallest child learns the stories about Jesus in Sunday school and we should never grow so old that we get away from these truths. The earliest creed of the church seems to have been—Jesus is Lord. And no one can have true Christian faith today without that confession.

Take the engine out of a car and it won't go. Remove the propeller from a ship and it is useless. Take Christ out of Christianity and you have only the shell left. For Christianity is a religion with a Savior and with a gospel that tells us that we can have eternal live through that Savior.

W. A. POOVEY

Lord, Jesus, be the Lord of my life. Amen

Prayer concern: Chronic worries

Daily Reflections_____

_____
_____
_____

The Name of Jesus

... who, though he was in the form of God, did not regard equality with God as something to be exploited ... ❖ Philippians 2:6 (NRSV)

Most of us have known someone willing to use their acquaintance with a powerful person to have a traffic ticket dismissed, to get passes for the big game, or to have some other problem solved without going through the usual channels.

Today's passage from Philippians reminds us of a powerful "name" who did not view power or authority as means for self-exaltations. That person was Jesus. We are reminded that our Lord chose to humble himself, enduring the challenges and difficulties of human life in order to accomplish God's will. For his humility and example of service, his death and resurrection, we honor Jesus' name above any other.

Jesus' example of humble service and obedience to God's will is an assurance that God is with us daily in our hearts. By it we are guided in the faith and mission that lie before us.

DONNA HACKER SMITH

I call upon the holy name of Jesus today. Dear Lord, help me to serve humbly and dedicate my life completely, as you did, to God's will. Amen

Prayer concern: Those who have not heard the name of Jesus

Daily Reflections_____

_____

_____

_____

In a Mirror Dimly

O Sovereign LORD, you have begun to show to
your servant your greatness and your strong
hand. ❖ Deuteronomy 3:24 (NIV)

With all our vaunted discoveries in the natural world we have
scarcely begun to see the glory and greatness of God. Each
of us sees only a piece of God's greatness. This is also true in
God's spiritual realm. The greatest spiritual leaders were
permitted to see only fragments of God's matchless glory.
Moses stood outside looking toward the promised land.

The apostle Paul rejoiced in the establishment of little
Christian beachheads in the Mediterranean world. He could
only trust and hope they would survive and grow.
Missionaries start small "colonies of the gospel" but the
triumph of the kingdom is delayed. Our lot is to know in part,
to see "in a mirror dimly." But with the mark of faithfulness
we can enter into the joy of our Lord now.

LAWRENCE D. FOLKHEMER

The mysteries of your creation, O Lord, surpass even our
powers of imagination. Although our vision is dimmed
by finiteness and sin, we are grateful that we can know
you as our Savior. Amen

Prayer concern: Spiritual mentors

Daily Reflections_____
_____
_____
_____

Freedom to Serve

You, my brothers, were called to be free.
❖ Galatians 5:13 (NIV)

There are two ways to look at freedom. It can be something to enjoy for oneself and it can be a way to use life in the service of others.

It is not wrong to enjoy freedom if you have it. God did not intend us to be slaves. The Bible depicts sinfulness as a form of slavery, as a lack of freedom. God wants us to be free people who are able to enjoy life and appreciate it to the full.

But there is something greater than enjoying freedom in a selfish way. That is to serve other people. The person who is most free is the person who chooses to do something he or she doesn't have to do.

Children often are free to play and not to help with household chores. But they are also free to do these things.

God is pleased when we make use of the freedom from the power of sin that he has given us through Christ to use our lives so that others will benefit. Christians are free to do good, as God wants us to.

SIDNEY A. RAND

Father in heaven, teach us both what freedom is and how to use it. Amen

Prayer concern: Those who live under tyranny

Daily Reflections_____

_____

_____

Our Savior's Name

On the eighth day, when it was time to circumcise
him, he was named Jesus, the name the angel
had given him before he had been conceived.
❖ Luke 2:21 (NIV)

What's in a name? The names we choose for our children are
labels. For the most part they are neutral and have no
intrinsic meaning. We usually choose them because we like
them, not because the root meaning of the name that we find
in a name dictionary has an aura or power.

Jesus' name, however, was deliberately chosen for its
meaning. "You shall call his name Jesus, for he will save his
people from their sins." Jesus offers us God's gift of
forgiveness. He has saved us from our sins, erasing our past
and opening us to our present and future. He recalls us to our
Baptism when God grafted Christ's name to us in accepting
us into his family, the church.

We have a choice now. What are we going to do about the
name *Jesus Christ* in our lives? Will it be only a label, or will it
involve us in mission for him who has saved us from our sin?

ROBERT R. STROHL

*Lord Jesus Christ, you have called us into your family
and have inscribed your name upon us. Help us to be
witnesses to your love throughout the year. Amen*

Prayer concern: Children

Daily Reflections_____
_____
_____
_____

I Get Scared

Restore us, O God Almighty; make your
face shine upon us, that we may be saved.
❖ Psalm 80:7 (NIV)

Tucked into bed for the night the small voice requested,
"Leave my light on, Mommy. I get scared when it's dark."
I smile and flip on the light that chases away the bogeyman
in the closet and the monster under the bed. Safe in the glow
of the soft light, the little one relaxes and sleeps.

Don't you wish it were so easy to chase away the darkness
in our own lives? This might entail disappointing
relationships, the downward spiral of empty possessions, the
loneliness, the suffocating sense of godlessness, and the
stark reality of evil.

I, too, get scared when it is dark. "The light shines in the
darkness, but the darkness has not understood it" (John 1:5).

BARBARA D. SORENSON

*Shine your light, O Lord, and chase away the darkness
and despair that lies lurking in our closets and under
our beds. Amen*

Prayer concern: The United Nations

Daily Reflections_____

_____

_____

In God's Classroom

Do not let this Book of the Law depart from your
mouth; meditate on it day and night, so that you
may be careful to do everything written in it.
❖ Joshua 1:8 (NIV)

When Moses died, Joshua was appointed by God to be
Israel's deliverer. Under Joshua's leadership, Israel was to
reach the promised land. The legal provisions of the book of
Deuteronomy would be the binding authority in Israel's life.
So Joshua was to be faithful to the will of God as he
understood it.

As Christians we are not today bound by the laws within
Deuteronomy. There is a higher law for us. It is the law of
love, interpreted by Christ, and focused clearly in him. What
could be more important for us than to be serious students of
Christ, as he is made known in the Bible. Each of us—from
age 3 through 103—will do well to be found in the classroom
of God, listening to the Spirit as our teacher and guide.

JOHN V. STROM

*Lord, come to us and enlighten our minds, so that we
many understand more of the will of God for our lives
today. Help us to see our Savior clearly mirrored in
Scripture. Amen*

Prayer concern: Courage for those facing trials

Daily Reflections_____

_____

_____

_____

Royal Service

For even the Son of Man did not come to be
served, but to serve. ❖ Mark 10:45 (NIV)

It has always been hard for people to understand that the
higher a person's rank the greater is the demand for service.
When James and John came to Jesus with a request that he
should give them the chief places when they entered his
kingdom, he told them gently that such places were not in his
power to give. Those places would be given to those to whom
God allotted them. Then he went on to say that while it was
true that some kings and other powerful people took pleasure
in lording over others, "it shall not be so among you; but
whoever would be great among you, must be your servant,
and whoever would be first among you must be the slave of all."

Peter later wrote, "All of you, clothe yourselves with
humility toward one another" (1 Peter 5:5). He had learned
an important lesson! An old badge of the Prince of Wales was
the three feathers with the motto: "I serve." That ought to be
the motto of the Christian, too; for the only true royalty is the
royalty of serving others. He is king indeed, who is servant of
all. Christ himself took a towel and girded himself and
washed his disciples' feet, and the disciples were told that
they must be as their Lord (John 13:1-16).

O. K. STORAASLI

*Make me as your servant, Lord, that as a free, forgiven
person I may serve others. Amen*

Prayer concern: Those who humbly serve

Daily Reflections

_____

_____

_____

A Family is Love

It always protects, always trusts, always hopes, always perseveres. ❖ 1 Corinthians 13:7 (NIV)

For better, for worse . . . for richer, for poorer . . . in sickness and in health . . ." According to traditional marriage vows, a husband and wife are to withstand such problems through love. And naïve is anyone who thinks that marriage and a family do not stretch love to its limits.

Love is what holds a family together. Not love in the sense of sentiment, but love as a pliable sharing of the adventures of life. Money, health, career, reputation, children help make that love more comfortable, but they are not the core of a family. It is only as long as family love is patterned after the love of God for his children that family solidarity holds up. God's love outlasts anything else, and true family love outlasts adversity. That is why the love within a family, as well as from God, bears, believes, hopes, and endures all things.

EDGAR R. TREXLER

Almighty God, we give thanks for families and homes that reflect the love that you have shown us, and pray that where such love is lost, that it may be regained. This we ask for your glory, and in the name of your Son. Amen

Prayer concern: Families

Daily Reflections_____

_____

_____

_____

Belonging to Another

You belong to Christ, and Christ belongs to God.
❖ 1 Corinthians 3:23 (NRSV)

"Who am I?" Many of us struggle with this question at different times in our lives. The question can come when a radical change occurs, such as the birth of a child or children leaving home. The change can be when bereavement occurs, a job dissolves, or a new occupation is found. It can come as we meet different points in the aging process—adolescence, young adulthood, middle age, and older age.

The question strikes most often when we feel the roots of our self-identity shaking. It grabs us when what we have counted on for our self-definition—a person, an activity, or a status—simply is no longer there.

The Christian has a refuge when the question comes around. First of all, we are our Lord's. We are Christ's baptized and forgiven people, his instruments of love to the world. However else our self-identity twists and turns, that much, by our Lord's own promise, will never change.

KAREN BATES

Lord, let our identity rest first of all on your love for us. Amen

Prayer concern: Peace in our world

Daily Reflections

A New Certainty

*Why are you troubled, and why do doubts rise in
your minds?* ❖ Luke 24:38 (NIV)

A huge billboard in London once announced the message,
"THE WAR IS OVER!" But the hitch was in the small print at the
bottom, which read, "IF YOU WANT IT." The whole thing was a
season's greeting from John Lennon and his wife, Yoko Ono.
It was intended, they said, to get people thinking about the
continuing violence in the world and to confront people with
the need to change.

Easter is the announcement of God's victory over sin,
death, and evil. There is peace for all because of what God
has done—if we want it.

The disciples were slow to grasp the victorious meaning of
the resurrection of Jesus. Even when he stood among them
in Jerusalem on Easter evening, surprised by the joy of his
presence, they still "did not believe it because of joy and
amazement" (verse 41). But slowly they understood. And
with understanding there came a new certainty of the peace
and power of Easter. That certainty is ours—if we receive it.

JAMES A. BERQUIST

*In our troubled world and questioning hearts, Lord,
by your risen presence grant us peace. Amen*

Prayer concern: Those who struggle with unbelief

Daily Reflections

A Friendly Church

Accept one another, then, just as Christ
accepted you, in order to bring praise to God.
❖ Romans 15:7 (NIV)

A congenial atmosphere is essential to a truly Christian
church. It requires more than a formal welcome from the
pastor. It develops when many other members habitually
welcome strangers to the service and make them feel at
home when they come. Saint John appreciated this, for he
wrote to his friend Gaius: "Dear friend, you are faithful in
what you are doing for the brothers, even though they are
strangers to you" (3 John 5).

Long ago Christ welcomed you into the fellowship of
believers in holy baptism. When Paul said, "one another," he
surely meant all humanity. The words must mean the same
for us today. A congregation is not intended to continue as an
exclusive circle of intimates and their descendants and
acquired relatives. Our Lord wants us to welcome all people
to share God's gift of salvation.

OSCAR A. BENSON

*We thank you, Lord, for receiving us so graciously into
your fellowship. Cleanse our hearts of the lurking desire
to deny to any fellow human that supreme privilege.
Hear us in Jesus' name. Amen*

Prayer concern: Visitors in your congregation

Daily Reflections_____

_____

_____

_____

Day 196 ❖ Deuteronomy 6:1-3

Pass It On

That you, your children and their children after
them may fear the LORD your God as long as you
live by keeping all his decrees and commands . . .
❖ Deuteronomy 6:2a (NIV)

Families create and pass on many traditions from generation
to generation. It may be something as simple as how to
prepare a special homemade wheat bread or as complicated
as how to run the family farm. Traditions produce strong
bonds between family past and present.

Of all the traditions that a family passes on, the most
important is the worship and reverence of the Lord. The
family that chooses to honor God in thought, word and deed
is building a strong foundation for the next generation.

If you haven't already done so, why not begin creating
traditions of faith that your children and your children's
children may pass on? Begin by worshiping in a Christ-
centered congregation. At home, have daily devotions in
which all family members participate. Develop some ways of
celebrating God's presence that become unique to your own
family. Help one another—and ask the Spirit's help—to read
and love and obey the scriptures. Build well, then pass it on!

JUDY HEVEEN

Father, help our family honor you. Amen

Prayer concern: Christians in Italy

Daily Reflections_____
_____
_____
_____

On Seeing Beyond a Small World

The LORD reigns, he is robed in majesty.
❖ Psalm 93:1a (NIV)

Our world is really a small world. It is bounded by our sorrows, pains, crises, joys, and triumphs. So it is that we take God into our world that he may help us in a very personal way.

Because of this, we are prone to see God as the Holy One who serves, rather than the Lord God who reigns. Yet the world of God encompasses the stars, the planets, the vastness of space, everything, everywhere. God created it. God established it. God reigns over it.

The miracle is that, specks though we are in a universe so vast that it staggers our imagination, God recognizes us. In Jesus Christ, God does this very thing. For God's entrance in Christ into our tiny world enables us to see beyond it and, in seeing beyond it, to be less anxiously and selfishly concerned about it. God grants us the peace that passes all understanding.

DWIGHT A. HUSEMAN

God, grant that, in seeing the vastness of the kingdom under your reign, we may entrust ourselves wholly to your care. For our world and our cares are ever so slight when placed beside the boundlessness of your love. In Christ's name, Amen

Prayer concern: Those who share God's peace

Daily Reflections

The Christian's Credentials

The people were amazed at his teaching, because
he taught them as one who had authority, not as
the teachers of the law. ❖ Mark 1:22 (NIV)

If a speaker wants a hearing today, he needs to be able to
show that he knows what he's talking about. His words then
have a ring of authority.

Jesus amazed people because he spoke with authority.
And this may be the key for us in our evangelism efforts. We
need to realize that speaking about love, forgiveness,
concern, acceptance, and other great and noble themes of the
church is not much use unless the one who speaks is loving
and forgiving and concerned and accepting.

Speaking with authority does not depend on our academic
qualifications. But it does depend on what sort of people we
are. Speaking the gospel is important, and to say the words
clearly and appropriately is a needed skill. But our words take
on authority only when the gospel takes on flesh and blood in
our own lives.

DANIEL A. DICKHART

*When we're discouraged about our ineffective evan-
gelism methods, Lord, remind us that we must both
speak and be the gospel. Help us to know him better,
whose word we are called to speak, Jesus Christ our
Lord. Amen*

Prayer concern: Christians in Pakistan

Daily Reflections_____

_____

_____

A Day of Good News

Let's go at once and report this to the royal
palace. ❖ 2 Kings 7:9 (NIV)

Samaria was under siege. Starvation stalked through the city.
Elisha made the bold prediction, that "about this time
tomorrow a measure of fine meal shall be sold for a shekel."

The king of Samaria refused to believe this. See what
happened. Four lepers, sitting at the entrance to the gate,
were also hungry. They might enter the city and starve. Or
they might remain where they were and starve. Or, the might
risk their lives by stealing food from the enemy.

They chose to enter the tents of the enemy. They found
them empty. Evidence showed that the enemy had fled in
haste, leaving provisions and arms behind. The lepers ate
their fill and sat down to think things over. They arrived at
the conclusion "This is the day of good news—let us go and
tell the king's household."

We have been called, enlightened, and sanctified. We have
fed on heavenly food. Thinking things over we, too, must
come to the conclusion, "This is the day of good news—let us
tell the king's household"

GEORGE W. KRUEGER

*Lord Jesus Christ, you have saved us. You have healed
and helped us. Help us to bring the good news of
salvation to all who sit in darkness. Amen*

Prayer concern: People who are hungry

Daily Reflections_____

Overcoming the World

> Who is it that overcomes the world? Only he who
> believes that Jesus is the Son of God. ❖ 1 John 5:5 (NIV)

In our day people lack security, we are told. In spite of having one of the world's highest standards of living, which should assure our happiness, we don't have it.

Young people of high school and college age want to know what to do with life, what occupation to plan, and whom to marry. And we all want the government to do as much as possible to ease the tensions and problems of life.

What we need is a sense of "overcoming." This does not mean always having it easy or never having problems. It does mean being able to live in this world without letting it overcome you. The Bible gives us a clear promise that faith in Christ equips us for life in this world. Our lack of assurance or security could well be due to a lack of faith in him.

Christians are not people with a magic wand for life's ills. They are, or ought to be, the most realistic folks there are. They know the problem: The world presents all kinds of possibilities for ill. But they possess a strategy to counter this. They know that a life dedicated to the Christ who overcame sin, death, and the world shares his power and his peace.

SIDNEY A. RAND

Gracious Lord, help us to overcome in you. Amen

Prayer concern: Those living in fear and insecurity

Daily Reflections_____

_____

_____

_____

Love's Ultimate

Greater love has no one than this, that he lay
down his life for his friends. ❖ John 15:13 (NIV)

You might remember the fairy story about the Deadly
Desert, where the sands would destroy any living thing. But
the desert was crossed by a magic carpet, which unrolled
before a person and rolled up again behind.

So we move in a perilous world that is destructive of true
humanity. The magic carpet that unrolls before us and rolls
up behind us is the demonstrated love of God in the actions
of our Lord.

To talk about a law of love and to try to apply such a law
makes us idealistic and vague. But there is nothing vague
about John 15:13. God has demonstrated his love in the Son.
This demonstration in the cross is carried out in the midst of
the disciples. The disciples themselves are swept into the
act—therefore they are now "friends." And as "friends" they
do what they are commanded to do.

HENRY E. HORN

O Love that will not let me go,
I rest my weary soul in you;
I give you back the life I owe,
That in your ocean depths its flow
May richer, fuller be. Amen

Prayer concern: The oppressed

Daily Reflections_____

_____

_____

_____

Exaltation from Humility

For everyone who exalts himself will be humbled, and he who humbles himself will be exalted. ❖ Luke 14:11 (NIV)

In the midst of Jerusalem is the Dome of the Rock, a rock sacred to three of the world's great religions. To Muslims, it is the spot where Mohammed ascended to heaven; to Jews and Christians, it is where Abraham endured the ultimate test of his faith when he offered to sacrifice Isaac. This rock is a cornerstone in the foundation of these religions. Can we really be so far apart in the religions of the world when we can find such a spot in such a country where history, politics, and religion blend together just as the ethnic mix of the people?

Remaining foremost, above all the history and all the politics and the religious heritage, is Jesus. His own humility triumphed over the cross. He is exalted as God's redeemer. Can we unite our lives in common fellowship with each other? Can our love reach out, as Jesus' did, to everyone? Can we share the joy of our faith with others? Then we, too, can be exalted.

RICHARD S. SCHWEIKER

Lord Jesus, make us humble as you were humble. Touch our lives so that your love will shine within us and radiate from us. Amen

Prayer concern: Humility

Daily Reflections_____

_____

_____

_____

Day 203 ❖ John 1:40-42

Jesus and Andrew and Peter

> The first thing Andrew did was to find his brother
> Simon and tell him, "We have found the Messiah" . . .
> And he brought him to Jesus. ❖ John 1:41-42 (NIV)

Andrew was a disciple of John the Baptist. Andrew listened to
John's preaching about Christ, and knew him when he came.
He was so thoroughly convinced that Jesus was the Christ
that he led his own brother Peter to be his follower.

Here is a feast of food for prayerful thought today. Do we
listen to gospel preaching? Does our listening lead to a
knowledge and a following of Christ? Do we live the truth we
know? Do the zeal and certainty of our faith persuade others
to come to the Savior? Do we win those of our own
household?

Andrew thought of others. He first brought Peter to Jesus.
Peter came to share with Andrew all the enriching intimate
experiences of Christ—on the mountain top, in the Upper
Room, in the garden of prayer.

Andrew could not have changed Peter from an ordinary
fisherman into a leader among the apostles. But he did what
he could—he brought his brother. Jesus transformed Peter
the Galilean into the man of God.

ANONYMOUS

*O God, draw us so near to you that we may draw to you
those who are near us. Amen*

Prayer concern: Your family members

Daily Reflections_____
_____
_____
_____

How Rich Are You?

> And my God will meet all your needs according to his
> glorious riches in Christ Jesus. ❖ Philippians 4:19 (NIV)

How rich was Jesus? On earth he appeared poor indeed—in a
borrowed manger, in a borrowed boat, on a borrowed colt.
Even in a borrowed tomb. Yet this was because he "humbled
himself," or "became poor" for our sake.

How rich was the Apostle Paul? His father, a Pharisee, was
probably a rich man. Paul, however, suffered the loss of all
things when he became a bond-servant of Christ. He doubtless
lost his earthly inheritance. He labored long and hard with his
own hands. He experienced hardship, hunger, and thirst. Yet
in union with Christ Paul was surely rich, as the portion before
us today clearly shows. He was filled with every needful gift
and blessing.

How rich are you? You might not have large bank accounts
or lavishly furnished homes. But those things do not make
one rich in the best sense. They belong to the category of
treasures that eventually perish. Are you "rich toward God?"
Are you daily enriched in every way. "In Spirit?" Are you able
to make others rich by your life and witness? If you experience
the blessed truth of our text (verse 19), you are rich indeed.

MILTON H. SCHRAM

O God, make us deeply grateful for your heavenly gifts,
for the riches of your grace. Amen

Prayer concern: The poor

Daily Reflections_____

_____

_____

_____

Command Performance

I was appointed a herald and an apostle and a teacher. That is why I am suffering as I am. Yet I am not ashamed, because I know whom I have believed, and am convinced that he is able to guard what I have entrusted to him for that day.
❖ 2 Timothy 1:11-12 (NIV)

When the President or Prime Minister summons an individual to offer him an appointment to an important post in the government, that person rarely declines. One doesn't lightly refuse his country's leader. It's almost like a command performance before royalty.

We ought to feel the same sort of reluctance to refuse God's invitations to work for him.

The writer of today's verse was willing to endure suffering, if need be, because God "appointed" him to proclaim the good news. He was even confident about it all: "I know whom I have believed."

The King of kings and Lord of lords has called us to proclaim his good news today. We dare not refuse.

PAULWYN L. BOLICK

Father, we hear your call to proclaim the good news in our community, but we don't always take it seriously. Impress upon us the gravity of our responsibility. Make us more willing because we know you in whom we have trusted. Amen

Prayer concern: Those who work in the media

Daily Reflections_____

_____

_____

_____

How to Meet a Crisis

The LORD will fight for you; you need only to be
still. ❖ Exodus 14:14 (NIV)

Crisis looms. Things are not going as expected. We are worse
off than before. What then shall we do?

There are many moments in history when just such
sentiments have prevailed in the hearts of people. It is sad,
but interesting commentary on humankind to relate the story
of how people have reacted in the face of crisis.

Moses reacted by reaffirming his faith in the Lord, thus
bringing all his Israelite children to his side. In Moses' day
and age, the crisis was an army of Egypt's Pharaoh; in our
day, it is ballistic missiles, and terrorism. But though the
shape of the crises may vary, the response of faith is still the
only answer. Other answers are false solutions and are built
on vain hopes. No array of political alliances or strategic
weapons can substitute for firm faith in the Lord, who
preserves and watches over his own.

ROBERT R. CLARK

*Dear heavenly Father, give us the will to fight our battles
faithfully, as sinners made righteous in your sight
through Jesus Christ our Lord. Amen*

Prayer concern: Those suffering from terrorism

Daily Reflections_____
_____
_____

Waiting in the Presence

Come up to me on the mountain, and wait there.
❖ Exodus 24:12 (NRSV)

Waiting is difficult. Minutes become hours in a hospital emergency waiting room. Time nearly stops while waiting for an overdue traveler. After years of captivity, the people of Israel waited for God to give the law to Moses. For six days they waited and watched the cloud-covered mountain. Finally, on the seventh day, God called to Moses. Even then, the wait was not over; Moses was on the mountain for another 40 days and nights.

Appointment books, day-planners, to-do lists, and schedules are ways to reduce our waiting time. Waiting, we say, is not productive; it is boring. Although we work hard to manage time, sometimes we find that we are on God's time. And God's time is full of waiting.

Noah and his family waited 40 days for the rain to stop and another 10 months for the water to subside. Abraham and Sarah waited decades for their promised son, Isaac. Jesus lay in the tomb for three days before the stone was rolled away.

"Come up to me on the mountain," God said, "and wait there." Amazing things happen when we wait on God's time.

THOMAS S. HANSON

O God, let my soul wait for you in joy and hope. Amen

Prayer concern: Those who seek peace of mind

Daily Reflections_____

_____

_____

_____

Your Turn!

Elijah passed by him and threw his mantle over
him. ❖ 1 Kings 19:19b (NRSV)

While a good novelist or screenwriter generally gives us
some background motivation and context for what the
characters in their stories do, there is an abruptness to many
biblical stories that is nothing short of disconcerting. The
story of Elijah calling Elisha is one of those stories.

Without a word, the prophet Elijah passes by Elisha, who
we are told was plowing a field, and draped his cloak over
him, symbolizing that God was passing the mantle of prophet
and leader from Elijah to Elisha. Elijah did not even stop for
a second to see what they surprised Elisha would do.

As readers of this story we have many questions: Were
Elijah and Elisha already acquainted? Why did Elisha
respond so quickly and willingly? Was this expected or
unexpected?

The suddenness of this story, like so many other Bible
stories, serves to remind us that God is constantly breaking
into our world in surprising ways and places. Elisha's quick
response further reminds us of how we are to respond when
God calls. Have you heard God's call yet? How did you or
how would you respond?

MARK HINTON

*Lord, grant us the wisdom to discern your call and the
strength to follow you. Amen*

Prayer concern: All mission workers overseas

Daily Reflections_____
_____
_____
_____

Christus Victor!

> Many people spread their cloaks on the road,
> while others spread branches they had cut in the
> fields. ❖ Mark 11:8 (NIV)

A Roman commander who won a great victory was honored with a triumph, a parade showing off his soldiers, his captives, and his booty. A similar honor today would be a ticker-tape parade. Fidel Castro once had such a parade down Fifth Avenue. People lined the street and shouted from windows, but few realized what he really represented.

Our Lord's entry into Jerusalem was comparable to a New York ticker-tape parade. He was the "Miracle Man" and "God's Anointed," who had come to deliver the Jews from the Romans. But few people realized what he represented.

Jesus' victory was beyond human understanding, for he overcame both death and sin. What a triumph he must have been given when his Father welcomed him home!

CLOSS PEACE WARDLAW

Help us, heavenly Father, to have some conception of the price your Son paid for victory. And show us how we may echo now his victory celebration. Amen

Prayer concern: Those in need of deliverance and hope

Daily Reflections_____

_____

_____

_____

Day 210 ❖ James 4:11-17

I Will—D.V.

Instead, you ought to say, "If it is the Lord's will,
we will live and do this or that." ❖ James 4:15 (NIV)

Did you ever get a letter telling you of the plans of the writer,
but in parenthesis were the letters D.V.? Being curious, you
probably looked them up and found that they stand for two
Latin words meaning "God willing." James says this should
be our practice in making and announcing our plans.

Can we ever be sure we are going to do what we plan to
do? A young lawyer was running for office, and his plans
were to be elected. One day he went for a physical checkup
and found out that he had cancer. It was a sad occasion when
he gathered his supporters to announce his withdrawal from
the race.

The simple truth is that, in these uncertain and fast-
changing times, no one can be certain what he will do or
where he will be tomorrow. When we make our plans, we
often put total reliance upon ourselves and forget God's plans.
We need to say with the psalmist, "My times are in your
hand," and thus acknowledge God as the determiner of our
destiny. "See you tomorrow at 9?" "Yes, D.V."

JOHN R. BROKHOFF

*Lord God, we thank you for reminding us that our times
are in your hand. May our plans be acceptable to your
will and purpose for our lives. In Jesus' name. Amen*

Prayer concern: Those who work with the homeless

Daily Reflections_____

Day 211 ❖ Psalm 138:4-8

God Preserves Our Life

Though I walk in the midst of trouble, you
preserve me. ❖ Psalm 138:7 (NRSV)

"You won't be able to think about anything else for many
months," a wise friend wrote distraught parents after a child's
sudden death. Life stops. Everything is questioned. Long-
held beliefs are examined. It is nearly impossible to find joy
or to see beauty and grace.

Slowly, perspectives change. Pain may remain, but God
leads us to a wider vision. We learn that suffering and
burdens occupy only a small portion of our life span.

We think of the years we have enjoyed without illness,
death, or disappointment; the years of full physical activity,
though now restricted; the times we were preserved from
accidents.

For many of us, a large portion of our lifetime has been
joyful. With the psalmist, we walk in the midst of trouble, but
say with thanks, "You preserve me."

ROLAND SEBOLDT

*Praise to you, O God, for preserving my life in pleasant
and troubled times. Amen*

Prayer concern: People who mourn

Daily Reflections_____

_____

_____

_____

The Power Source

Grace and peace to you from God the Father and
the Lord Jesus Christ. ❖ 2 Thessalonians 1:2 (NIV)

I once spent several days on a lonely island off the coast of
Scotland. The house where I lived was modern in every way.
It had proper wiring, attractive light fixtures, and well-located
electric switches. But we had to use kerosene lamps for
illumination because the house hadn't yet been hooked up to
the power source outside.

Sometimes we are like that house. We seem to have all the
proper Christian attributes, but we are weak and helpless, the
victims of doubt and temptation. We have failed to attach
ourselves to the power source. Paul says grace and peace
come from God and from Jesus Christ. Jesus told his
disciples that apart from him they could do nothing, and we
are in the same situation. We must be attached to God, the
source of all power. We are dependent on him for all good
things.

W. A. POOVEY

*Father, fill my life with your power. Give me your grace
and peace. Amen*

Prayer concern: Hypocrites

Daily Reflections_____
_____
_____
_____

So Now?

So now I bring the first of the fruit of the
ground that you, O LORD, have given me.
❖ Deuteronomy 26:10 (NRSV)

Action. Response. The history of God's relationship with us
follows this sequence. God acts, we respond. The people of
Israel also recounted this history. "The Lord brought us out
of Egypt, so now . . ." Deliverance and gratitude, God's
generosity, human gratitude. This pattern we can trace
throughout the Bible.

Where do you experience God's action in your own life?
Unless we prayerfully can recount our own faith history of
deliverance, blessing, comfort, and hope, our gratitude is
likely to be perfunctory. Have you felt the hand of God
leading you from death-like life to the fullness of joy?
Whether leading us through our own droughts, or subtly
prodding us toward maturing wisdom and faith, God's
restless Spirit continues to work for blessing in our lives. So
now, after the harvest God has helped to bring about, what is
our response?

CAROLYN MOWCHAN

*Dear Lord, we ask for the eyes of faith to trace and trust
your presence in our lives. Help us to respond as faithful
stewards. Amen*

Prayer concern: Those who feel hopeless

Daily Reflections_____
_____
_____
_____

Day 214 ❖ Matthew 20:8-16

God's Gift of Grace

So the last will be first, and the first will be last.
❖ Matthew 20:16 (NIV)

In this fast-paced, high-tech, commercialized world, many strive to achieve material wealth. With this material wealth we hope to satisfy our egos, and to clamber up the social and/or economic ladders of success.

As we get caught up in the treadmill of success, we must continually be cognizant of our stewardship. We should be good stewards because we want to be, not because we feel we must in order to maintain our status. Remember, all service ranks the same with God. Our stewardship is not measured in neat units of this or that. It is the love through which our stewardship of time, talent, and treasure is given, that is all-important.

How sobering. All God gives us his grace. No matter how much we give, we cannot earn what God gives us.

CARL K. G. SHAPPERT

Dear Lord, help us to understand the joy there is in giving, in being good stewards in your vineyard. May we be willing workers in your kingdom. Thanks be to you for all the blessings you have showered upon us! Amen

Prayer concern: Generosity in our stewardship

Daily Reflections_____

The Qualified Yes

He who is not with me is against me, and he who does
not gather with me, scatters. ❖ Luke 11:23 (NIV)

Have you ever met the "almost, perhaps, maybe" Christian?
Most of us would recognize one on the spot because we
ourselves fit that description—at least in part. Whenever the
influence of the gospel is weak, we can be sure that such an
area is populated by Christians who habitually respond: "I'd
like to, but!" or "I would if . . . !"

During his time on earth, Jesus knew his associates well
and recognized that most of them had a rough time
answering "yes" to his invitation: "Follow me." So Jesus also
understands our nature but he also speaks directly to our
need: "Either you're with me or against me; there's no middle
ground." We appreciate these firm words because it is easy to
compromise, to postpone, to let others sacrifice, to allow our
hearts to house divided loyalties.

As we respond to Christ with growing singleness of
purpose, we'll enjoy the wonderful experience of seeing the
effect our deep loyalty has on others.

LAWRENCE M. REESE

*O God, whose Son shared the misery of a divided spirit
and overcame temptation: grant us the measure of grace
sufficient for the healing of our divided hearts. Amen*

Prayer concern: Those struggling with mental illness

Daily Reflections_____
_____
_____
_____

The Sign of Life

Therefore the Lord himself will give you a sign.
❖ Isaiah 7:14a (NIV)

Several years ago, I took our son and several of his friends to a basketball game that was played at a school in a rural section of the county. I wasn't familiar with the road, so I asked some friends to let me follow them home. After driving several miles, we noticed that we were following the wrong car. We thought we would be able to find our way home, but we soon realized we were lost. We had traveled many miles, so we knew we would need directions to find our way back. However, there were no service stations open, and all the homes were dark. Eventually, we saw a sign that had a name we recognized. What a joy and comfort we felt at that moment!

God knew the needs and frustrations of the people in the days of King Ahaz, so God said that he would send a sign. God fulfilled that promise through the birth of Jesus. What joy-filled lives we would have today if we would only follow the true Sign of life—Jesus Christ.

JOYE A. WHITENER

Help us, O God, to be still and know that you are God. Forgive us for not listening carefully to your directions. Amen

Prayer concern: Christians in Guatemala

Daily Reflections

Bearing Each Other's Burdens

I long to see you so that I may impart to you
some spiritual gift to make you strong—that is,
that you and I may be mutually encouraged by
each other's faith. ❖ Romans 1:11-12 (NIV)

A famous minister met a stranger on a train. The stranger
was carrying a small aluminum cross. He explained that a
number of men carried them. When they found some
strength by thinking about this spiritual reminder, they
passed the cross to other strangers in order to help them
overcome their weaknesses. If such encouragement can be
found in a simple act between strangers, how much more the
bonds of brotherhood in the church should bind us to aid
each other.

The apostle Paul wrote to his friends in Rome that he
wanted to see them; not only to bring his spiritual service to
them, but also to receive their comfort. By our faith we can
strengthen our pastor, our missionaries, and our church
teachers. When we are yoked together in Christ, we bear
each other's burdens.

THEODORE A. YOUNQUIST

*Heavenly Father, help us who enjoy fellowship of the
church to strengthen each other in love and helpfulness
through our mutual faith. In the name of Jesus, our
refuge in every trouble. Amen*

Prayer concern: The healing ministry of the church

Daily Reflections_____

_____

_____

We Surrender Our Children

> The path of the righteous is like the first gleam of dawn, shining ever brighter till the full light of day. But the way of the wicked is like deep darkness; they do not know what makes them stumble. ❖ Proverbs 4:18-19 (NIV)

A familiar sight is the school crossing guard. He or she guides small feet and delivers them to the safety of the other side of the street. My daughter still chuckles at the daily admonition she received as a child: "Look both ways!" Certainly every parent wishes all dangers ahead were as easily pointed out. Many parents grieve because they did not see the shining light in time to point out the sin lurking in the shadows. The writer of Proverbs is talking about this very thing: "Do not set foot on the path of the wicked or walk in the way of evil men."

In our city the chief of police recently asked everybody to leave an outside light burning at night. This will reduce crime. "But the way of the wicked is like deep darkness; they do not know what makes them stumble," the writer of Proverbs cautions. If our children stumble, is it because we have not left the light burning? Maybe the shining light was only a 20-watt bulb instead of God's complete light! Maybe our children aren't learning to walk in the light of God's word.

LEE TOLLEFSON

Lord, we surrender our children! Amen

Prayer concern: Parents of teenagers

Daily Reflections_____

_____

_____

_____

Having a Bad Day

I saw all the deeds that are done under the sun;
and see, all is vanity and a chasing after wind.
❖ Ecclesiastes 1:14 (NRSV)

When a man I know is told, "Have a good day!" he responds, "I have other plans."

The writer of Ecclesiastes was having much more than a bad day. His thoughts were rushing in a downward spiral about all the things that we think are so important—our ambitions, our strivings, our rivalries, our hard work, our egos. He concluded that all the strivings of humankind are like chasing after wind. The reason? Death, the great equalizer, comes to all alike—wise and foolish, rich and poor, honest and dishonest, diligent and slothful. Death reduces all human strivings to vanity and emptiness.

Everyone occasionally has a bad day. How could it be otherwise in this life? If we enter a downward spiral of depression, we might need professional help. At other times, our family and friends can function as healing agents of God. In either case, our trust in the faithfulness of God can be medicine for our souls and bring joy to a bad day.

MARSHALL D. JOHNSON

Heal us, O God, from our own thoughts. Amen

Prayer concern: People struggling with depression

Daily Reflections_____
_____
_____
_____

When All Is Said and Done

*. . . if I only may finish the race and complete the task
the Lord Jesus has given me.* ❖ Acts 20:24 (NIV)

"The End" is often associated with high drama and tension.
Whether "The End" comes as the last few scenes of a movie,
the last few pages of a book, or the last few breathes of life—
endings carry great import and impact.

Like many early Christians, the apostle Paul contemplated
a dramatic end to his ministry and life. He must have realized
his days on this earth were numbered. His zeal for the gospel
drew the wrath of many. "The End" had not yet come, but
already it gave such meaning to the present.

Each moment in a believer's life can be marked by love,
purpose, and impact, even though thoughts of the end are
never far from us. The daily headlines, global and local,
remind us how fragile life is. When that time comes, what do
we want to say of our work and witness? May our concern for
a good ending bring goodness to the beginning, middle, and
close of each day we are yet granted to live.

JON TEMME

*O God, Alpha and Omega, the beginning and the end,
keep us faithful unto life everlasting. Amen*

Prayer concern: People who have terminal illnesses

Daily Reflections_____

_____

_____

Christ Overcame—So Can You

No temptation has seized you except what is
common to man. ❖ 1 Corinthians 10:13 (NIV)

Temptation is universal, but temptations need not cause us to
sin. Christ was sinless, and wants to share with us his power
to resist.

Most Christians are not tempted by the more conspicuous
sins such as murder or burglary. Rather, our sins are inside
us—resentments, grudges, selfishness; withholding from
God the time, capabilities, or money he deserves.
Withholding is a form of robbing God, a sin of omission.

Verse 13b in today's text says, "God . . . will not let you be
tempted beyond your strength, but with the temptation will
also provide the way of escape." One "way of escape" is to
think about God, not about the sin that is tempting us. Try it.
For example, instead of letting your mind go in circles of
resentment for a real or fancied offense, think of the many
times Christ has forgiven you, and thank him for them. There
will be no time left to dwell on your grudge.

VERA J. NELSON

*God, give me the grace to see my sins and confess them,
so that you can forgive me. Then show me how to overcome them. Thank you. Amen*

Prayer concern: Those struggling with temptation

Daily Reflections_____

_____

_____

_____

First They Prayed

After they prayed. ❖ Acts 4:31 (NIV)

We are not told in so many words how long it was after the early church had been launched that these early Christians were at work in Jerusalem. But we do know that later on persecution scattered them abroad.

This persecution was the best thing that could have happened. It stirred them and set them out on the road spreading the gospel across the world. Meanwhile in Jerusalem they were doing their best by meeting with one another. Thus they were able to weather the storm sweeping around them, and keep the lamp burning.

Three things happened in this particular gathering that the church of today might take to heart: they prayed, they were filled with the Spirit, and they lost all fear.

What is it we pray for? What is it that most deeply interests us? To examine ourselves in these two areas should show us what it is that mostly holds our hearts. The little band of men and women whom the storm had driven into hiding, instead of shivering with fear, prayed for courage to stand up against their persecutors. Prayers like that let God's Spirit in. That is what happened on the first Pentecost.

O. K. STORAASLI

Lord, teach us in the unity of the Spirit to pray, and then expect your blessing. Amen

Prayer concern: Those who feel challenged in their faith journey

Daily Reflections_____

_____

_____

_____

An Expensive Plan

This is what is written: The Christ will suffer and
rise from the dead. ❖ Luke 24:46 (NIV)

Twenty centuries of Christianity come out of one grave.
From Jerusalem, the places where the last flicker of hope
had gone out, a plan was to emerge. The tale of tragedy and
woe that the disciples had witnessed when their loving Lord
was taken from them and nailed to the cross had a happy
ending after all.

The happy news of salvation is too good, too wonderful to
be kept to yourself. The extinction of Christianity is always
just one generation away and is saved from extinction only as
long as new generations are being taught about the Savior by
those who know him. The ceaseless impact of your life on
others is vital to God's plan. Be assured that the Holy Spirit,
moment by moment, will equip you with divine strength for
the task to which you are called.

WILLIAM GORDON JOYCE

*Almighty God, you show us our error and give us the
light of truth. Amen*

Prayer concern: Christian education programs

Daily Reflections_____
_____
_____
_____

Discipleship

Going on from there, he saw two other brothers, James son of Zebedee and his brother John. They were in a boat with their father Zebedee, preparing their nets. Jesus called them, and immediately they left the boat and their father and followed him. ❖ Matthew 4:21-22 (NIV)

Jesus called James and John to be full-time disciples. Not many of us can leave our work the way they did. We cannot all be pastors. In fact, Jesus does not call everyone to full-time service. Many of us are like Zebedee, who stayed with his nets. What can we do?

We can still be profitable servants of God. We can still be witnesses to his love. We can encourage others in their calling to full-time service. We can help our pastors instead of obstructing their work. We can offer our prayers for our pastors and for all leaders of the church.

In the midst of this part-time labor for the Lord, the time may even come when we are called to more extensive service in God's work. Maybe we too can fish for people.

JOHN. R. ALBRIGHT

Help us to recognize your call, O God. Grant that we may know the correct portion of our efforts to devote to your service. Be with our spiritual leaders. Help us all to walk with you. Amen

Prayer concern: Christians in Saudi Arabia

Daily Reflections_____
_____
_____
_____

Resting with Jesus

The apostles gathered around Jesus and reported to him all they had done and taught. Then, because so many people were coming and going that they did not even have a chance to eat, he said to them, "Come with me by yourselves to a quiet place and get some rest." ❖ Mark 6:30-31 (NIV)

The apostles had returned from their first preaching mission—excited and tired from the strain of their unusual and wonderful experiences. They told Jesus all that they had done, and what they had taught. Knowing the effect of their work upon them, with loving wisdom Jesus saw the need of withdrawing for a while from the crowd and resting with him. The people were thoughtless in their constant demands on his divine power of healing, and he and the apostles had no leisure so much as to eat. So he sought seclusion and rest.

There was need for a brief period of quietness and undisturbed fellowship with the Lord. Faithful labor deserves rest and the opportunity of getting new power for one's work in life. Like Mary, who chose that good part, we also must get away from our regular activities and sit at Jesus' feet and hear his word.

ANONYMOUS

Lord, we thank you for the blessed privilege of knowing you through our knowledge of your Son, Jesus. Amen

Prayer concern: Those who feel unworthy of Jesus

Daily Reflections_____

_____

_____

_____

The Way of the Cross

Each of you should look not only to your own
interests, but also to the interests of others.
❖ Philippians 2:4 (NRSV)

We were all tired under the hot Jerusalem sky as we traveled
the "Way of the Cross," the traditional route of Jesus on the
day of his death. But my 4-year-old brother was on the verge
of causing us to drop out of the tour group altogether.

"David, can you carry Jay for a while?" my mother asked.
"Your dad's back isn't up to it."

I didn't want to do it, but I was a proud teenager. I carried
him just to prove that I could do so.

Now, years later, I understand in my bones a bit more
about Jesus' carrying our sins along that path long ago. Yet
how much greater was the weight that he carried and how
much more willing was he to look beyond his own interests
to care for others.

DAVID A. SORENSON

*Lord Jesus, we thank you with all our heart for your
willingness to become a vulnerable human being, that the
message of your saving love would be clearly understood.
Amen*

Prayer concern: People of the Middle East

Daily Reflections

Day 227 ❖ Genesis 18:10b-14

Not Too Hard for God

Is anything too hard for the LORD?
❖ Genesis 18:14a (NIV)

One of the hardest things for an artist to decide is when a painting is finished. The artist's critical eyes can always see one more little touch that's needed—a highlight here, a bolder stroke there. It can make it very hard to know when to stop. We're like that about ourselves, too, aren't we? We're close enough to ourselves to know about our flaws and imperfections. A sensitive Christian is well aware that he or she is not perfect and that there's always more growing to be done.

But sometimes we take that a few steps too far. Since we know about our imperfections and can't accept them, we jump to the conclusion that God can't really accept us until we're perfect.

But, as the Lord reminded Abraham and Sarah, nothing is too hard for him. If something suits his purposes, it will be accomplished. And God has shown us that it is his will to accept us, even with our flaws and imperfections. Nothing is too hard for him!

TOM KADEL

O Lord, in the deep mystery of your ways you accepted us in spite of our failings. Strengthen us to accept our neighbor as you accept us. Amen

Prayer concern: Families

Daily Reflections_____

_____

_____

_____

Before and After

But God demonstrates his own love for us in this:
While we were still sinners, Christ died for us.
❖ Romans 5:8 (NIV)

Karen gets it. She knows she hasn't always been a nice person. Widowed young, she raised her three girls in an alcoholic stupor some days. It wasn't what she had planned. She remembers herself before Jesus and after. It was the love that saved her. Talk to anyone who has been pulled from his or her brokenness by God's grace and given undeserved favor and unconditional acceptance. It's life-changing. Those who are touched by grace in this way don't forget it.

In some ways, Christians like Karen have an advantage over Christians who have grown up always knowing God's love. They remember the before and after. Some people who endure their own self-imposed darkness for a long time are overwhelmed by hope pouring into their hearts, convincing them of their own worth.

We need to listen to their stories; hear about the before and after. We need to remember our own brokenness as we listen and give thanks to God that suffering and endurance produce character, hope, and overflowing love. Just look at Karen.

BARBARA DEGROTE SORENSON

Lord Jesus, remind me of my own brokenness, that I may better see your light. Amen

Prayer concern: People who are involved in Alcoholics Anonymous and other Twelve Step programs

Daily Reflections_____

_____

_____

_____

Forgive Me

Jesus said, "Father, forgive them; for they do not know what they are doing." ❖ Luke 23:34 (NIV)

When I was younger, I was sure of what sin was. Now that I'm older, things seem more complicated. Those whopping sins are easy to spot. They require immediate apologies to friends and family members, and confession to God. But it seems I find myself in situations more and more often where there's no clear way out. I want to excuse myself by claiming that the lesser of two evils can be virtue rather than sin. Or I try doing right, only to see others get hurt.

I'm not so different from the people who crucified Christ. The horrible part of their story is that they thought they were doing the right thing. The high priests were preserving religious purity, Pilate was ensuring civil tranquility and the soldiers were just doing their jobs.

The beautiful part of their story is that Christ asked forgiveness for them even before they recognized and confessed their sins.

INEZ SCHWARTZKOPF

Jesus, forgive my unwitting sins. Amen

Prayer concern: Campus ministries

Daily Reflections_____

_____

_____

_____

The Chosen

These are the names of the twelve apostles . . .
❖ Matthew 10:2 (NIV)

What a strange crew Jesus picked for his disciples! They weren't religious scholars; they weren't even particularly spiritual men. They seemed so riddled with weakness! Peter was boastful and rude. James and John were vainly concerned with position. Thomas had an uncertain faith. Judas later betrayed him. Would you pick these men? Jesus did.

Jesus could see through the appearance these men gave. He knew what each man might do for the kingdom, and, of course, he was right. They went into forgotten corners of the world. They gave their lives for Jesus' sake. And now the company of believers has grown until it embraces the whole world.

Jesus can make use of all kinds of people in his kingdom. He can use you no matter what your age or circumstance, no matter what your strengths and weaknesses. You have been chosen to take your place among the saints. Once you give him your life, he will accomplish much through you.

EDITH A REUSS

Lord, you know my strengths and weaknesses. Use me in your kingdom. Amen

Prayer concern: Christians in the United States

Daily Reflections_____

_____

_____

_____

Day 231 ❖ Isaiah 12:1-6

Water of Life

With joy you will draw water from the wells of
salvation. ❖ Isaiah 12:3 (NRSV)

My aunt, "Tante Lena," had a well with an old-fashioned
pump on her farm in New Jersey. Pump, pump, and then,
splash, the water would come! How cool it tasted on those hot
summer days! Isaiah might have had a similar thought as he
wrote to his people facing oppression and captivity in
Babylonian exile. His people would soon know the heat of
forced march and the dryness of oppression. Yet Isaiah
prophesied deliverance by a root of the tree of Jesse, and
return to the homeland.

We Christians, who claim Jesus, believe that we are
liberated from the oppression of sin and evil. This is marked
in the waters of our baptism, that through Jesus' agony on
Golgotha we may know the splash of God's forgiveness!

JOHN F. HAZEL JR.

*Dear God, thank you for the liberation of our lives by the
life, death, and resurrection of Jesus, the well of our
salvation. Amen*

Prayer concern: Those suffering from drought

Daily Reflections_____
_____
_____
_____

The Cross and the Curse

Christ suffered for you, leaving you an example, that you should follow in his steps. ❖ 1 Peter 2:21 (NIV)

We look upon people in pain, affliction, or hardship and say it's "a cross" they have to bear. But it is not a cross, it's a curse—the curse that fell upon all of us when the human race rebelled against God in the person of Adam.

This curse, a result of sin in the world, is no respecter of people. It falls upon rich and poor, and on the just and the unjust. Affliction and hardship are part of being human and are not necessarily laid upon us by God.

Neither is a cross. A cross is something we take up when we choose to follow in the steps of Jesus. The cross usually involves rejection, isolation, sometimes persecution, or even death. The cross happens when we, like Christ, seek help for the poor, aid the defenseless, and demand justice for the oppressed.

When you ask people who have everything to share with people who have nothing, you are often asking for a cross for yourself. But don't despair. Christ accomplished his mission and so will we, if we take up our cross and follow him.

DENNY. J. BRAKE

Lead on, O King eternal. Amen

Prayer concern: Oppressed people

Daily Reflections_____

_____

_____

_____

Sleepy Christians

Could you men not keep watch with me for one hour? ❖ Matthew 26:40 (NIV)

Have you ever found it hard to keep awake in church? Did you miss some of the sermon because you were sleepy? Are there times when you do feel like your soul is drowsy?

Jesus left the other disciples and took Peter, James, and John with him farther into Gethsemane. "Watch with me," he said and went on a little farther and fell on his face and prayed. Three times he came back to find them asleep. He spoke the words of our text to Peter, "Could you men not keep watch with me for one hour?" They were too sleepy to see Jesus in this great struggle in the shadow of Calvary. They were too sleepy to pray in this critical hour.

Today, too, Christians become drowsy. They become careless about their daily Bible reading. They do not witness with joy because their flesh deadens their desire and lessens their burden for others to be saved. They do not pray much because they are too sleepy from running and forgetting to "be still before God." To every drowsy Christian, Jesus says, "Could you men not keep watch with me for one hour? Watch and pray!" Keep your eyes with open to Jesus in his word!

OSCAR C. HANSON

O God, wake us up to see Jesus. Keep our eyes open to see people in need of a Savior. Amen

Prayer concern: A wideawake faith

Daily Reflections

Day 234 ❖ Acts 9:26-31

Signs of Growth

So Saul stayed with them and moved about freely
in Jerusalem, speaking boldly in the name of the
Lord. ❖ Acts 9:28 (NIV)

Paul was not trusted by the disciples in Jerusalem. He had
been known and feared as a persecutor of the young
Christian community. Then on the Damascus road the risen
Lord himself confronted Saul and he became Paul the
apostle. But was the change real? Was it lasting? When he
attempted to join the disciples in Jerusalem they were
suspicious. Not until Barnabas spoke for him was Paul
accepted. He had changed. The disciples saw signs of his
conversion and growth.

We may not preach like Paul, as the old hymn has it. But
what is the sign of newness in our lives? A former British
Minister of Education stated three tests of an "educated
person": Can you entertain a new idea? Can you entertain
another person? Can you entertain yourself?

To grow as a Christian is not simple. It means to grow in
our ability to accept God's new life, to care for others, and to
know by experience that we have been made new.

JAMES A. BERQUIST

*We search for newness in ourselves and sometimes find
little evidence. Lord help us to grow and demonstrate the
signs of growth. Amen*

Prayer concern: Christians in harm's way

Daily Reflections_____

Surprised by Joy

*Then they spoke the word of the Lord to him and
to all the others in his house.* ❖ Acts 16:32 (NIV)

When the jailer asked, "What must I do to be saved?" he may
not have had in mind what Paul and Silas were about to
suggest.

Just a moment before, he had been ready to kill himself.
He knew that, had his superiors found an empty cell the next
morning, he would have been executed. Slaying himself
would have "saved face."

But miracle of miracles! The prisoners had not fled! How
could he persuade them to stay until he devised a workable
means of freeing them?

Yet Paul and Silas wanted more than freedom from prison.
Moreover, they had something more to give the jailer than
continued life on earth. Not claiming to be holy themselves,
they told their good news of the new life in Christ. That night
in Macedonia the jailer accepted both life and New Life from
those he had held prisoner.

LAVONNE ALTHOUSE

*Lord of Life, give us that new life in Christ that surprises
us with the joyful certainty that no adversity nor prison
nor even death can separate us from you. Amen*

Prayer concern: Those affected by suicide

Daily Reflections_____

_____
_____
_____

Going to Church

I was glad when they said to me, "Let us go to the
house of the Lord!" ❖ Psalm 122:1 (NRSV)

How do you view Sunday mornings? Are you eager to get up
and go to church, or do you scrounge around for excuses to
stay home and sleep in?

I came across a pamphlet that said on the outside, "Ten
Good Reasons for Staying Home from Church." When I
opened up the pamphlet, I found it was completely blank! The
message was clear. Except perhaps when a person is sick, is
there a *good* reason for staying home from church.

When we love other people we can't wait to be with them,
talk to them, and listen to them talk to us! We anticipate our
moments together and plan to make the most of them. We
need to cultivate that same attitude toward church
attendance. We go to fellowship with God and his people. If
we plan ahead to participate by praying, listening, taking
notes on the sermon, and applying God's message to our
lives, we will enjoy churchgoing all the more!

JANICE L. HANSON

God, I love to meet you in church! Amen

Prayer concern: Someone in college

Daily Reflections_____
_____
_____
_____

More than Moralism

Teach me your way, O LORD, and I will walk in your truth. ❖ Psalm 86:11 (NIV)

A mischievous boy named Nicholas tries hard to learn all the rules. When his parents correct him, he repeats their words and asks if he has understood. Through careful reflection, he has amassed a great list of rules that, he believes, will keep him out of trouble.

As a boy, I imagined that the Christian faith was a matter of learning the correct rules and living by them. Walking in the truth, however, is not knowing the right rules, but knowing on whom we can depend.

As Christians, we walk in the truth by trusting and following Jesus who is the way, the truth, and the life. That truth brings not fear, but hope and joy.

DAVID L. MILLER

Lord, teach us the truth that we may be free to live fully. Amen

Prayer concern: Someone feeling self-condemnation

Daily Reflections_____

_____

_____

_____

Our Beloved Son

"You are my Son, whom I love; with you I am well pleased." ❖ Mark 1:11b (NIV)

Today is our son 18th birthday. He is a man. In one sense, our job as Kurt's parents is over. We are no longer legally responsible for his support and training. Yet our relationship is lifelong. I will still worry about Kurt when he retires and I'm 90.

In 18 years, some of our brightest moments with Kurt have been those times when he has done something to please us. We shouted our pride and told him how much we love him. He was happy to have pleased us, because he loves us.

Jesus' baptism was just such a beautiful moment in his continuing relationship with his Father. Jesus was ready to begin his work of preaching, teaching and healing. He was doing so out of love for us and obedience to his Father.

And the Father burst with pleasure at Jesus' obedience. He gave him the praise that every child needs and deserves.

INEZ SCHWARTZKOPF

Father of all, teach us to love our children and to please our parents. Amen

Prayer concern: Ministries for social justice

Daily Reflections_____

Not by Sight

So Abram went, as the LORD had told him; and
Lot went with him. ❖ Genesis 12:4 (NRSV)

The Bible is so impressed with Abraham's faith it calls him
the father of those who believe. When it comes to faith,
Abraham is held forth as top example. When called upon to
explain such accolades, the Bible says Abraham went out
without knowing where he was going. God called and
Abraham went, not by sight but by faith.

However, Abraham's faith was not a plunge into the dark.
It was a plunge into the light. He'd heard God speak and that
was enough for him because what God said had substance.
Five big promises punctuated the divine oratory. Abraham
trusted the promises and hit the road. He had heard from
God about the future. When there is faith in the future, there
is power in the present. Much is possible when we trust God.

Moving to a new town, I learned about a man some
likened to Abraham. I was soon on his doorstep seeking an
interview. After we sat down, my first words were, "I hear you
have a big faith."

"No," he corrected me, "I have a little faith in a big God."

PHILLIP A. BARNHART

Almighty God, you are sufficient for me. Amen

Prayer concern: Those facing an uncertain future

Daily Reflections_____

_____

_____

_____

Day 240 ❖ Luke 22:1-6

Betrayals

They were greatly pleased and agreed to give
him money. ❖ Luke 22:5 (NRSV)

This verse refers to Judas Iscariot. We are all familiar with
Judas, one of the twelve disciples, a follower of Jesus. We are
also familiar with his betrayal of his Lord.

Judas's motives for betrayal are not clear. He received 30
pieces of silver. Whether that motivated him, we do not know.
Recent plays and movies have attributed to him various
motivations.

What should concern us, however, is *our* betrayal of our
Lord—the betrayal that occurs each time we forget, or
ignore, his commandments to love God and to love one
another. When we deny God, and when we hate or ignore our
fellow human beings, we are as guilty as Judas is of betrayal,
no matter what our reasons may be.

LINDA WEIMEISTER

*Jesus, we all betray you daily. Forgive us these betrayals.
We pray for strength to live lives more pleasing to you.
Help us to love all others, to care about them—friends
and enemies. Let us realize that our love of God begins
with our love for others. Amen*

Prayer concern: Faithfulness when we are tempted to
betray Jesus

Daily Reflections_____
_____
_____
_____

Burning Hearts

Were not our hearts burning within us while he
was talking . . . and opened the scriptures to us?
❖ Luke 24:32 (NRSV)

It would be the ultimate experience to have Jesus walk with
us and tell us all the mysteries of life. Our hearts would truly
be burning within us. But until that day when he returns,
Jesus is present to us in the scriptures and in our prayers.
That may not seem like much to the ordinary person who
looks at religious people with caution and skepticism. But to
people who have believed all their lives, the scriptures and
prayer become the whole armor of God.

A life of devotion sustains us and carries us through
difficult times. How many times in our lives has it seemed that
Jesus was far away? How many times have we wished we
could sit face-to-face with him and ask the great questions that
plague our souls? Until the day we meet Jesus, we have the
scriptures and prayer to guide our questions and provide
answers.

We all struggle to reach into the depth of our faith to meet
God. And each time we discover a truth in the Bible or feel the
presence of God in prayer, we are sustained for the long
journey.

CLARK MORPHEW

*Show us your merciful presence, O God, as we walk the
Emmaus with you. Amen*

Prayer concern: Those who haven't walked with Jesus

Daily Reflections_____

_____

_____

_____

But What Can I Do?

He dug it and cleared it of stones, and planted it
with choice vines. ❖ Isaiah 5:2 (NRSV)

"I would love to do more to give thanks to God, more
volunteer work, more affirming of others, more work for
good causes, if I only had . . ."

How easy it is to think of the things that we cannot do,
because of the resources that we do not have. We do not have
enough food to feed all they hungry on a city's streets. We
may not have the skill to create a work of art for our church.
We may not have time to be foster parents to children born to
parents who abandon them because of drug addiction.

But then again, God does not ask mangoes to grow on
grape veins.

God has provided us with all that it would take for us to
grow and bear fruit. In fact, God has give us more than
enough resources to do his will. God has given each of us
particular skills and talents, with opportunities to use them
for God's glory.

SERENA SELLERS LEE

*Lord, teach us to dig our roots deep into your promises,
and to know that we are choice vines. Help us to daily
remember and be renewed by our baptism, and moved to
serve you in others. Amen*

Prayer concern: Opportunities to serve

Daily Reflections_____
_____
_____
_____

Day 243 ❖ Romans 14:5-6

Beauty in Differences

One man considers one day more sacred than another; another man considers every day alike. Each one should be fully convinced in his own mind. ❖ Romans 14:5 (NIV)

While hiking, we came across a meadow. It was covered with several varieties of flowers, ablaze with a full prism of color. Each color added to the beauty of the other.

It is good that God rather than humankind created that meadow. We don't always appreciate differences. I'm afraid that if we had designed the meadow, the flowers would all have been the same height, shape, and color. A bit dull.

God has created a variety of Christians. We would be more comfortable if everyone were the same. But our differences highlight each other's beauty and demonstrate the richness of the gospel.

God does not call others to be like us. Rather, God calls us to be confident in our beliefs and live out our lives in faith.

KEVIN E. RUFFCORN

O God, thank you for differences. Through them may we bring you glory rather than disgrace. Amen

Prayer concern: Someone who is hospitalized

Daily Reflections_____

God's City

Great is the LORD and greatly to be praised in the
city of our God. ❖ Psalm 48:1 (NRSV)

As a pastor of a congregation in the heart of the city, I
welcome our brothers and sisters from the suburbs and from
small towns who participate in our ministries. I am thankful
that many of them do come, willing and eager to share the
gospel. However, sometimes I need to remind them that their
role is not to "bring Jesus or God" into the city—God is
already there. Instead, they are to help uncover, unmask, and
reveal the presence, justice, and love of God that are often
hidden behind people's poverty, heartaches, and crisis.

As an inner-city pastor, I take great comfort in the
knowledge that God loves the cities and its people. Such love
and presence empowers me to witness and minister to my
inner-city neighbors. God's steadfast love is in God's people,
wherever they may be. God's love is with you today.

LALAHERY ANDRIAMIHAJA

*O God, let your constant love and presence forever be
known and felt in our cities around the world. Amen*

Prayer concern: Protection and safety in our cities

Daily Reflections_____
_____
_____
_____

Growing Up

Into your hands I commit my spirit.
❖ Psalm 31:5a (NIV)

Most young children trust their parents implicitly. As they grow older, however, children are encouraged by parents and educational systems to rely on themselves. While such an attitude may go far toward achieving worldly success, it can be a stumbling block to Christian growth. We have been taught to rely on ourselves so much that we often have to struggle to rely on God.

The psalmist comes to God with complete trust. His trust is like the implicit trust of a child in his parents; but it is also more than that. It reflects a total and conscious submission to the will of God. Such was the trust and submission of our Lord on the cross.

As growing children, we learn to rely less on our parents and more on ourselves. As growing Christians, we learn to put our trust in God. Christian maturity is trusting him with our whole lives.

MARJEAN BAXTER

Lord, we want to put our lives into your hands. Help us to trust you, both in our living and in our dying. Amen

Prayer concern: Christians in Brazil

Daily Reflections

His Eye Is on Us

Do not hide your face from your servant; answer me
quickly, for I am in trouble. ❖ Psalm 69:17 (NIV)

He was afraid of the dark. As his mother tucked him into bed
she promised to sit there and look at him in the darkness
until he fell asleep.

In the benediction we hear the reassuring words: *The Lord
bless you and keep you. The Lord make his face shine on you,
and be gracious to you. The Lord look upon you with favor and
give you peace.*

If his eye is "on the sparrow," surely it will be on us, his
children, even when the darkness of loneliness or fear of
hopelessness engulfs us.

And there are moments like that in every life. Our dearest
friends may not know the anxieties and depression we feel.
It may not be easy for us to express these concerns, and we
may we want to let them be known. At such times, there is
One who knows without being told. Jesus' face is soft with
compassion and strong with courage. Knowing that his eye
never leaves us is the ultimate comfort.

ALVIN ROGNESS

Thanks, O Lord, for keeping me always in view. Amen

Prayer concern: Broadcasting ministries

Daily Reflections_____

_____

_____

_____

Good People among a Wicked People

This is the list of the descendants of Adam.
❖ Genesis 5:1 (NRSV)

Eve considered her son Seth to be a gift of God. She mothered this life as a precious link with God. She and Adam were so successful in rearing Seth that he in turn reared a generation that "began to call upon the Name of the Lord."

This was a great triumph, considering their failure in Cain, their loss of Abel, and their own rejection of God's way. These repentant parents who again sought God and his help became the progenitors of a select group of people who worshiped God in the midst of a wicked generation. The godly home can triumph over a wicked world.

The godliness of Seth lived on down through the many generations that followed until it produced Enoch, who "walked with God" (5:24). Enoch was the product of a praying people living in the midst of a godless generation. An evil day need not defeat the function of the family to produce godly characters.

The great grandson of Enoch lived in the spirit of his ancestor. Noah became the morning star of a new era. And one wonders how many of the unnamed sons and daughters born to these ancestors in the faith also lived in and walked with God.

ANONYMOUS

Our Father in heaven . . .

Prayer concern: Parents

Daily Reflections_____
_____
_____
_____

A Living Sacrifice?

> I appeal to you therefore, brothers and sisters, by the mercies of God, to present your bodies as a living sacrifice, holy and acceptable to God, which is your spiritual worship. ❖ Romans 12:1 (NRSV)

What a strange thing Paul requires of us, that our bodies should be offered as a living sacrifice. In days when so much is made of the sacrifice of human life, it rubs us the wrong way to read that our faith requires such a sacrifice as well. The difference is that this living sacrifice ends in life and service, not in death and defeat.

Paul calls upon us not to end our life for our faith's sake; but to renew, recommit, and reinvigorate that life in the service of God and God's people.

The sacrifice is not in giving up our life, but in the giving up of those things in our life that might cause us to fail to serve God's people to the fullest extent of our abilities.

RICHARD C. PANKOW

O God, the giver of life, help us ever to be aware of the gift of life that you have bestowed upon us, that we may ever use this gift to your glory and for the service of your people. Through Christ, the servant of servants, we pray. Amen

Prayer concern: Those who serve and sacrifice

Daily Reflections_____

_____

_____

_____

Not in My House!

*Why does your teacher eat with tax collectors
and sinners? ❖ Matthew 9:11b (NRSV)*

"I'll never allow so-and-so in my house, never!" Have you ever heard someone say this?

The act of bringing someone into our home and sharing a meal is a very significant one. Our home is a place of shelter and security, the place where we try to live out the values that we hold dear. A meal is our daily source of nourishment for physical life.

In Palestine, tax collectors and sinners were ostracized as "Gentiles." The people of Israel would have nothing to do with them—certainly they would never bring them into the sacred place of home and meal. Here we see Jesus giving a very basic lesson in the hospitality of discipleship. We are to open our hearts and homes to those whose lives are in need of healing. Our community of faith is not to be an elite club of "Good Christians Only," "Middle Class Only," or "Employed Only." Our doors are to be open to all in need of healing—and that is all of us.

JEAN M. BLOOMQUIST

Jesus, so often we fear to open ourselves to others because they don't fit our expectations of what people of faith should be. Touch our hearts and open our eyes, that we may reach out in mercy for all whose lives cry out for your healing. Amen

Prayer concern: People who are homeless

Daily Reflections_____

_____

_____

_____

Day 250 ❖ Psalm 34:1-10

Shelter Secure

O taste and see that the LORD is good; happy are those who take refuge in him. ❖ Psalm 34:8 (NRSV)

In our state, a winter traveler may find that blowing snow and icy roads make safe progress impossible. A driver may be stranded in a tiny town with no accommodations. When this happens, the inhabitants often take in strangers, offering them food and shelter. Even those accustomed to the best motels are thankful for refuge, however humble.

David knew about humble refuge. In the years that the soldiers of King Saul pursued him, he stayed in many a mountain cave with only surrounding rocks to protect him from the elements.

Without hidden shelter provided by God, he might have been found and slain.

Yet more than physical shelter, God gave David spiritual refuge. David, the sinner, loved God, prayed to God, and relied on God's promises. We should praise God that this lesson of David has been preserved over the ages: When we approach despair, God is there to protect us from all that endangers and assaults us.

NANCY LEE SASSER

Heavenly Father, I seek safety. Shield me and hold me in your everlasting arms. Amen

Prayer concern: Safety from storms

Daily Reflections_____

_____

_____

God Still Speaks to Us

And having been warned in a dream not to return to Herod, they left for their own country by another road. ❖ Matthew 2:12 (NRSV)

God uses a variety of ways to speak. He used a star to tell the wise men when and where the Savior was born. He used a dream to tell Joseph and Mary to flee with Jesus into Egypt.

You and I may feel a bit envious of such sure and direct means of divine communication. But we are not left without the means of having God speak to us. Read and study the scriptures so that God's presence in your life becomes a reality. Pray. Live with Christ in mind. Seek first God's rule. Than the problem will not be whether God still speaks so surely and directly to us today, but whether we will be obedient to what God tells us to do.

Fortunately, Joseph and Mary heeded the warning of God. The child must be given a chance to grow up, both in body and wisdom. Joseph and Mary were no match for the evil that is in the world. Only Jesus was. The time would come when Jesus at last would say, "Listen, we are going up to Jerusalem."

ROBERT H. THURAU

Lord God, we thank you that we are not left without directions from you. Only help us to have ears to hear, and then to do, whatever is your will for us. In Jesus' name. Amen

Prayer concern: Translators of the God's word

Daily Reflections_____

_____

_____

_____

Joy in Everything

Rejoice in the Lord always. I will say it again:
Rejoice! ❖ Philippians 4:4 (NIV)

The Philippians were knowing difficult times. There was external pressure (perhaps even persecution) and internal division. Paul, who called them to rejoice, was also knowing hard times. He was a Roman prisoner awaiting execution. Yet the keynote of their lives, Paul wrote, was to be joy. At all times, they were to be rejoicing and giving thanks to God.

Why not? Isn't all life—the pain as well as the pleasure, the enmity as well as the friendship—a gift from God, a meeting with God? In pleasure, God is the giver of good gifts; in pain, our comfort and fellow sufferer. When we know friendship, God's love is our deepest bond. In enmity, God is our reconciler, the bridge to those we cannot otherwise reach. Rejoice and give thanks—always!

LOUIS A. SMITH

We thank you for being our God in good and evil circumstances. Open our eyes and ears, that we may never miss you in our world. In Jesus' name. Amen

Prayer concern: Those who rejoice in Christ

Daily Reflections_____

_____

_____

_____

Drop Your Conceit Here

Therefore no one will be declared righteous
in his sight by observing the law; rather,
through the law we become conscious of sin.
❖ Romans 3:20 (NIV)

A large wastebasket stood near the entrance to an art gallery.
A visitor asked the guard at the door what it was for. He
answered with a smile, "That is where the students drop their
conceit when they leave." He had noticed over the years that
many students, when they go to the gallery and see the work
of great painters, leave having given up conceit over their
own work.

Paul reminds us that no one can come to the gallery of the
Law of God and go away conceited. It makes us realize our
sin. When we admit our sinfulness, God can deal with us. We
can't be forgiven unless we realize we need it. Drop your
conceit, and let God show you what real life is like.

C. DANIEL LINDSTROM

Help us, O God, to see our inability to live as we should.
Forgive us and lead us to the new way of living for you.
Amen

Prayer concern: Show us daily that we need your grace

Daily Reflections_____
_____
_____
_____

A Teaching Moment

On one occasion when Jesus was going to the house of a leader of the Pharisees to eat a meal on the sabbath, they were watching him closely.
❖ Luke 14:1 (NIV)

Many who were interested in Jesus were simply curiosity-seekers. Others, like the Pharisees, were concerned that Jesus might be leading people astray. So this group of Pharisees invited him to share a meal, not entirely out of curiosity, but also out of a fear that could quickly turn to hostility.

Still Jesus came, without fear, without evidence of any anxiety at all. And he used this moment, filled with tension for some, as a teaching moment. In a few brief moments, Jesus brought home a simple teaching about humility.

How many of us have jobs or positions in which we are also observed by many people? Bishops and pastors, teachers and administrators, public officials and elected represent-atives all do public work. Often the feeling is not one of a readiness to be forgiven, but more like "one mistake and you're dead." For those of us being so observed it is good to walk with a forgiving and loving brother in Jesus. All of us can learn from him.

PETER BECKSTRAND

Lord of life, take our tension-filled moments and turn them into teaching moments. Amen

Prayer concern: People who serve in the public eye

Daily Reflections_____

_____

_____

_____

Healing

... and heals all your diseases. ❖ Psalm 103:3b (NIV)

Long before modern medicine recognized that interaction between mind and body, the psalmist sensed this connection. A mind that is at leisure from itself, resting in God's peace, disposes the body to live in health. This is not to say that the peace of God automatically confers bodily wholeness. Some people are born healthy and strong while others are born weaker or with serious illnesses. Whatever the native gifts in physical strength that each person may have, they may be enhanced by God's healing power. Therefore the psalmist boldly reminds himself that God heals all his diseases.

In listening to the psalmist, some might want to claim him as a forerunner of Christian Science. But note carefully: the reality of disease is not denied. God has endowed the human body with marvelous powers of recovery. These powers can be inhibited and blocked by fretfulness, worry, hatred, and resentments. And they may be released when peace and love live in the heart. Therefore, Paul wrote, "Let the peace of Christ rule in your hearts" (Colossians 3:15a).

FREDERICK A. SCHIOTZ

O Lord, fill our hearts with trust in you, that your healing work may not be hindered. Amen

Prayer concern: Wholeness of body, mind, and spirit

Daily Reflections

_____

_____

_____

Could This Be the Christ?

*Come, see a man who told me everything I ever
did. Could this be the Christ? ❖ John 4:29 (NIV)*

Who am I to tell people of Christ? Some of us feel that
because of our past we are not qualified to witness. We are
sinners. Who will listen to us?

The woman at Jacob's well did not hesitate. Once she had
heard the life-giving words of Jesus, she went to witness to
others. Jesus had said, "Woman believe me." She believed
and invited those who didn't think much of her.

The stream of living water cleansed her soul. She
remembered those who avoided her. The people of the city
had likely called her "that woman." But she left her water jar
and invited them. "Come, see a man who told me everything
I ever did. Could this be the Christ?"

This most comforting account of how Jesus saved a sinful
soul should encourage us to go and tell what we know of
Christ. We have been washed and cleansed. We have been
saved for such service. Nothing should keep us from going
even to those who may despise us for our past misdeeds. Let
us say to them, "Come see him who changed my life and
made me his own. This is truly the Christ."

GEORGE W. KRUEGER

*Wash and cleanse me, Savior, and give me grace to go
and tell what you have done for me. Amen*

Prayer concern: Those who boldly proclaim Christ

Daily Reflections_____
_____
_____
_____

Set Free

The LORD has taken away the judgments against
you, he has turned away your enemies. The king
of Israel, the LORD, is in your midst; you shall fear
disaster no more. ❖ Zephaniah 3:15 (NRSV)

The enormity of the Lord's love, forgiveness, and protection
is such that we hardly can take it in. Over and over again God
rescues his people, showers them with blessings, protects
them from enemies, and even forgives their forgetfulness.

While God's mercy is truly beyond human understanding,
it is revealed to us as we become more aware of God's
presence in our lives. Little by little, we grow and mature in
our faith. As this happens, the implications of God's grace in
our lives open avenues of service to others.

What a privilege it is to be set free from sin! Our God
loves us so greatly that he comes to us where we are and as
we are to transform our lives with love and forgiveness.

MARY BRAUCH

*God, remind me daily that your grace sets me free to
serve and love. Help me conform to your will. Amen*

Prayer concern: Those in prison

Daily Reflections_____

_____

_____

_____

Worship the All-Pervading God

> The God who made the world and everything in it
> is the Lord of heaven and earth and does not live
> in temples built by hands. ❖ Acts 17:24 (NIV)

"Mommy, does God live in the church?"

"Yes, Tony," answered his mother "the church is God's house and so we go there to worship him every Sunday."

"But Mommy, why did my Sunday school teacher tell us then that God's home is in heaven?"

Tony's predicament is easy to sympathize with. Paul found the same kind of thinking among the Greek philosophers in Athens. All of us must admit that we, too, often think of God as being just a man. We think of him as being some sort of super person, but still as having many of our limitations. Often we feel that God is localized, usually at some spot where we don't happen to be.

Let us rather think of God as God really is—all-powerful, all-knowing, and present everywhere. While we think of a church building as God's in a special way, still the hallowed walls in no way confine God's activity or presence. God is with us wherever we happen to be. Even if we were to go on a trip to the moon or to one of the planets, God would accompany us also there.

JOHN F. SIEVERT

Lord, you are present everywhere. Help us always to feel that you are very near us, within our hearts. Amen

Prayer concern: Those who feel far from God

Daily Reflections_____

_____

_____

_____

A Gate to . . .

> I am the gate; whoever enters through me will
> be saved. He will come in and go out, and find
> pasture. ❖ John 10:9 (NIV)

We go through a lot of doors, or gates, every day of our lives.
We go into the house, into the car, into the grocery store, into
the backyard, into church. This door is different. "I am the
gate." What a bold statement! The door to what? Would you
believe, the door to everything else that matters? Jesus opens
the door to life for all who will look to him.

Many doors open to temptation to be this or that, or to buy
this or that. Jesus invites us through a door that frees us to be
as God created us to be. He invites us to live in community.
He invited us to the security of salvation. He invites us to
come in and accept our identity as daughters and sons of God
who live for others because he lived for us. Jesus promises
that his door is always open, His invitation is always there,
reminding us, supporting us, welcoming us.

RICHARD A. MAGNUS

*Christ, thanks for your always-open door. Help us
remember each day that you call us through the door of
life as God would have us live it. Strengthen us to be
your free people. Reminds us of the salvation you have
won, and help us to share that good news with others.
Amen*

Prayer concern: Church missions

Daily Reflections

_____

_____

_____

Authority

Then Jesus came to them and said, "All authority
in heaven and on earth has been given to me."
❖ Matthew 28:18 (NIV)

Who or what is in back of you? By what authority do you
believe, speak, and act? Someone or something controls you
because you were made to serve a cause and to obey a
master.

Anything that keeps you from believing in and from
serving Jesus will lead you away from God, for Christ is "God
of God and Light of Light." "All authority in heaven and on
earth" has been given to him by the heavenly creator. Jesus
bought you with a price, with his precious blood shed on the
cross. He is in truth the Savior of all people and the Lord of
the nations.

The problem of authority has been solved for you and me
as believers. Jesus is our authority. He is able to help, heal,
and save. If he is the focal point of our faith, we are backed by
the most important authority in the world—God himself. And
in this assurance we can live victoriously.

MARTIN E. LEHMAN

*We thank you, blessed Savior, that you have full
authority in heaven and on earth. Gratefully we confess
your lordship over our lives. Help us but the Holy Spirit's
indwelling to bear witness to you as the world's true
hope. We ask it in your name. Amen*

Prayer concern: Boldness in proclaiming the gospel

Daily Reflections_____

_____

_____

Getting Out of a Trap

So Peter was kept in prison, but the church was earnestly praying to God for him. ❖ Acts 12:5 (NIV)

When one is trapped and there is no rational means by which he can escape, what can he do?

Miguel Asturias, in his Nobel-Prize-winning novel entitled *El Señor Presidente,* dramatizes a husband's and wife's reactions when trapped. The husband knows that he is a marked man for execution, and he attempts to escape from the country by craftiness. But he is circumvented by the dictator's henchmen, who outwit him and shoot him.

His young Christian wife has her infant son baptized and endures the oppressive dictatorship. She trains her child and hopes that something will break to free them from the oppression. The only hope she has is that some prayer-like miracle will enable them to prevail.

Ever since early Christianity, this trust in the miraculous power of God has motivated prayer. God has effected many miracles such as the one that released Peter from prison.

HAROLD H. ZIETLOW

Fill us with the profound faith and insight that can unite us to your miraculous power, dear God, and save us by your compassion. Amen

Prayer concern: Those who feel trapped

Daily Reflections

A Love Beyond

God is love, and those who abide in love abide in God, and God abides in them. ❖ 1 John 4:16b (NRSV)

A young man went to college, where he found values and a way of life unfamiliar to his parents. The result was quarrels and bitterness, particularly between father and son, to the point where the son did not wish to come home and the father did not really want to see him.

But one day the son did come home and said, "I love you, Pop."

And the father was able to say, "I love you, Son."

Their love grew, and was able to overcome and endure and express itself once again. "God is love, and those who abide in love abide in God, and God abides in them." The love of God will express itself, in different ways with different people. But it will show. It will give us courage to declare ourselves, to share that love with others. Love does not demand; love gives.

JOHN R. QUANBECK

God of love, we pray that our love may grow more and more. Help us to give that love to others. Help us to see that in the giving is the growing of love. Help our love to endure all things as Christ's love endured. Amen

Prayer concern: Christians in Sweden

Daily Reflections_____
_____
_____
_____

Bit Players

Now there was a disciple in Damascus named Ananias. The Lord said to him in a vision, "Ananias." He answered, "Here I am, Lord."
❖ Acts 9:10 (NRSV)

I thought I knew the story of Paul's conversion on the road to Damascus pretty well, but I had forgotten about Ananias. Without this willing "bit player," Paul's story could have turned out very differently.

Ananias knew all about Paul's fanaticism. But Ananias obeyed God anyway. It was not until after Ananias lay his hands on Paul and healed his vision that Paul proclaimed Christ as Lord. The first great mission of the Christian church began because one Christian said, "Here I am, Lord," to a job that didn't seem to make sense.

Perhaps Ananias should be proclaimed the patron of Sunday school teachers and nursery workers, of janitors and quilt makers. There are so many important people who rarely get to see the results of their work in the church. But how they're needed!

INEZ SCHWARTZKOPF

Thank you, Lord, for Ananias and for all his spiritual descendants in our time. Amen

Prayer concern: All theological schools

Daily Reflections_____
_____
_____
_____

An Appointment with Yourself

Come away . . . by yourselves and rest a while.
❖ Mark 6:31 (NRSV)

The days had been busy for Jesus and the disciples in the towns and villages of Galilee. After hours devoted to meeting the needs of people, they had reached feelings of stress and fatigue. Jesus sensed that a change was essential.

"Come away by yourselves and rest a while," was his invitation. The disciples needed time to reflect. They needed private time to replenish their spiritual batteries, time alone and time for prayer.

One observer said of George Bernard Shaw, "He walks as though he had an appointment with himself and might be late for it." That sentence suggests an idea: Make an appointment with yourself. To make an appointment with yourself can be to make an appointment with God. These words of Jesus are an invitation to rest as God rested on the seventh creation day. Make an appointment with yourself—and meet God there.

LUTHER ABRAHAMSON

Make our worship today, Lord Jesus, an appointment with ourselves and with you. Amen

Prayer concern: Your nearest neighbor

Daily Reflections_____

_____

_____

_____

Extra Mile

So you also, when you have done everything you were told to do, should say, "We are unworthy servants; we have only done our duty." ❖ Luke 17:10 (NIV)

Christianity is a religion of "going the extra mile," of "turning the other cheek," of "service above and beyond the call of (ordinary) duty."

No one can exceed their potential, and no one, except Christ, has ever equaled it. There is so much unused energy, so many unused brain cells, so much of the available potential that never gets used. Some researchers say that most people utilize at the most 15 percent of their potential. We are so used to this that when much more is used, on occasion and in emergencies, we are inclined to cry, "Miracle!"

Dr. Leslie D. Weatherhead tells of a woman with a "bad heart," who during one of London's "Blitz" bombings, and upon hearing that her son had been wounded, ran the eight miles from her home to London, and was none the worse for it. Nor did she wish to take any credit for it, but rather gave "thanks to God."

KENNETH R. ANDERSON

Keep us, O Christ, ever sensitive to the fact that every good and perfect gift comes from above, from the Father, so that when we do what is right, we may always give the glory to him from whom all blessings flow. Amen

Prayer concern: All those who crave peace

Daily Reflections

The End

I am . . . the Beginning and the End.
❖ Revelation 22:13 (NIV)

Not only is God the source of our being, but God is also the end of our being. We are made for life with God.

We most easily see God as the end of our existence when we contemplate our own earthly end, our death. Jesus' promise, "I will come to receive you unto myself," enables us to see our Lord waiting to receive us when we depart this life.

God is not the end of our being only in that final way, however. Our present life is to be lived with God as the end. A medieval cook in a monastery, Brother Lawrence by name, has left us a marvelous testimony as to what this can mean in a piece called *The Practice of the Presence of God.* For Brother Lawrence, the rattle of the pots and pans, the aroma of cooking food, and the hustle and bustle of the kitchen were the ways by which he praised and thanked God. The food met the needs of his brothers, and the preparation of it and the cleaning up after if pleased God.

What greater thing can family members do for each other than to help each other love and serve God? Our earthly relationships are deepest when our actions toward each other help us to live unto God, the end of our being.

DAVID PREUSS

Help us to know that we need not wait till we die to direct our lives to you. Amen

Prayer concern: The ability to serve and praise

Daily Reflections_____

_____

_____

_____

Childlike Faith

Therefore, whoever humbles himself like this
child is the greatest in the kingdom of heaven.
❖ Matthew 18:4 (NIV)

In *Paradise Lost*, John Milton tells of the angels who fell as
committing the sin pride, and he calls their leader "proud
Lucifer." Dante describes the deliverance of the soul from
purgatory as the steep ascent of a mountain where at
intervals the deadly sins are purged away. The first of these
sins to be burned away on the road back to paradise is the sin
of pride.

These poets are recognizing the truth that Jesus so often
taught. At the door of the entrance to the heavenly kingdom
is a humble childlike spirit. The angels are those who do
God's bidding. They do not proudly assert themselves or
insist upon their own will. They obey the will of God.

Becoming as a little child means becoming docile,
teachable, trusting. It means resigning oneself to God as the
child rests trustingly in the parent's arms. Unless we are
willing to humble ourselves thus, no matter what our other
virtues may be, we shut ourselves out of his kingdom.

ANONYMOUS

Open us to the door of your heavenly kingdom, and give
to us the lowliness of heart and submissiveness of soul
that shall enable us to enter, through Jesus Christ our
Lord. Amen

Prayer concern: Childlike faith

Daily Reflections_____

_____

_____

_____

Voice of People, Ear of the Lord

O LORD our God, you answered them; you were
a forgiving God to them. ❖ Psalm 99:8 (NRSV)

The book of Psalms is the hymnbook and prayer book of the
people of God. The psalms contain the whole range of human
experience with God and the whole range of human
experience with God. Nothing is held back. There are psalms
of joy and sorrow; repentance and defiance; and mercy and
vengeance. A thread that runs through all the psalms is that
God hears the voice of the people and answers them.

Sharing one's fears, joys, and sorrows—and knowing that
someone really is listening—brings peace and assurance.
Getting it "off our chest" goes a long way in bringing healing,
even if trouble continues. When we share with another, we no
longer bear the burden alone.

The psalms witness that God hears our cries, even those
we cannot utter. There is nothing we experience or think that
is foreign to God or from which God recoils. And in listening,
God answers. Sometimes God's answer is "wait'; sometimes it
is "no" or "tell me more." As a child of God, know that God
hears your cries and your shouts of joy. Know that God will
not remain silent. God forgives and answers.

THOMAS S. HANSON

*Dear Lord, loosen my tongue to speak, and open my ears
to hear. Amen*

Prayer concern: Those who are alone in their troubles

Daily Reflections_____

_____

_____

_____

Sent

And how are they to proclaim him unless they
are sent? ❖ Romans 10:15 (NRSV)

There is a chicken-and-egg quality to the cyclical nature of
the proclamation of God's word—send, preach, hear, believe,
call, and send again.

For the individual believer the process begins with
hearing God's word preached and ends with being sent.

For the church as a whole, the process begins with
sending believers to preach God's word and ends with
sending again. No wonder this text is chosen for so many
ordination services.

There is a renewed sense of urgency in the church for
people who are willing and able to be sent. There is a shortage
of pastors, missionaries, and lay workers of all kinds.

Who do you know who should be encouraged to consider
training for ministry—as a pastor or teacher, evangelist,
leader, scholar, writer, artist, musician, missionary, mission
volunteer? The calling and sending of ministers is crucial, for
God's word needs to be proclaimed in order for people to
hear it, believe it, and call upon the name of the Lord.

KAREN HANSON

*Raise up proclaimers of your word, O God, that all the
people might call on your name. Amen*

Prayer concern: Missions

Daily Reflections_____

_____

_____

_____

Entertaining Angels Unawares

Abraham looked up and saw three men standing
nearby. ❖ Genesis 18:2 (NIV)

Hebrews 13:2 refers to this story about Abraham and tells us
to practice hospitality. Abraham was fortunate to be a
gracious host that day, because he "entertained angels
unawares."

Etiquette books aren't much help here. There is no proper
protocol for receiving angels. But even if there were, I doubt
that it would help, because angels are, in Bill Graham's
words, "God's secret agents." God's messengers cloak
themselves in the ordinary. We are not likely to recognize
them for what they are unless they appear in glory as they
did in the fields of Bethlehem. That is most rare!

Most often, God's messengers are mortal, but as
messengers they are still like angels. Jesus even said that
whatever we do to the lowliest believer, we do to him! Can we
learn to recognize angels—and Christ—in those we meet,
especially those in need?

FREDERICK W. BALTZ

Lord, help me be a friend to everyone. Amen

Prayer concern: Christians in Cameroon

Daily Reflections_____

_____

_____

Day 271 ❖ Acts 4:5-22

The Secret Power

Then know this, you and all the people of Israel:
It is by the name of Jesus Christ of Nazareth,
whom you crucified but whom God raised from
the dead, that this man stands before you healed.
❖ Acts 4:10 (NIV)

Here is a group of men so astonished at the disciples' deeds
that there is wrung from them the involuntary question, "By
what power or in what name did you do this?" The answer is
the most natural and most obvious one for Christians. "By the
name of Jesus Christ." Wherever Christ is proclaimed, he
enters new strength to a new heart and a new way of life.

In the name of Christ we find the personal rule, the saving
power, and the very presence of God. What is the greatest
miracle and the greatest gift to us is that we may call upon
this name. In Christ, God's heart is wide opened to us with its
fullness of grace and forgiveness. We find power in the name
of Jesus Christ when we call upon him in worship and prayer.

GUNARS J. ANSONS

*Lord Jesus Christ, make God's presence and saving
power known also in us, so that others my be forced to
ask about the quality of our lives, "By what power or in
what name do you do it?" Amen*

Prayer concern: Those who struggle with laziness

Daily Reflections_____

U-Turns

Repent, and believe in the good news.
❖ Mark 1:15b (NRSV)

After traveling in circles for nearly an hour, we suggested that our driver stop and ask for directions to get us home. Our plea fell on deaf ears and he continued driving. He could not or would not admit that he was lost. Finally, after passing a bright red barn for the third time, we boldly blurted, "Stop. Look. Listen to us. You are lost. Admit it. Turn around and get some directions!"

He slammed on the brake, mastered a grand U-turn, returned to the highway, and drove into the nearest service station. There, he asked for and received the directions that led us safely home. "Repent," said the prophets of old. "Repent," said John the Baptist. "Repent," said Peter. "Repent," said Paul. Jesus says, "Repent."

The word *repent* may sound old-fashioned to our ears. It may sting our ego or wound our pride. But, it would be wise for us to slam on our brake, stop, look around us, listen to Jesus, and make a giant U-turn. Let's admit it; without the good news we are lost. With it, God's Son can and will lead us safely home.

BARBARA HARKINS STEINWART

We are forever grateful to you, Lord, for allowing and encouraging U-turns of repentance and faith. Amen

Prayer concern: The desire and strength to repent

Daily Reflections_____
_____
_____
_____

Come to the Light

But whoever lives by the truth comes into the light,
so that it may be seen plainly that what he has done
has been done through God. ❖ John 3:21 (NIV)

How often our newspapers reveal the evil that has been done the evening before. It is not just a figure of speech that evil loves darkness rather than light.

You and I have been called to live and walk in the light. We have been called to be honest (do what is true). This means first, honesty with ourselves. So often we try to hide from ourselves our true motives and feelings only to have them break out at inappropriate times. It also means to be honest with others, both in thought and deed. Such honesty can show us that there is more evil in us than we admit. Than must come honesty before God: the cry, "Lord, be merciful to me, a sinner."

With God's forgiveness comes a flood of light and the power of God to work in us his deeds. It is to change darkness into light that Christ died for you. It is because God loves you, that God would make you whole again, to live in the light.

OSWALD ELBERT

Lord, send your Holy Spirit that he may take my life of darkness and transform it into light. Amen

Prayer concern: Those who fear the darkness

Daily Reflections_____

_____

_____

_____

The Christian Host

If you consider me a partner, welcome him as you
would welcome me. ❖ Philemon 1:17 (NIV)

Scott was having a bad day. When the waitress did not keep his coffee cup full, he lost his temper. He told the waitress angrily what a bad job she was doing. But it did not matter because she was only a waitress.

Shirley didn't have time to stand in the long line at the bank. When she got to the window she told the teller how slow he was. But it didn't matter because the young man was only a teller.

We often react to people according to what they do rather than considering who they are. We see people as garbage collectors, secretaries, and waiters. Paul challenges Philemon and us to see people for what they are.

Paul wanted Philemon to receive Onesimus not as a slave but as a brother in Christ. We are challenged to see people as people whom God loves and as brothers and sisters in Christ. Then we are to act toward them in love.

KEVIN E. RUFFCORN

Father, help me to see people through your eyes, as people
you love. Amen

Prayer concern: People working in the service industry

Daily Reflections_____

_____

_____

The High Priest Who Understands

Therefore, since we have a great high priest
who has gone through the heavens, Jesus the
Son of God, let us hold firmly to the faith we
profess. ❖ Hebrews 4:14 (NIV)

Jesus sympathizes with our temptations. He knows what it is
to feel thirsty, to walk hot roads, to cry, to be disappointed,
even to die in the fading afternoon sun. The wonderful thing
is that God loved us so much that he came down in Christ to
share this human life with us.

Some writers have said that God came in Jesus to show us
what human life can be like. He took us back for a moment of
history to a time long ago, before a serpent in a garden
deceived a man and a woman and all their kin since.

How easy to use God as a crying towel, begging off from
the challenges of faith because we are too weak. God knows
that, but he knows much more. By God's love we can be born
anew into a fresh, stronger life. Yes, even when we can "hold
firmly to the faith we profess" and do things for God we think
are impossible.

JOHN. S. KERR

*Blessed God, hear us when we cry in our weakness. But
open our ears also to hear the rush of our Spirit as it
brings your power to fill us and empower us to serve
others in love. Amen*

Prayer concern: Those who confess Christ

Daily Reflections_____

_____

_____

_____

All Are Welcome

> My house will be called a house of prayer for all nations. ❖ Isaiah 56:7b (NIV)

Our family was traveling through Ontario one Sunday morning while on vacation. We looked for a church to attend and found one in a small town, arriving just in time for Sunday school.

Although we were strangers, we were greeted cordially at the door. The people of the Sunday school also welcomed us. We worshiped in a building that had been built by people we did not know. We were led in prayer by a pastor who voiced concerns that were also ours. We enjoyed the fellowship of those Christians at a coffee hour afterward. They were people we never had seen before and probably never would see again, but they made us feel welcome.

The doors of Christian churches are open to all who care to step inside. This is as it should be. God's house is a house of prayer for all people.

WILLIAM LUOMA

Lord, help us to open the doors of our churches and of our hearts to everyone. Amen

Prayer concern: World Christian cooperation

Daily Reflections_____
_____
_____
_____

A Gift Is for Giving

And he is not served by human hands, as if he needed anything, because he himself gives all men life and breath and everything else. ❖ Acts 17:25 (NIV)

A popular expression says that the best things in life are free. Such a statement is much too vague to be generally accepted. What are the *best* things in life and what is meant by *free*?

Strictly speaking nothing is absolutely free. Everything has its price. However, our beautiful world with its challenging mountain peaks, fertile valleys, winding streams, mysterious seas, interesting sounds, and satisfying colors was brought into being and given by God for our use and enjoyment. Waste and misuse will prevent us from giving it to future generations.

There is such waste and misuse. People are selfish. They mistrust, hate, and kill each other. We need trust, patience, love, forgiveness, hope, and faith. These are also given us without cost. The cost has been paid by him who died for the sins of all people. This good news needs to be told to everyone for it is the way God has chosen to change people. The only way people can really be changed is from within.

We are to be good to people not because they are good to us but because God always has been and still is good to us. We have received. We should give. It's only fair.

ALFRED H. EWALD

Heavenly Father, help us to be thankful and give. Amen

Prayer concern: Grateful hearts

Daily Reflections
_____

_____

_____

_____

Jesus, the Teacher

Jesus answered, "My teaching is not my own. It comes from him who sent me." ❖ John 7:16 (NIV)

"Run that through again" is a popular way for many of us to ask for repetition. Likewise, the disciples wanted to "run through" the events of Jesus' ministry. Now those events—seen through resurrection eyes—took on new dimensions and meanings.

We, too, can benefit from reflecting on Jesus' ministry. Jesus was a master at telling parables. When asked about being a neighbor, he told a story of a Samaritan—who might not have been welcomed in the neighborhood. Yet he showed love to a victim (Luke 10:25-37). When teaching about God's love, he told a parable of a prodigal son who was forgiven (Luke 15:11-32). When asked for a way to relate to the world, he said "Love your enemies" (Matthew 6:44). Later when hanging on a cross, he asked that those involved be forgiven. Jesus' teachings, and his actions, reflected his love.

Those same teachings speak to the world today. As we think about Jesus' teachings, we know that this is God's word to us.

ALICE L. SCHIMPF

Help us to not only reflect on Jesus' teachings, but to follow them in a world that needs love and compassion. Amen

Prayer concern: Teachers

Daily Reflections_____

_____

_____

Love Somebody Today

Do to others what you would have them do to
you, for this sums up the Law and the Prophets.
❖ Matthew 7:12 (NIV)

It is amazing how our feelings, our likes and dislikes, shine
through our words and our actions. Every day we are doing
"for others" something that reveals our love or hate, and our
tolerance or prejudice. People soon learn from us what we
think of them, and they usually reciprocate in kind what they
have received from us.

Christ is very much concerned about our attitude toward
people who are in need of the essentials of life but who are
unable to reciprocate, let alone respond, to our concern, our
love for them. What we do for the hard-to-love children of
God can be our finest witnessing for Christ.

KLAUS G. W. MOLZAHN

*O Lord, help us to reveal greater love and concern for
those with whom it is so difficult to communicate, but to
whom we want to offer what we have received from you.
Help us, O Lord, to show the love that is in our hearts.
Help us now. Amen*

Prayer concern: Christians in Japan

Daily Reflections_____
_____
_____
_____

Not Guilty? Really?

Therefore, there is now no condemnation for those
who are in Christ Jesus. ❖ Romans 8:1 (NIV)

Most of us have seen enough TV programs about the law or
had some experience in a court to have some idea of what the
declaration, "Not guilty!" must mean to the one who is
accused. But if we have never been in the position of being
judged guilty or innocent, we can only guess at what those
feelings might be.

All of us are aware that our lives are being judged. Paul
tells us that our whole life is examined by God. Measured
against the intention that our lives be lived with God as the
center, all of us have missed the mark.

Surprisingly enough, there is a verdict addressed to us as
sinners that is the occasion for neither despair or pride. It is
God's declaration of "Not guilty!" spoken to us in Christ:
"Therefore, there is now no condemnation to those who are
in Christ Jesus."

PHILIP A. QUANBECK

Forgiving Lord, we are grateful for your declaration of
"no condemnation." Help us receive the gift with thanks,
that we may live in it. Amen

Prayer concern: Thankful hearts

Daily Reflections_____

_____

_____

_____

Our Illumination

> The Word became flesh and made his dwelling
> among us. We have seen his glory, the glory of
> the One and Only, who came from the Father, full
> of grace and truth. ❖ John 1:14 (NRSV)

The transfiguration of Jesus turned out to be an illumination
for the disciples. The light that radiated from Jesus reached
them and broke in upon them. They took this light *in*; they
were enlightened. Jesus was continually transfigured in the
presence of his disciples. They continued to be enlightened
by his presence.

We should understand that the instances of illumination
that the disciples experienced did not remain detached in
their minds. When Jesus revealed his divine light to his
disciples by his deeds, and his discourses, one grand
enlightenment came out of all. One grand enlightenment
came to the disciples when they recognized Jesus as both
the *Son* of God and the *Sun* of God.

The Bible teaches us that the inner illumination becomes
ours by the help of the Holy Spirit.

EDGAR P. EBERT

*Dear Lord Jesus, induce us to pray for the best gift, the
gift of the Holy Spirit. Amen*

Prayer concern: Our nation

Daily Reflections_____
_____
_____
_____

Love Means Serving

If I have prophetic powers, and understand all
mysteries and all knowledge, and if I have all
faith, so as to remove mountains, but do not have
love, I am nothing. ❖ 1 Corinthians 13:2 (NRSV)

In this passage, the apostle Paul is speaking to a church that
does not know the gift of love in God but is filled with the
talent with which God blesses us.

Love is a physical act for most people today. Our economy
sells its merchandise preying on this concept of love. But it
takes little deep thought to realize its superficiality—most
people are not fooled for long.

No, love is much more. We can be the most talented
people that God has made, filled with the gifts of apostles,
prophets, and teachers—but if we do not use those gifts to
serve those who are hungry, dying, cold, thirsty, orphaned,
or in need in other ways—in short, if we do not love—all
those gifts are for nothing. Love means serving.

STEVEN C. KANOUSE

*Our Lord, you are the God of the cross, and you have
shown such loving as we have never seen. Fill our hearts
that we may follow in your footsteps of giving, through
your Son. Amen*

Prayer concern: Those who are married

Daily Reflections

Will We Get Out of Grade School?

> Therefore let us leave the elementary teachings
> about Christ and go on to maturity, not laying again
> the foundation of repentance from acts that lead
> to death, and of faith in God. ❖ Hebrews 6:1 (NIV)

It is of real concern when a child of six still has the mind and actions of a baby. It is also true in the soul life that some people are baptized and even confirmed in the Christian faith but really never do grow into Christian maturity.

Today's text speaks of land like the dry lakes in Arizona that often become flooded but because of the alkaline soil produce only cactus and catsclaw—thorns and thistles. It is worthless and near to being cursed; its end is to be burned. This is grim language when we realize that so many individuals who have received so much in Sunday school and in worship still curse, lose their tempers, cheat, and gossip.

The writer hastens to assure his beloved readers that he expects better things of those who take time to worship and study the Word of God. "For God is not so unjust as to overlook your work and the love that you showed for his sake in serving the saints." In Christ by faith, we have a sure anchor for our soul.

CHARLES SCHMITZ

O God, forgive the many times we have carelessly heard but ignored your word. Amen

Prayer concern: Those who have wandered away from the faith

Daily Reflections

Love Is Expansive

Then Peter began to speak: "I now realize how
true it is that God does not show favoritism."
❖ Acts 10:34 (NRSV)

God used a stranger and a foreigner to teach Peter a difficult
lesson. The Christian mission for the world might have been
blocked had not the Roman army officer, Cornelius—and
later Paul—helped Peter learn that God's love is not limited
to the religious insiders. Nor is it limited to those who
conform to the cultural traditions of the "home" group. The
gospel breaks all barriers of race and distance as it works its
new way in the world.

What do we want most for the world? Certainly justice for
those suffering hunger, poverty, and oppression. Will love
provoke us to make the sacrificial changes in our lives
necessary to work for human good everywhere?

Do we not also, and most basically, long for God to be real
to every man, woman, and child? When that happens,
miracles takes place. A fighting love and genuine care takes
the place of bitterness and weak sentimentality. Expansive
love forms new people who are prepared to work for a new
and better world society.

JAMES A. BERQUIST

*Forgive our ingrown complacency, Lord. Change us, and
through us the world. Amen*

Prayer concern: Our complacent hearts

Daily Reflections_____

_____

_____

_____

Intermission Time

Very early in the morning, while it was still dark,
Jesus got up, left the house and went off to a solitary
place, where he prayed. ❖ Mark 1:35 (NIV)

In recent years many young Americans have been attracted
by Eastern religions that place great emphasis upon
meditation. Western Christians sometimes forget that on
numerous occasions our Lord went apart from his disciples
and from all human contact for prayer and meditation. Jesus
felt the need for refreshment and renewal even in a time
when life moved at a much slower tempo than today.

In the early days of my ministry, it was my privilege to go
on retreats to a well-known retreat center just north of New
York City. One of the rules what that each attendant was
required to spend a rather large part of time in complete
silence. I have never forgotten the meaningful hours that I
spent there in prayer and meditation.

Day-to-day life for many of us tends to be ordinary and
hectic. We all need to take intermissions from the pressure of
daily routine.

ROBERT LONG

*Praise to you, O God, for preserving my life in pleasant
and troubled times. Amen*

Prayer concern: Christians in France

Daily Reflections_____
_____
_____
_____

United in Faith

There is one body and one Spirit . . . one Lord, . . .
one God and Father of all, who is over all and
through all and in all. ❖ Ephesians 4:4-6 (NIV)

In a family, each person must do his or her part in order that
there may be harmony. One member of the group can, by his
or her actions, disrupt a harmonious spirit. This is true in
regard to church life also.

For this reason the apostle Paul makes an urgent and
eloquent plea for unity in the church. Calling upon Christians
to be "eager to maintain the unity of the Spirit in the bond of
peace," he points them to the unifying power of the Holy
Spirit. "There is one body and one Spirit."

Our faith unites us in this one body under the lordship of
Christ. Such oneness, effected by the Spirit of truth, is
completely in harmony with the Savior's vision and prayer,
and with the purpose of Paul's prayerful longing and
sacrificial labors. Let us also pray and labor earnestly for the
unity of God's people. We shall be richly blessed in doing this.

MARTIN E. LEHMAN

*O God, we thank you that we—as the body of Christ, the
church—can labor in the unity of the Spirit for the
coming of your kingdom. Amen*

Prayer concern: Christian unity

Daily Reflections

In the Home of Happiness

> On the third day there was a wedding in Cana of
> Galilee, and the mother of Jesus was there. Jesus
> and his disciples had also been invited to the
> wedding. ❖ John 2:1-2 (NRSV)

There was something about this wedding that we often forget
in our weddings today. "Jesus was invited." When we prepare
our invitations, we fail to send him one, and only think of him
when the pastor mentions his name in the service. He is not
one to come uninvited. He must be invited if he is to be
present.

Jesus had been invited, which would indicate that this
couple thought of Jesus long before the actual service. We
ought to, also, for he should be with us in the choice of our
life partner, then he will be at the wedding, and will be an
ever-present member of our family afterward.

Take not, that when a problem arose at this wedding,
Jesus was there to solve it in his gracious way. It is a picture
of the manger in which he can dissolve all our family
troubles. Be sure he is near always! He keeps happiness alive
in the homes of his children!

ROBERT R. CLARKE

*Gracious Lord, grant that those who enter holy wedlock
may have the blessing of your presence in their courtship,
marriage, and throughout their lives. We pray in your
name, O Lord. Amen*

Prayer concern: Those engaged to be married

Daily Reflections

This Endless Forgiveness

Then Peter came to Jesus and asked, "Lord, how
many times shall I forgive my brother when he sins
against me? Up to seven times?" Jesus answered,
"I tell you, not seven times, but seventy-seven
times." ❖ Matthew 18:21-22 (NIV)

God does not stop forgiving. We may stop asking God for
forgiveness, or we may refuse to accept this forgiveness, but
God never stops forgiving. Until the end of our lives, God's
door is open for us to come. Sometimes a mother's love is
like that. No matter how many times her son has sinned, she
always takes him back and never stops forgiving.

Many of us don't have too hard a time forgiving someone
the first time they let us down or harm us. But, how about a
second, third, or even twentieth time? Are we able to keep on
forgiving? The Bible says we must try. Because we are to
forgive as God forgives, and his forgiveness is endless.

Suppose God should grow tired and stop forgiving us. He
could well grow tired. How often do we not offend him? How
often do we not go against his will and displease him? Every
day we must come back to God to be forgiven all over again.
How wonderful if we, like God, can keep on loving someone,
no matter how often he has hurt us or sinned against us?

ALVIN ROGNESS

*Forgive us our trespasses, as we forgive those who trespass
against us. This is hard, O Lord, but help us. Amen*

Prayer concern: The power to forgive

Daily Reflections⎽⎽⎽⎽⎽⎽⎽⎽⎽⎽⎽⎽⎽⎽⎽⎽⎽⎽⎽⎽⎽⎽⎽⎽⎽⎽

⎯⎯⎯⎯⎯⎯⎯⎯⎯⎯⎯⎯⎯⎯⎯⎯⎯⎯⎯⎯⎯⎯⎯⎯⎯⎯⎯⎯⎯⎯⎯⎯⎯⎯⎯⎯⎯⎯⎯

⎯⎯⎯⎯⎯⎯⎯⎯⎯⎯⎯⎯⎯⎯⎯⎯⎯⎯⎯⎯⎯⎯⎯⎯⎯⎯⎯⎯⎯⎯⎯⎯⎯⎯⎯⎯⎯⎯⎯

⎯⎯⎯⎯⎯⎯⎯⎯⎯⎯⎯⎯⎯⎯⎯⎯⎯⎯⎯⎯⎯⎯⎯⎯⎯⎯⎯⎯⎯⎯⎯⎯⎯⎯⎯⎯⎯⎯⎯

Faithfulness in Small Things

Whoever is faithful in a very little is faithful also
in much. ❖ Luke 16:10 (NRSV)

A woman was shocked when she left the bank and discovered
that the teller had given her $900 for a $9 check. She hurried
back into that financial temple and hesitantly said that she
wanted to report an error.

First, she had to assure the bank employees that the
mistake favored her. Then she was brushed aside because
the employees assumed that the error was only a matter of
pennies, and they did not want to bother with such a small
correction. When she mentioned the true amount of the
discrepancy, they suddenly were willing to hear her story.

Her honesty in a financial matter indicated that she would
be honest in other ways as well. Faithfulness in doing what
these minor tasks usually arises out of one's relationship to
God. Great accomplishments are the product of consistent
faithfulness in daily living and doing.

NORMAN V. JOHNSON

*Make us faithful in praying, heeding your voice, and
doing your will, O God. Amen*

Prayer concern: Business and economic leaders

Daily Reflections_____

_____

_____

_____

God's Insatiable Hunger for Sinners

"For this son of mine was dead and is alive again;
he was lost and is found!" And they began to
celebrate. ❖ Luke 15:24 (NRSV)

We have ambivalent feelings about the word *sinners*. While it may not be a problem for us to join with the congregation to confess that we are sinners, if someone classifies us with sinners we might be uncomfortable. While tax collectors and discernible sinners crowded up close to listen to Jesus, we'd be more comfortable standing at the edge with the Pharisees and the scribes.

Well-publicized sinners aren't popular. A star athlete may lose all endorsements if caught in a scandal. A politician will lose votes if caught up in fraud. Our first impulse is to shun such people.

The parable Jesus told about the ungrateful son is both comforting (when we think of our sinfulness) and provocative (when it pushes us to reach out to sinners). God is the hero. God's insatiable love for sinful child could not be repressed. With a similar insatiable hunger, God reaches out to us when we fall to our own wayward living, whatever shape it takes.

LOWELL C. HESTERMAN

Forgive us, Father, and receive us in our love. Amen

Prayer concern: Thankfulness for God's forgiveness

Daily Reflections_____
_____
_____
_____

A Stone Church

You also, like living stones, are being built
into a spiritual house to be a holy priesthood.
❖ 1 Peter 2:5a (NIV)

"I love God but I hate the church." said a teenager. If you
know what the church really is, how could you hate her?
Today's text comes from Peter's definition and description of
the church. The church is a "spiritual house"; she is not a
physical building, a budget, or a body of doctrine. She is a
spiritual reality built of the building blocks of believers.

The church is a living organism. Members are "living
stones." Ever see or hear a stone breathe, or talk, or move?
Nothing could be more inanimate than a hard, cold stone.
But the church is alive because her members are living
stones. They live because they live in Christ.

The church is a "holy priesthood." Like a priest, she lives
to serve. A priest's job is to offer sacrifices to God. As priests,
church members offer themselves as living sacrifices.

JOHN R. BROKHOFF

*Lord, for the church we give you thanks. Grant that she
may be all that you want her to be and do. In the name
of him who loved the church, Jesus Christ our Lord.
Amen*

Prayer concern: People who are hospitalized.

Daily Reflections

Umbrellas

Our soul waits for the LORD; he is our help and
shield. ❖ Psalm 33:20 (NRSV)

On a rainy day I can go outside with confidence—as long as
I take my umbrella,

Pouring rain, blowing wind, or puddles all around make
no difference. Under my umbrella I remain safe and secure,
prepared for the weather and protected from the rain.

There are, however, many days when I wish that my
umbrella were big enough or strong enough to protect me
from other trials of daily life: the devastation of a lost
relationship, or the pain of a single, lonely tear. But my
umbrella cannot offer protection from those trials.

In quiet moments I realize that my true umbrella is the
protection of the creator. The strong shield of God protects,
heals, and even saves. Then truly I can go outside every day
with confidence in the Lord, my help and my shield.

STEPHEN J. WEISSER

*Teach me, O Lord, the confidence and strength that can
be found by merely resting in you. Amen*

Prayer concern: Those who mourn

Daily Reflections_____
_____
_____
_____

Getting Something Out of Church

My son, give me your heart. ❖ Proverbs 23:26 (NIV)

One in a while we hear people complain that they get nothing out of church. But this is really not the point. The church is a place where we have opportunity to put in, as well as take out. Perhaps it could truly be said that we only get as much out of church as we put in. You don't get money out of the bank until you put some in.

Does your idea of church membership simply mean attending one service per Sunday? Has it ever struck you that the congregation has every bit as much to do with the preaching of the sermon as the preacher has, that people who come prepared to worship, people who have prayed for their pastor, are the very dynamic of the church's service? Has it ever struck you that it is grossly unfair to expect the church to do exactly what you demand if you, as a part of it, do nothing at all for it?

A well-known minister remarked pungently and almost despairingly that the trouble with most churches was that so many people connected with them were not really members but only "registered customers." We are the church, you and I believe in Christ. We are a part of the great Communion of Saints. Put in your heart, and you will reap rich blessings.

O. K. Storaasli

All that I have, O Lord, is thine alone. Amen

Prayer concern: Preachers of the word

Daily Reflections

The Lord Provides

These forty years the LORD your God has been
with you, and you have not lacked anything.
❖ Deuteronomy 2:7b (NIV)

The Bible is religious history. That is to say, it is always
history related to God's purpose. It is never history for
history's sake. We read the Bible because we want to know
what God is saying to us. One thing God is saying here is that
his goodness and love have never failed. God has always
provided for our physical and spiritual needs. Some people
find that hard to believe. Does not half the world go hungry
each night? What provision has God made for them? But
where is the failure? In God or in us? There is provision
enough to spare. There is bounty but not benevolence. There
is grain but not goodwill. The fault is in sharing and
distribution. The Israelites were required to buy food and
drink from Esau's people, not because they were in need of
them but in order that the inhabitants might benefit from
their presence and be assured of their goodwill. Are we our
brothers' keepers? God is gracious enough but are we?

LAWRENCE D. FOLKEMER

*O Lord, you have answered all our needs of body, mind,
and spirit. Make us continually aware of the needs of
others, and self-sacrificing enough to answer them,
through Christ our Lord. Amen*

Prayer concern: World hunger

Daily Reflections_____

_____

_____

_____

To Tell the Truth

He came as a witness to testify to the light.
❖ John 1:7 (NRSV)

The idea of testifying to our faith is uncomfortable for many of us. We can't imagine speaking in front of a group for fear that we might push our faith on people who find us intrusive.

Almost everyone has a negative impression of the people who knock on doors and try to convert others at random. Yet the Bible asks us to bear witness to the light!

A witness in a court of law is not there to browbeat or even persuade the jury, but simply to give a true account of what the witness saw or heard. We don't have to "preach" to anyone. We can honestly and simply tell others of the times and ways our faith has helped or made a difference in our lives. In this simple storytelling we witness to the light. We tell the truth.

KAREN BATDORF

Lord Jesus, when the occasion arises, give us the heart and words to bear witness to our faith. Amen

Prayer concern: Those who are searching for faith

Daily Reflections
_____

_____

_____

_____

Help!

Happy are those whose help is the God of Jacob,
whose hope is in the LORD. ❖ Psalm 146:5 (NRSV)

It is not only when we hear an ear-piercing shriek in the night that someone is crying out for help. Sometimes the cries come in puzzling ways.

A person may come to visit and not know when to get up and go home. They could be saying, "Ask me why I really came. I need someone to talk to."

A person may pester—even torment—us, until we think they are downright rude. Sometimes we call that "attention getting." It is really a cry for help.

Some people deliberately get themselves into trouble. Sometimes they leave such explicit clues it would take a miracle not to be caught. It's a cry for help.

Can we help at such times? God may have given us the skill to listen and suggest, help and heal. If not, there are others to whom we can turn such a hurting person. However we help, we do it in the name of him who first helped us— "the God of Jacob," our Lord.

P. L. KVITNE

Lord, help us to help others. Amen

Prayer concern: Peacemakers

Daily Reflections_____
_____
_____
_____

Day 297 ❖ Romans 6:23

The Unmerited Gifts

For the wages of sin is death, but the gift of
God is eternal life in Christ Jesus our Lord.
❖ Romans 6:23 (NIV)

In a culture where self-attainment is a highly sought prize, it
is surprising that many fail to grasp the dynamic for a
morally responsible life that Christianity offers. There is an
honesty about Paul's description of the human condition that
deserves our utmost attention. Our totally self-directed
efforts to achieve status before God are doomed from the
start. Through Jesus Christ we receive what we need but
cannot obtain by ourselves.

Through baptism and the work of the Holy Spirit, we are
enabled to grow in faith and life, and the four are inseparable.
Our discipleship involves obedience. God's love for us gives
us the needed motivation for Christian living according to
God's will.

ERNEST D. NIELSEN

*Lord Jesus Christ, we thank you for the gift of an endless
life, and for the call to discipleship. Grant that our lives,
by your grace, may be constantly renewed. Empower us
to withstand the temptation to do that which is evil or
wrong in your sight. Amen*

Prayer concern: True Christian obedience

Daily Reflections

All Generations Will Call Me Blessed

> . . . for he has been mindful of the humble state of
> his servant. From now on all generations will call
> me blessed. ❖ Luke 1:48 (NIV)

Every Sunday we confess, "He was conceived by the Holy Ghost, born of the Virgin Mary." Does this exalt God or Mary? Mary thought it exalted God; so when she realized that she was to be the mother of the Messiah, she broke forth in a glorious hymn of praise.

God chose to come to us through a human birth so that he could get down on our level and reveal himself to us. This is a God we can learn to know and love and who is our friend and brother on our earthly pilgrimage.

Many critics in denying the virgin birth of Jesus point out that Asian religions and Greek mythology are filled with incarnations. The Greek gods often entered into marriage with beautiful women on earth and begat children. But the characters created were as corrupt as the imagined unions.

But Mary gave the world the only perfect son and character. He could ask his enemies, "Who among you can convict me of sin?" So we call Mary blessed for being the mother of our Lord.

JOSEPH L. KNUTSON

Almighty God, we thank you that you came to us through the Virgin Mary as our Lord and Savior. Amen

Prayer concern: Expectant mothers

Daily Reflections_____
_____
_____
_____

The Name of the Lord

Let the name of the LORD be praised, both now
and forevermore. ❖ Psalm 113:2 (NIV)

A line from William Shakespeare's *Romeo and Juliet* makes
the point that what we call a rose "by any other name would
smell as sweet." Names, in other words, do not tell much
about true identity.

But that is not always the case. Our text speaks of the
"name of the Lord," and that name is one to be honored
indeed. That name truly describes the one who is our God.

What is the Lord's name? For the Israelites, it was
Yahweh. The name signified God as "I am who I am" (Exodus
3:14), the Holy One who cannot be defined by any others. For
us, the Lord's name is Jesus, God's Son, the one who, as his
name notes, will save God's people (Matthew 1:21).

It is from the Lord's name that we know he is to be
blessed. From it, we learn of God's great power, and of the
love the all-powerful God.

KATHERINE BATES

Lord, may we respect your great name. Amen

Prayer concern: Language that honors God

Daily Reflections

The Only Safe Foundation

For no one can lay any foundation other than
the one already laid, which is Jesus Christ.
❖ 1 Corinthians 3:11 (NIV)

In the construction of a building, a solid foundation is crucial. Everything else depends upon it. If the foundation is weak, a one-story house can collapse. On the other hand, the Parthenon has stood securely on its foundation for more than two millennia.

The Christian church has an even stronger foundation. It has endured for centuries and has withstood incredible stress (false teachings, persecution, and so on) because of its foundation. Samuel Stone expressed it well when he wrote: "the Church's one foundation is Jesus Christ, her Lord."

As we build up the church in our generation, everything we do must rest on the foundation of Christ. Otherwise our time and energies will be spent in vain. If we build on the sure foundation of Christ, our efforts will be blessed and the kingdom will be enhanced.

CHARLES KNORR

Lord of the church, may our efforts to build for you be founded on you. Amen

Prayer concern: Christians in China

Daily Reflections_____

_____

_____

_____

Shelter

> For in the day of trouble he will keep me safe in
> his dwelling. ❖ Psalm 27:5 (NIV)

One evening a famous minister was walking in the beautiful
grounds of a home, meditating upon his message for the
evening. Suddenly he was startled by the appearance of a
hawk in swift pursuit of a skylark. The frightened bird darted
among the trees with cries of terror. The hawk was steadily
gaining upon its helpless prey, bent upon its life. Presently the
bird espied the minister, who was standing a silent and
interested watcher. At once every instinct of timidity toward
humans forsook it. Turning quickly, the bird flew straight into
his bosom. There it nestled with wild beating heart, while the
minister sheltered it from its baffled foe. "Do you think," he
said, "that for one instant I would give up to its enemy this
helpless bird that had sought refuge in my heart?"

A relentless foe is pursuing us, bent upon the ruin of our
souls. We feel so alone, so sure of ultimate defeat. This is the
devil's lie. God's promise is that he will never leave or forsake
us. The psalms of David tell over and over again of the
protecting care of God. This is because he spent so much of
his turbulent life under enemy attack. "Thou art a hiding place
for me," he says. "You protect me from trouble and surround
me with songs of deliverance" (Psalm 32:7).

JOHN EVERETT

Lead me, Lord, to the security that is you. Amen

Prayer concern: Those who long for security

Daily Reflections

To See Jesus

"Sir," they said, "we would like to see Jesus."
❖ John 12:21 (NIV)

On either side of the chancel in one of our great churches stands a tall marble pillar. Pastors who climb a the few steps to enter the pulpit face this marble column and are confronted by these words: "Sir, we would like to see Jesus." This is the message of the Christian church, the proclamation of the gospel—the good news of salvation. People in Jesus' day and throughout the centuries since have been seeking Jesus, in need of his love and compassion.

Certainly each minister called to proclaim the love of Christ must proclaim this message. But the proclamation is not limited to ordained ministers. The message we hear from the pulpit should become alive in each of us so that we also proclaim it throughout the week. In each person we meet we should see the question: "Sir, we would like to see Jesus." If we have been with Jesus then we ought to demonstrate that we know him. In our lives they will see Jesus.

Are we willing to ask how we may use the sermon, the hour of worship, the Sunday school lesson in our daily lives? How may we be sure that our neighbors, our friends, and our companions at home see Jesus in us?

ELWIN D. FARWELL

Lord, permit the message of the gospel to show in our lives so that others may see Jesus. Amen

Prayer concern: All who pray

Daily Reflections_____
_____
_____
_____

The Unashamed Christian

> Do not be ashamed, then, of the testimony about
> our Lord or of me his prisoner, but join with me
> in suffering for the gospel, relying on the power
> of God. ❖ 2 Timothy 1:8 (NRSV)

What could possibly make us ashamed of the gospel?
Perhaps Timothy was ashamed that Paul was in prison.
Certainly it was no great honor to suffer in prison. Yet Paul
was not ashamed of his call to be an apostle and a teacher.

Christ endured ultimate suffering and death on the cross.
He was humiliated and defeated by both the religious leaders
of the day and the power of Rome. It is not easy to proclaim
the good news of Christ in a world that is increasingly
indifferent, even hostile, to Christianity. Nor is it pleasant to
think that we might have to suffer because we believe in
Jesus Christ and choose to follow him.

We may be embarrassed when our church body takes a
stand on an issue that ruffles some of the feathers of the
establishment. But Jesus is not ashamed of us even when we
retreat into safety rather than boldly proclaim the gospel.

CAROL A. BURK

*God of mercy, let me not feel ashamed to proclaim your
word. Amen*

Prayer concern: Those who feel ashamed

Daily Reflections

_____

_____

_____

Is It Unlawful?

Tell us then, what is your opinion? Is it right . . . ?
❖ Matthew 22:17 (NIV)

In 1900, Boston decreed that automobiles could not enter city parks between 10:00 A.M. and 9:00 P.M. Those "dangerous contraptions" were considered a threat to women and children.

In 1904, the first driver was arrested for speeding and sentenced to five days in jail. His crime was traveling in excess of eight miles per hour.

What is lawful at one time may not be legal in a different circumstance. We would be ticketed today for driving only eight miles per hour on most streets.

Rules and regulations may change, but one law has never changed. Jesus said, "A new commandment I give to you, that you love one another; even as I have loved you" (John 13:24).

The law of love applies to all our questions about what we are allowed to do. What is lawful is whatever love like Jesus' love compels us to do.

RONALD L. HEDWALL

Lord, your law of love binds us so tightly, yet frees us so completely. Amen

Prayer concern: People with cancer

Daily Reflections_____

_____

_____

_____

A Time for Growing

And the boy Samuel continued to grow in stature and in favor with the LORD and with men. ❖ 1 Samuel 2:26 (NIV)

Growth and change are marks of life. When they cease, life also ends. Today's text summarizes the growth of the boy Samuel, who was to be one of the great leaders of God's people in Old Testament times. The words are appropriate in the season of Epiphany for they are also used to summarize the early years of our Lord and his development (Luke 2:52).

What kind of growth do we enjoy? We do grow up in stature up to a point, and in years. Only physical death ends this type of change. Samuel also grew in "favor with the Lord and with men." The life in the presence of God and in his continued mercy resulted in this growth. This is what Paul encourages us to be about when he speaks of "growth in grace and holiness."

This movement will never end for those in Christ. We look to the time when all will be fulfilled in him and we will see him face to face. Until then we struggle and grow. Then we shall praise him perfectly in a new life—and continue to grow.

WALTER HUFFMAN

Dear Lord, let me grow forever in your presence. Amen

Prayer concern: Christians in Ireland

Daily Reflections_____

_____

_____

_____

Waiting Out the Storm

*Each man will be like a shelter from the wind and
a refuge from the storm, like streams of water in
the desert and the shadow of a great rock in a
thirsty land. ❖ Isaiah 32:2 (NIV)*

God has probably spared most of us from weariness in a
wilderness wandering, but picture in your mind a person lost
in a desert. How refreshing and life-giving would be a
windbreak, a stream of fresh water, or the shade of an
overhanging rock!

Life can be wearisome for any of us at times. The tumult of
war, riots, and disturbances swirls about like a tempest.
Neither defeatism nor an aggressive frontal attack is a
prudent course of action. Like prairie blizzards, the storms of
life eventually blow themselves out. We need shelters for the
moment where we can take refuge while we wait to go on.
God is always our refuge and strength, in whose sheltering
arms we can find rest.

KENNETH L. NERENZ

*O God, refresh my soul this day. If the darkness of doubt
and sorrow comes, be my guide until the day dawns
again and the shadows flee away. In Jesus' name I pray.
Amen*

Prayer concern: Those who long for sanctuary

Daily Reflections

Celebrate!

God has gone up with a shout, the LORD with the
sound of a trumpet ❖ Psalm 47:5 (NRSV)

The pitter-patter of a few palms echoed through the massive
sanctuary. Unsure of whether an outburst would raise
eyebrows, the resonating applause remained soft for a while;
and then the excitement grew, spurring everyone on to clap
vibrantly.

Sometimes it's difficult for us to uncork our celebratory
urges. Sensitive to what it may look like, we become stifled
and stiff. Sometimes we almost seem to be desensitized to
what it means to feel good and to share it.

Yet our God encourages us to do just the opposite. "God
has gone up with a shout." These words are part of an ancient
Old Testament hymn that celebrated God's victory as King
over all the nations. God is still victorious over all! Yes, we do
have reason to celebrate. As the first few lines of this psalm
begin, because of his victory we are enabled to "clap hands"
and to "shout to God with loud songs of joy!"

ANNE VAN WAGONER

*Our God, we praise you and thank you for your almighty
victory. May we always praise you as the source of all
that we enjoy. Alleluia! Amen*

Prayer concern: Church musicians

Daily Reflections_____

_____

_____

Hope in the Wilderness

For the LORD will comfort Zion; he will comfort all her waste places, and will make her wilderness like Eden, her desert like the garden of the LORD. ❖ Isaiah 51:3 (NRSV)

The voice of Isaiah spoke good news to the exiled people of Israel. They had been in the wilderness of exile in Babylon for more than 50 years, but Isaiah spoke to them a word of hope, "For the Lord will comfort Zion [Israel]." Isaiah spread the good news that soon they would be homeward bound.

On our walk with God, we experience times of despair, loss, and loneliness. It seems easy to be angry about the world's inconsistencies. Why are some people wealthy but others poor; some well-fed but others starving; and some comfortable but others homeless? We know all too well that it's a wilderness out there. How come? We cannot explain the harshness in some people's lives. We can only believe that God abandons *no one*, and the wilderness moments can be God's great opportunity to move in closer to us. God is not out to punish us. Rather, God seeks to capture us, to comfort us, to never let us go. Not even death can separate us from God. In this certainty, there can always be real hope.

JOHN COFFEY JR.

Holy God, reach deep into our hearts in those moments of despair, loss and fill us with patience and hope. Amen

Prayer concern: Those coping with change

Daily Reflections_____

_____

_____

_____

Aftershock

If you really knew me, you would know my
Father as well. ❖ John 14:7 (NIV)

The aftershock of the events of September 11, 2001, in America left few people untouched. People began to reach out to each other and to God in sorrow and fear. Christians struggled to make sense of tragedy. These questions often surface when disaster strikes: "Where is God and what is God doing?"

It didn't surprise me, then, to hear people ask, "Is God punishing us for our sins?" Behind that question is the same questions the disciples asked Jesus, "What is God really like?"

Jesus answered the question clearly and directly. There is no separate personality hiding behind Jesus ready to wreck vengeance on the world. Rather, keep your eyes focused on the one who hung on the cross and cried, "Father, forgive them, for they know not what they do!"

The God who suffered and died is a God who used infinite restraint to allow us the freedom of choice, even when our choices are heartbreaking. This amazing love is the only way our human hearts are broken open to love.

CAROLYN M. MOWCHAN

Merciful God, help us to trust in the promises of your Son. Amen

Prayer concern: Those with fearful hearts

Daily Reflections

Christ in Isaiah

Then Philip began with that very passage of
Scripture and told him the good news about
Jesus. ❖ Acts 8:35 (NIV)

Philip was a successful preacher of the gospel in the city of
Samaria. Many people there believed and were baptized. Then
Philip did a rather strange thing. Led by the Spirit, he left that
city and went along a desert road to preach to just one man,
an Ethiopian.

Returning from his worship in Jerusalem, this Ethiopian
was reading the prophet Isaiah. He had reached chapter 53,
which tells of a lamb suffering in silence, but he did not
understand the meaning. He needed a guide or an
interpreter. He gladly accepted Philip's explanation and thus
found Christ in the book of Isaiah; for Christ is the Lamb of
God, who dies for the sin of the world. Believing, the
Ethiopian was baptized and went on his way rejoicing.

In Ethiopia today one can get a copy of the Bible. That is
fine, but it is not enough. Many Ethiopians cannot read. Even
those who do read cannot by themselves find Christ in the
book of Isaiah. So we send missionaries to prepare Ethiopian
Christians to become teachers of God's word and lead others
to a saving knowledge of the Lamb, the Savior of the world.

MILTON SCHRAM

Holy Spirit, enlighten the minds of many more to find
Christ in the scriptures. Amen

Prayer concern: Christians in Ethiopia

Daily Reflections_____

_____

_____

_____

Look! You're Transparent

> Nothing in all creation is hidden from God's sight. Everything is uncovered and laid bare before the eyes of him to whom we must give account. ❖ Hebrews 4:13 (NIV)

On damp autumn days I enjoy the aroma of freshly baked cookies. On one such day I was sliding a dozen steaming chocolate chip cookies onto a cooling rack, the doorbell rang. When I opened the door I was greeted by our 8-year-old neighbor dressed in a clear plastic raincoat. As she scurried into the hose and plopped onto a kitchen chair, she proudly asked, "How do you like my new raincoat?"

Before I could reply, the phone rang. After answering the phone, I returned to visit with my guest. Although she was still sitting in the same position as when I had left, something had changed. There, stuffed in the right-hand pocket of her raincoat, were two freshly baked cookies. My guest had forgotten that her new raincoat was transparent.

We foolishly try to hide our thoughts and actions from God, forgetting that he can see right through us. But God's living presence does more than expose our sin it also heals and forgives.

JUDY HEREEN

Thank you, Father, for knowing the real us and for loving us in spite of our mistakes. Amen

Prayer concern: Christians in Spain

Daily Reflections_____

_____
_____
_____

Listen . . . for a Change

Morning by morning he wakens—wakens my ear
to listen. ❖ Isaiah 50:4 (NRSV)

If you, like me, want to take every opportunity to explore the many things that present themselves to you in the course of a given day, maintaining a discipline of regular prayer can be a challenge. Or maybe your challenge is not to be disciplined about prayer, but to find enough prayer time to lay before God the long list of needs you become aware of each day.

Isaiah reminds us that prayer is two-way communication. Prayer is not calling in an order for certain items we expect to have delivered within five to seven business days. When we enter into this conversation with the holy one, we bring our joys and concerns. But we also open ourselves to receive what God has to say to us.

It has been said that we do not pray to change God, but in order that we might be changed. Perhaps the ear is connected to the heart; when God wakens one, the other is opened, too. With open ears and hearts, we can hear and feel God beside us at all times and in all places, and our ears and hearts will be filled with the wisdom and goodness of the Lord.

LORI RUGE-JONES

Dear God, waken my ears and heart to fill them with wisdom and joy. Amen

Prayer concern: Offer thanks for one who taught you to pray

Daily Reflections_____

_____

_____

_____

Power to Endure

> Being strengthened with all power according to
> his glorious might so that you may have great
> endurance and patience, and joyfully giving
> thanks to the Father ❖ Colossians 1:11-12 (NIV)

Paul prays that we might be given power, not only to endure, but power for "all endurance with patience and joy." Most Christians, even new converts and young people, soon experience the joy of "knowing" more about Jesus and the rewards of serving him. But when we speak of "endurance and patience, and joy" we are stepping into deeper spiritual waters.

Many of us can put up with a great deal. Often, of course, this is because we have no choice. We can be stoic, or brave-hearted, and do a minimum of grumbling and complaining. But seldom do we "endure" with patience and joy. This seems to be expecting just too much! Patient endurance is a fruit of the Spirit that ripens slowly and only after we have learned to surrender more fully to the power within us. Life holds much that is unpleasant, difficult, annoying, and sad for each one of us. Christians are asked to endure with patience and joy. Why? "To the praise of his glory and grace" (Ephesians 1:6). How? "According to his glorious might."

S. D. FAWHE

Almighty God, teach us patient endurance that we might show forth your glory and power. Amen

Prayer concern: Christians in Cuba

Daily Reflections

_____

_____

_____

Witnessing

The harvest is plentiful, but the laborers are few.
❖ Luke 10:2 (NRSV)

Witnessing is never easy. In this passage, Jesus sends out 70 of his followers to spread the gospel to towns and villages where he himself intends to follow. Jesus offers these first evangelists some words of instruction. This advice is appropriate for modern-day evangelists as well:

❖ *Don't go alone.* Jesus gives us brothers and sisters in the faith to support us in our witnessing. We all need the prayers and encouragement of other Christians.

❖ *Eat what is put before you.* A modern-day translation might be, "Speak the language of those you want to reach." Be a good listener. Feel the pain of non-believers. Hear how the church has failed them. Don't pretend to have all the answers.

❖ *Don't condemn.* Faith doesn't come overnight. Pray for those you hope to reach. And know when it is wise to back off. You can't bring anyone to faith—only the Holy Spirit can do that.

MARSHA ERICKSON BATES

God of the harvest, help us to witness with compassion and understanding. Amen

Prayer concern: Missionaries

Daily Reflections_____

_____

_____

_____

Two Sons

Which of the two did what his father wanted?
❖ Matthew 21:31 (NIV)

A vinedresser had two sons. He bids them work in his vineyard. "Go, work today."

The first son refuses. He gives his father a harsh answer. Perhaps he has some other engagement or he doesn't like picking grapes. He sets out to leave the way of duty, to forget his father's invitation. But the sense of duty follows him. His conscience pricks him; he turns back. He goes to work in the vineyard.

The second son agrees to go. Alas, his eagerness is only in appearance. His obedience is only of the lips, not of the hands. He never gets near the vineyard. Obedience or profession—which shall it be? Lip service or a life devoted?

"Go, work today." The Lord's work is urgent. Delay is tragic. Think of those who died from the cold or hunger this past winter because we delayed our giving. Think of the souls that are lost daily because we have not yet gone into all the world, to preach the gospel. Think of the good we might do but don't.

ANONYMOUS

O Christ, send us forth—into the vineyard, the city street, the country lane, factory and shop, store and foundry, home and school, everywhere, among all people—to work for you. Amen

Prayer concern: Show us the work you want us to do

Daily Reflections

For the Man Who Has Everything

We tell you the good news. ❖ Acts 13:32 (NIV)

Every Christmas some of us anguish over what gifts to buy for people who seem to have everything. We know for a fact that they have everything they need. We know for a fact that they have an ample supply of the things that would be useful to them, so we often end up by buying them a frivolous gadget that will collect dust and perhaps be stored away indefinitely.

When Paul went into the synagogue at Antioch, he was aware of the rich religious heritage of his listeners. They were the chosen of God who had been promised a living, victorious Messiah. What Paul brought them was good news because it was the fulfillment of the promise.

In our day the good news is the perfect gift for our friends who seem to have so many of the things that perish and so little of that which endures. We need never hesitate to give the good news for no one has ever had too much of that. If we have enough of the good news to give away, we have everything.

ROBERT W. LONG

Thank you, dear God, for the gifts of the good news, which you shared with us that we could give it to others. Amen

Prayer concern: The strength to share our faith

Daily Reflections_____

_____

_____

_____

Deepening Shadows of Death

> Even though I walk through the darkest valley, I fear
> no evil; for you are with me. ❖ Psalm 23:4 (NRSV)

In our world, the shadow of death can fall suddenly in war, in street violence, in accidents, or in strokes and heart attacks. More often, the long, deepening shadows gather slowly, inexorably around the quiet beds of nursing homes or hospital intensive care units. Death is contained—experienced in little enclaves outside of the routines of "real life."

Family members and medical personnel watch with waning hope and wait in fear, sorrow, and resignation for the ultimate outcome. For those who are dying and those who love them, the walk through the valley is long and lonely.

But Jesus is there, too, hearing our anger and sorrow, knowing the evil that is the enemy, knowing too, our pain at separation and loss. God goes with the departing soul, receiving it into life. God stays with the mourners and promises eventual joyful reunion.

INEZ M. SCHWARTZKOPF

Lord of life and death, keep us close to you in life so we will know your presence in death. Amen

Prayer concern: Those who grieve

Daily Reflections

Day 318 ❖ 1 John 3:1-2

The Greatest Gift

See what love the Father has given us.
❖ 1 John 3:1 (NRSV)

It's a funny thing about love—we seem to think that we own it and it's our to do with as we please. Of all the gifts that God has given us, perhaps our poorest stewardship is displayed in the way we handle God's gift of love.

In the early day of the church, the love the Father has given us was freely shared by all who professed the name of Christ—so much so that "Behold, how they love one another!" became a descriptive statement about Christians.

Sharing this love in Christ's name has to be the first priority of the modern-day church, from the local congregation right up to the highest ecclesiastical officers. It begins with and in each of us. We cannot afford to hoard love selfishly in a world that needs it so badly. Sharing God's love will not only promote his kingdom, but it will also safeguard the world until his appointed time of judgement.

LANE L. KNOUSH

Dear Lord, help me always to share freely the love that is yours. Amen

Prayer concern: Newlyweds

Daily Reflections_____

Give Thanks

The earth has yielded its increase; God, our God,
has blessed us. ❖ Psalm 67:6 (NRSV)

Most Bible scholars consider this psalm to be one of communal thanksgiving for a bountiful harvest. God was seen as the source of blessings resulting in a year of plentiful agriculture. The psalms have been the focus of Jewish and Christian worship since early times. They speak to modern readers in completely different circumstances just as powerfully as they spoke to their original audience.

Even today farmers are dependent upon things over which they have little or no control. Too little or too much rain can have devastating effects on their crops. Prayers of thanksgiving are still offered by rural communities of faith during harvest.

For those who live in urban areas it may be more difficult to see a connection between God's blessings in nature and their daily lives. Yet, even with a sense of independence, there are things urban Christians cannot control. Just as farmers cannot control the rain, none of us can control job layoffs, poor health, crime, and financial hardships. We may even take our blessings for granted rather than thanking God for them.

SUZANNE SMITH LAMMI

Gracious God, we give you thanks for our many blessings. Amen

Prayer concern: Farmers facing drought

Daily Reflections

Shaped by God

We are the clay, you are the potter; we are all the work of your hand. ❖ Isaiah 64:8 (NIV)

For a self-reliant person, the attitude of complete dependence on God comes with extreme difficulty. We are, after all, human beings, not unthinking, immobile clay pots! But in respect to our genetic inheritance, our physical appearance, our intellectual potential, even our security from accidents, we are, in a sense, like clay pots, shaped by a destiny greater than our will or desire.

Contentment and purpose in life both rest in large measure within the circumference of recognizing our potential, accepting our limitations, and rejoicing in our achievements within that sphere. How important, therefore, to believe that he who shapes us to be what we are is wise and good.

In that sense, we are in right relationship with God when we acknowledge God as our creator, when we humble ourselves before him, when we seek him in prayer and wait for his direction, when we walk in the light as he is in the light.

JEAN SWEIGERT

Dear God, keep us from hurtful pride and, most of all, keep us humble in your presence. Amen

Prayer concern: Christians in New Guinea

Daily Reflections_____

_____

_____

_____

Break Up the Fallow Ground

Break up your unplowed ground; for it is time to
seek the LORD, until he comes and showers
righteousness on you. ❖ Hosea 10:12 (NIV)

Unbroken, fallow ground will bear no harvest. It has not been
plowed. Therefore the life-giving rains and sunshine cannot
penetrate and become absorbed. In many people the Spirit
never gets deep enough to make religion a reality. The
religious life of many, even of those who go to church, lies
only on the surface. It was to such people that Hosea the
prophet was speaking. As George Adam Smith once put it,
"They expect religious privilege without religious discipline."
The beginning of a real religion, a vital faith, is what Hosea
describes as breaking up the fallow ground so that God's light
and power can penetrate our lives.

Christ wants our hearts, not only our lips, our busy hands,
and our minds for an hour on Sunday. None of us knows what
treasures are waiting in the dark soil of our hearts until we
open them up to his light and his love. Jesus came to give us
life "abundantly." Therefore, we all long for greater fellowship
with him.

O. K. STORAASLI

Dear Lord, break up the fallow ground of my life so that
great fruit may result. I offer myself to you for whatever
purpose you have for me. Amen

Prayer concern: Open hearts

Daily Reflections

How Firm a Foundation

That foundation is Jesus Christ.
❖ 1 Corinthians 3:11 (NRSV)

It is easy for all Christians to forget that the foundation of the church is not Martin Luther, Philipp Melanchthon, John Calvin, or John Wesley. It is tempting for us all to confuse our denominational points of view with the universality of the church. It is easy to begin to believe that we have a corner on the market of truth, of true faith.

The Corinthians had the same difficulty. The church at Corinth was divided. Some were claiming to follow the apostle Peter, some Paul, some an evangelist name Apollos. In all the fighting, the unity of the body of Christ was threatened. Paul wrote to the Corinthians to remind them that the foundation of the church is Christ.

Paul's reminder is for us as well. Christ is the sure and certain foundation. What we build on the foundation of Christ will surely last. But when we build on the shifting sands of denominational prejudice, arrogance, and ignorance, whatever we build will certainly be lost, exposed in the end for what it is.

MARK HINTON

Gracious Lord, help us to build in love and in your name. Amen

Prayer concern: Ecumenical under-standing

Daily Reflections_____
_____
_____
_____

So That You May Believe

Thomas answered him, "My Lord and my God!"
❖ John 20:28 (NRSV)

Have you ever been called a "doubting Thomas?" Usually it is meant to be negative, suggesting that questions or doubts are somehow wrong or that one's faith is weak. But doubt is not necessarily the absence of faith.

Questions and doubts are a part of human existence. They serve a purpose. Just as our knowledge grows when we ask questions, so our spiritual life grows. To question or doubt is to look for something more than we now know. In our search, what we believe becomes clearer to us, our faith increases, our relationship to God deepens.

Jesus doesn't condemn Thomas for having doubts, nor does he condemn us. Rather he says, in effect, "Come to me. Touch me. Let me show you that I am real and alive, so that you may believe." Jesus invites us to look to him for new growth. Our searching provides an opportunity for the Holy Spirit to speak and work in us, and our faith increases.

Then we can say in confidence along with Thomas, "My Lord and my God!"

LINDA HOXTELL

Lord God, strengthen our faith and help us to look to you for answers to our questions. Amen

Prayer concern: Those suffering and wavering

Daily Reflections_____

_____
_____
_____

The God Who Acted

For Christ died for sins once for all.
❖ 1 Peter 3:18 (NIV)

Take a map and locate Erie, Pennsylvania, or Los Angeles, California. There's only one place on the map for each of these cities. Or look at the dates in a history book— Columbus's first voyage, 1492; Pearl Harbor, 1941, and so on. Each event happened at a specific time.

The salvation of humanity is just as definite. It happened in Palestine in the first century when Jesus died on the cross. It happened once for all.

Some people don't like this definiteness. They resent the idea that they owe their salvation to something that happened long ago in a far off land. But God is not a God of generalities. He is the God who acts and he does things when and where he chooses. He chose to redeem humankind through Christ's death.

And we can be happy that this was God's way. For human beings can cover up ideas with a fine blur of words. We can talk around a subject. But the death of Christ on the cross is clear and precise, just as definite as Los Angeles or 1492. Thank God for a God who doesn't shilly-shally but says, "This is it. My Son has died for your sins, once and for all."

W. A. POOVEY

Lord, may I always see in Christ my Lord and Savior— and in his death my only hope of escape from sin. Amen

Prayer concern: Our unbelief

Daily Reflections_____
_____
_____
_____

Praising the Lord

Let them exalt him in the assembly of the people and praise him in the council of the elders. ❖ Psalm 107:32 (NIV)

A most neglected exercise in the Christian life is praise and thanksgiving. We are much more prone to complain and grumble. Instead of being thankful for what we have, we deplore a multitude of things: high prices, the weather, physical ailments, the church, the pastors, our spouses, our children, our lack of time, the pressures of life. All who read this must admit that they've complained about one or all of these items at some time.

In today's reading, the psalmist lists just a few things for which we should be thankful. First, as Christians we should be thankful for our salvation in Christ. It is life's most precious gift, and we so often take it for granted. Daily safety from known and unknown dangers is another. And when did you last thank God for his love and for the love of family and friends? Do it now.

CLARA BERNHARDT

Thank you, Lord, for countless blessings showered upon us. May we be more quick to recognize them and to return thanks for your goodness. Amen

Prayer concern: Christians in Argentina

Daily Reflections_____

_____

_____

_____

Recognizing the Resurrection

> When he was at the table with them, he took
> bread, gave thanks, broke it and began to give it
> to them. ❖ Luke 24:30 (NIV)

The high point of any dramatic piece is the "recognition scene," in which the divergent elements of the plot suddenly reveal a pattern and design. The hidden and the obscure suddenly congeal and this miniscule reflection of life makes sense in the eyes of the characters of the play. Some move to despair and suicide, others to relief and even humor. The road to Emmaus is a recognition scene from the drama of human redemption. Perhaps these men needed special attention or special education. The scriptures say simply that he interpreted God's law in the light of himself. But what a difference his being there made! They recognized him! They beat it back to Jerusalem. The resurrected Lord had been seen outside the city! He was not bound by time and space anymore! Their recognition added to the accumulating proof of God's caring.

ROGER F. COOPER

Blessed Lord Jesus, I want to walk with you. Help me not to be afraid when we meet. Amen

Prayer concern: Those who wish to walk with Jesus

Daily Reflections_____

_____

_____

_____

God—the Source

For us there is one God, the Father, from
whom all things came and for whom we live.
❖ 1 Corinthians 8:6 (NIV)

Every day we are called upon to make choices as to how our
times will be spent. Work, household chores, family
obligations, club or athletic commitments, volunteer groups,
and community groups all lay claim to our lives. Our personal
ambition, talents, and interests will determine the amount of
time we spend at any one thing.

How often do you relate everyday activities to God? Paul
says that all things are from God and that we exist for him.
This close relationship is possible if we accept the idea that
all of life is a gift from a gracious God.

Just think what it would mean for each activity of your life if
you were able to recognize it as an opportunity to serve God.
Work might not be the dreadful bore it sometimes becomes.
Household chores might lose their burden. Family obligations
might take on the fullness of expressions of love. All our
activities would be opportunities for thanksgiving to God.

E. FREDERICK HOLST

*God, help us to experience your closeness to us and to
recognize and accept you as the one who makes life
possible, the one for whom we live each day. Amen*

Prayer concern: Eyes to see God in all we do

Daily Reflections_____

_____

_____

_____

How Grateful Are You?

Let us not become weary in doing good.
❖ Galatians 6:9 (NIV)

Have you ever been tempted to grow weary in your concern for the needs of others? Who hasn't? As Christ "went about, doing good," so the Christian is characterized by generosity, praise, and gratitude.

There is a story that tells how a crowd was watching a disaster that had befallen a peddler and that had wrecked his cart. Among them was a Quaker man. Many were the expressions of sympathy for the poor peddler in his loss. Amidst all the words the Quaker stepped forward: "I am sorry five pounds," he said, handing a five-pound note to the peddler. Then he turned to the crowd: "Friend," he said to each, "how much art thou sorry?" Always for the Christian the sympathy of words must be accompanied by sympathy of deeds. "Let us not grow weary in doing good."

Christ's followers will also be characterized by gratitude. "O give thanks unto the Lord, for he is good," said the psalmist (Psalm 106:1). One of the most common sins is the failure to say thanks for all the benefits we have received both from others and from God. It is a graceless thing always to be taking and never to acknowledge with gratitude the debt that we owe.

O. K. STORAASLI

Lord, help me to do good. Amen

Prayer concern: Those who work for a better society

Daily Reflections

Christic in the Home

> Jesus left the synagogue and went to the home of
> Simon. Now Simon's mother-in-law was suffering
> from a high fever, and they asked Jesus to help
> her. ❖ Luke 4:38 (NIV)

Something always happened when Jesus came to town. The
sick, the lame, and the blind would gather around him. And
when he entered a home, there was an attitude of expectancy;
for he was always kind and compassionate. In his presence,
fevers departed, sinners confessed, and demons fled. The
tears of the penitent and the praise of gratitude alike were
proof of devotion.

Sometimes homes actually change in appearance when
Jesus is welcomed: floors are scrubbed, rugs are put down,
rooms are tidied, and flowers are set to bloom in the
windows. But what is more, language becomes clean, faces
are kinder, hands are more helpful, and hearts are more
loving. The open Bible now appears on the table and there is
family unity, because everything revolves around one
common center: Christ, the Lord. And when trouble, sickness
or sorrow comes, he bids us cast our care on him; for he
truly cares for us.

ANONYMOUS

Lord, we thank you for sending your Son to dwell among
us, and to be our Savior and our friend. Abide with us,
O Lord, and bless our home. Amen

Prayer concern: Inviting Christ into our homes

Daily Reflections

The Axis of Faith

God has called us to live in peace.
❖ 1 Corinthians 7:15b (NIV)

Shalom! The beautiful Hebrew word for peace has now become an international word, used in many cultures and languages. It means satisfaction, fulfillment, and contentment. Paul inserts this appeal for peace into the midst of a long discussion about many problems of marriage. He was tackling the tough problems that these early Christians were confronting. Faith must deal with these problems, and central to their solution is the peace that can keep steadiness and bring fulfillment.

That quality of peace is not easily won. It requires a conscious effort to keep it our center for life. Peace is not death, nor the absence of fighting, nor an escape from problems. It is the axis of the gyroscope of faith, keeping us on course and steady as we deal with life's hard problems. Peace be with you. Shalom!

RALPH W. LOEW

God of all the ages, steady us with an understanding of your purpose. Be a companion to us in all that we try to do, and then, beyond our understanding, grant us peace, through Christ our Lord. Amen

Prayer concern: Christians in Philippines

Daily Reflections_____
_____
_____
_____

The Direction We Are Going

Repent, then, and turn to God, so that your sins may be wiped out, that times of refreshing may come from the Lord. ❖ Acts 3:19 (NIV)

It may strike us like lightning that Peter's words are addressed to us, too: "Repent, then, and turn to God" (or, "Change your mind and your direction," as the Greek may also be translated). Of course, like any person, we concede that we make mistakes and take some wrong turns, but we all assume that basically we are on the right track. We have not killed Jesus the way those did who cried, "Crucify him!"

But we are betraying Jesus by passing him by and turning our backs on him day in and day out on the merry-go-round of our lives. The faster we go and less time we have for him, the dizzier we get from the ups and downs of our successes and failures, and our vision gets so blurred that we lose him all out of sight as we are rushing after our goals. We have to stop, to get off this merry-go-round, and find him in whom life is real and full of joy and purpose.

GUNARS J. ANSONS

O Lord, who knows the emptiness of my days and the fruitlessness of my efforts: Send your Son, Jesus Christ, to bring new life to this wasteland of mine, that it may abound with forgiveness, mercy, and love. Amen

Prayer concern: Those who need a break from the busyness of their lives

Daily Reflections_____
_____
_____
_____

Abram's Lint

And he believed the Lord; and the Lord reckoned
it to him as righteousness. ❖ Genesis 15:6 (NRSV)

Compared to Abraham, we have centuries of history with the
Lord. We have the rest of the Bible and the story of the early
church and the witness of millions of people who have
testified that God has kept his promises. Abram could plunge
his hands into the pockets of his history with God and find
less than lint. And yet, at God's word of promise, Abram left
to go to a far country. Along the way, Abram showed that he
was more accustomed to taking care of himself and his own
family than trusting anyone else. Abram's journey of faith was
not so smooth, but what faith he had compelled him to move
in God's direction. Those tiny steps were enough for God to
call Abram a righteous man.

To each new life, God renews his promise of community
and steadfastness. Armed with a history of God's faithfulness
to people like Abram for thousands of years, we who move in
tiny steps of faith in God's direction can be confident of God's
applause and delight even when we feel ourselves to be less
than lint.

DEBRA GRANT

Holy God, receive our steps of faith toward you. Amen

Prayer concern: Those who haven't heard God's voice
in their heart

Daily Reflections_____

_____

_____

_____

Fear and Trust

> See, the LORD your God has given you the land.
> Go up and take possession of it as the LORD, the
> God of your fathers, told you. Do not be afraid;
> do not be discouraged. ❖ Deuteronomy 1:21 (NIV)

Fear is one of our bitterest enemies. It is subversive and paralyzing. It eats away at faith and weakens the will to act. As anxiety, it runs wild and plays all kinds of havoc with personality. It distorts life badly. The Israelites had every reason to trust God, who had delivered them out of bondage and sustained them in the wilderness. But fear, the deadly enemy within, rocked their faith. It took hold of the 12 spies who explored the land and made the enemy Amorites look like giants. The real giants (fears) were inside the mind. Fear is contagious. It can be transmitted to others. So, the hearts of the people also "melted" with fear. A whole people became immobilized through fear.

People can only take possession of the promised land when they trust in God. All the promised lands of peace, brotherhood, forgiveness, and salvation are waiting to be conquered by fearless trust in God.

LAWRENCE D. FOLKHEMER

O Christ, whose life was perfect love and in whom no fear resided, dispel from our hearts the crippling blows of anxiety. Make us to love you as we ought to love. Amen

Prayer concern: Those who suffer from anxiety and with phobias

Daily Reflections_____

_____

_____

_____

Day 334 ❖ Luke 2:25-40

Simeon's Vision

> For my eyes have seen your salvation, which you have prepared in the sight of all people, a light for revelation to the Gentiles and for glory to your people Israel. ❖ Luke 2:30-32 (NIV)

In some cultures, people believe that not only do a person's eyes reveal his inner thoughts, but that they are a path into the depths of the self. Simeon's little song, which we call the Benedictus, shows us a person caught up in expectation and submission to God's will. It is also clear that Simeon has received a great gift as be beholds the child. It is as if nativity starlight and transfiguration brightness has filtered into his inmost being. Truly, here is an enlightened man!

His song reminds us of a multitude of other scriptural events, such as Andrew bringing Peter to Jesus, or the woman by the well calling to her neighbors, "I have seen—come see." We remember the words of the first witnesses to the risen Lord when they breathlessly claimed, "We have seen the Lord!" Indeed, the history of the Christian church might well be written under such a title as "my own eyes have seen the salvation."

WALTER HUFFMAN

Open our eyes and our lives, O Lord, that we might again behold the beauty of your saving love shining in the life, death, and resurrection of Jesus your Son, our Lord. Amen

Prayer concern: Christians in Denmark

Daily Reflections

The Townspeople or the Good Guy?

For the LORD will not reject his people; he will never forsake his inheritance. ❖ Psalm 94:14 (NIV)

A western town was in turmoil. The outlaw gang had ridden in and taken over. The townspeople sought refuge in their homes, hoping the evil band would somehow disappear from view. Then the good guy with the white hat rode in. He valiantly fought the outlaws and subdued them. Peace once again came to the little town.

So often it seems that when Christians are confronted by the onslaughts of life—its sin, its evil, and the tragedy of its consequences—they seem to resemble the townspeople hiding out rather than the good guy in the white hat. And this may seem natural until you consider that Christians, among all people, have the strongest defense and strength and power that will ever exist. They need only respond and act as those who place their whole trust and lives in the Lord their God in Christ. Against such a force, evil and sin cannot stand.

DWIGHT A HUSEMAN

Lord, grant that we the people of God may become the people that you have called us to be. May we not shrink in fear at the onslaughts of life. May we rather advance victoriously, trusting solely in the strength that you provide us through Christ our Lord. Amen

Prayer concern: People who are afraid to act

Daily Reflections

The Beginning

In the beginning God . . .❖ Genesis 1:1 (NIV)

Lurking somewhere near our surface is the question, "What is in back of it all?" Children are only a few years old when they begin probing. "Where did it come from?" they ask. Relentlessly they drive you back to the beginning—to God.

God is the one who always has been. God is the guarantor of existence. If God ever stopped creating we would stop existing. Night and day, the sun, the stars, the earth and all its inhabitants are called into being and are maintained in existence by God. God is the parent of us all, and because that is so we address him as "Our Father."

Life has a way, like "Ol' Man River," of just rolling along. The generations roll endlessly by and we take things for granted. It should not be so. The air we breathe, the bodies we inhabit, the family we love, the colors we see, and the sounds we hear are all products of God's handiwork.

As individuals, as congregations, as members of a church, and as members of the all-encompassing body of Christ, we are called to live in constant awareness of our beginnings. It is not all we are meant to do by any means. It is the necessary point of beginning.

DAVID PREUSS

O you who are the beginning, we praise you for your creative power, and we thank you for your creative goodness. Amen

Prayer concern: God's creation

Daily Reflections_____

_____

_____

_____

The Great Empire

I do not understand what I do. For what I want to do I
do not do, but what I hate I do. ❖ Romans 7:15 (NIV)

We know that the very foundation and the stability of our
democratic society rest upon law. Yet however strong the
hoped-for restraining influence of the law, the law itself is not
able to stop violations. The same observation applies to the
law of God. The question "Why did I do this?" haunts all of
us. Conscience-stricken, we often delude ourselves and
others into believing that our wrongdoings were caused by
extenuating circumstances beyond ourselves.

The apostle Paul's whole stance is exceedingly helpful. He
deals with the problem of sin in a morally responsible
manner. He has no doubt about the power of sin; it is
inseparable from the human condition. The battle between
good and evil cannot be won by him, but only by the risen
Christ.

ERNEST D. NIELSEN

*Heavenly Father, in your infinite love and mercy, forgive
us our sins. Heal us from the wounds of guilt. When we
are tempted, let the Holy Spirit show us the mind of
Christ. Help us to forgive others. Aid us in our desire to
live responsibly. Amen*

Prayer concern: Those you have wronged others

Daily Reflections_____
_____
_____
_____

Wisdom and Money

I tell you, use worldly wealth to gain friends for yourselves, so that when it is gone, you will be welcomed into eternal dwellings. ❖ Luke 16:9 (NIV)

The steward in Jesus' parable was sharper than a tack, but he got no further than his dishonest head would let him. As Benjamin Franklin said, "He that is of opinion money will do everything may well be suspected of doing everything for money." Having no conscience, he made a mess of his life, was suspected, accused, found guilty, and fired. Clever as he was, he did not know that making men his partners in fraud would not make them reliable friends.

As "sons of light" (John 12:36), we are to be wiser than "the sons of this world," whose best friend is the dollar. "Unrighteous mammon" is Jesus' name for money made as this swindler made it. But he also says that there is a right way of doing business, which will make friends who will be glad to live with us forever in heaven. If we are wise, we will put all our know-how into God-pleasing ways of making and spending our money.

RAYMOND R. STAMM

O God, to whom we owe all that we have and are: help us to use material things for spiritual ends. By honesty and kindness may we draw all with whom we do business to Jesus, so that they and we may dwell together as his friends forever. Amen

Prayer concern: Those who struggle with greed

Daily Reflections

New Every Morning

His compassions never fail. They are new every
morning. ❖ Lamentations 3:22b-23a (NIV)

After being released from a Vietnamese prison camp, an
American prisoner of war had a rather unusual way of
celebrating. Every morning for several weeks he would think
about how fortunate he was as he put on either new clothing
or some that had been freshly laundered.

In so doing, this free man desired to erase from his
memory the filthy, vermin-infested rags that he had worn for
months on end during his incarceration. It also was a way for
him to express his thanks for having the privilege of new and
clean apparel.

This could be a picture of our own Christian lives. We
many times come to the close of a day with regrets, shame,
and guilt toward God and people with whom we are
associated. But we, too, can put on the new and the clean
every morning. Each day is a new beginning, a new life given
to us by our Savior, Jesus Christ. His mercies never come to
an end. Let us lay aside our sins and be clothed with that
newness at every daybreak.

GERALD D. A. ENGELHARDT

*We praise you for your mercies, O God, that are new
every morning. Amen*

Prayer concern: Christians in Germany

Daily Reflections_____
_____
_____
_____

Day 340 ❖ 1 Peter 3:15-18

In Your Hearts

> But in your hearts set apart Christ as Lord. Always be prepared to give an answer to everyone who asks you to give the reason for the hope that you have. But do this with gentleness and respect. ❖ 1 Peter 3:15 (NIV)

In the Bible, the person we are in our innermost self is identified as heart, or soul, or mind, or spirit. But in Psalm 103:1 the author is not content to identify the inner person with one word alone. The psalmist seems to be talking to himself in the presence of God when he says, "Bless the Lord, O my soul; and all that is within me, bless his holy name." In a lightning moment of understanding that no one word can properly identify the inner person, he uses a whole phrase: "All that is within me."

Peter says, "In your hearts set apart Christ as Lord." It would not be amiss to apply the psalmist's inclusive phrase: All that is within me . . . reverence Christ as Lord. Deep within the person that is *you*, you know whether you allow Christ to be your Lord. The Spirit himself testifies with our spirit that we are God's children. An occasional disobedience does not cancel this commitment.

FREDERICK A. SCHIOTZ

Father, you know that in our hearts we would reverence Christ as Lord. Amen

Prayer concern: Repentant and faithful hearts

Daily Reflections_____

_____
_____
_____

Our Mediator

> For there is one God; there is also one mediator
> between God and humankind, Christ Jesus,
> himself human. ❖ 1 Timothy 2:5 (NRSV)

Time and time again the Old Testament emphasizes the fact that the God of Israel is the one and only God. This emphasis is the greatest contribution that Judaism has given the world. Alongside of this fact is Paul's word to Timothy, that there is one mediator between God and humanity, Jesus Christ. Sometimes a child wants something. He asks mother for it. Often she says, "Go, ask your father." But his plea is, "You ask him, please." Mother becomes the mediator and the intercessor.

The book of Hebrews frequently refers to Christ as our mediator. It says, "He always lives to make intercession for them that draw near to God." Christ does this because as human he knows the needs of humanity, and, as our Savior, he alone has the right to plead for us with the Father. That is why we properly pray "in Jesus' name." To seek any other mediator is vain, and slights the redemptive work of Christ. "Ask, and you will receive."

HENRY W. SNYDER

Father, we thank you for the gift of Jesus Christ, who ever lives to make intercession for us. Grant us daily life and strength that by your grace we may serve you acceptably. Amen

Prayer concern: Those who long for peace

Daily Reflections

_____

_____

_____

Forgetfulness

> Praise the LORD, O my soul, and forget not all his
> benefits. ❖ Psalm 103:2 (NIV)

As the psalmist reflects on the presence of the Spirit, he
recognizes that one of the great barriers to voicing simple
gratitude is forgetfulness: "Forget not all his benefits."

No matter how brilliant a person may be, he or she will
still forget some things. For the young it may be because of
preoccupation with new interests. For the old it may be due
to physical changes in the brain. Unfortunately, God's
blessings can be easily forgotten by young and old alike. The
psalmist's prayer-soliloquy is actually a confession that
forgetfulness robs him of the incentive to thank God. This is
no morbid confession that the psalmist uses to flay himself.
It is rather an honest acknowledgement.

A church can forget blessings as easily as an individual
can—perhaps even more easily. The changing world in which
we live can easily obscure for us God's abundant blessings.
What a wholesome experience it would be today to begin
counting our blessings.

FREDERICK A. SCHIOTZ

*O Lord, remove the forgetfulness that obstructs our flow
of praise. Amen*

Prayer concern: Church historians

Daily Reflections_____

_____
_____
_____

With Thanksgiving

> . . . one God and Father of all, who is above all and
> through all and in all. ❖ Ephesians 4:6 (NRSV)

How dull life can become! All the little and big events can feel
purposeless unless two ingredients are added: the wonder of
creation and the zest of thanksgiving. These two make all
things warm and personal. Thanks involves wanting the giver
as well as the gift. Anything we have becomes meaningless
if no one else sees it.

Our relationship is dead if we do not thank the creator.
If, to your requests, you add thanksgiving, you are in a
meaningful relationship to God through Christ. Christ makes
thanks possible. The Bible says much about thanksgiving,
but the greatest is found in Revelation 1:5b-6: "To him who
loves us and has freed us from our sins by his blood . . .
to him be glory and power forever and ever. Amen" (NRSV).

Gratitude is learned by example. The disciples heard
Jesus give thanks many times. In the New Testament the
word *repent* occurs only about 47 times, while just one form
of the word for thanking is found at least four times as often.
The word translated as "thanks" is the same word that is
translated *grace*. How closely these two thoughts are inter-
woven in the Bible!

HERB G. LODDIGS

Thank you, God, for your innumerable favors. Amen

Prayer concern: Those who feel without purpose

Daily Reflections_____

_____

_____

_____

The Future

You hypocrites! You know how to interpret the appearance of earth and sky, but why do you not know how to interpret the present time?
❖ Luke 12:56 (NRSV)

The weather in Jesus' day was sultry with impending revolution. His followers were praying for the day when the Christ would take vengeance on the hated Romans. Men of violence were doing their evil best, and they wanted Jesus to set the date for his D-Day. Instead, he warned them to stop hating and begin to love God with all their heart and their neighbors, including the Romans, as themselves.

When storm signals go up we prepare for the hurricane, and meteorologists hope to some day prevent dangerous weather. Jesus offers abundant resources of faith, hope and love to control this world's spiritual climate so as to substitute his way for humanities chaos of self-defeating revolutions. As the barometer rises and falls it is not easy to adjust to changes that are not to our liking. But as wise stewards we have God's promise: "As your days may demand, so shall be your strength."

RAYMOND T. STAMM

O God, help us to have faith in things not seen. Keep us mindful that you are able to do for us far more than we ask or think. Amen

Prayer concern: Those people who feel anxious about the future

Daily Reflections_____

_____

_____

_____

Day 345 ❖ Philippians 1:19-27

Enjoying Our Work

If I am to live in the flesh, that means fruitful
labor for me. ❖ Philippians 1:22a (NRSV)

Every now and then you might see a newspaper article about
some successful business leader or politician who is giving
up a career to become a rancher, a writer, or perhaps the
owner of a resort. Whatever the change, it is usually drastic;
with the person giving up a secure income and a set future
for a more tenuous position.

I have known two people who made significant career
changes: one wanted to become a police officer and another
wanted to be the operator of a nursing home. The reasons for
such changes are always interesting, and seeing people's
dedication in their new fields is refreshing.

We make changes in what we do either when we become
disenchanted or when we are sure that we will find greater
satisfaction in another area. No matter what our occupation,
though, we can find real meaning in our lives by realizing that
our Lord has a worthwhile job we can do for him. Through
that labor can come full enjoyment.

JAMES C. ALLISON

*Thank you, Father, for the tasks you want to give us.
Help us see the marvelous plan you have for each of our
lives. Give us daily renewed enthusiasm, enduring
strength, and steady hands, that we might labor long and
well for your cause. Amen*

Prayer concern: Those who work to ease suffering

Daily Reflections_____

_____

_____

_____

Day 346 ❖ John 10:11-14a

The Good Shepherd

I am the good shepherd. The good shepherd lays
down his life for the sheep. ❖ John 10:11 (NIV)

Have you every driven through one of the western states and
seen a shepherd's hut on a high meadow or plateau? Or have
you ever seen the shepherd himself in the midst of his sheep?

Not may Americans know much about sheep or
shepherds. Only a small percentage of Americans live on
farms and few of the farmers have much to do with sheep. So
for most of us it would seem that the biblical description of
the good shepherd does not have much to draw on as far as
our experience is concerned. We don't know much about
either shepherds or sheep.

Nevertheless, Psalm 23 and the picture of Jesus as the
"good shepherd" are firmly fixed in our minds. We can surely
recall pictures of Jesus with the lamb on his shoulder. What
we remember when we read of the good shepherd is love and
care. In this word-picture we are the ones watched over and
cared for. That is good to remember not only when things go
well, but also when things don't go at all well for us. We are
cared for—by the good shepherd.

PHILIP A. QUANBECK

*Help us to remember with thanksgiving your loving
care for us. Amen*

Prayer concern: Joyful hearts

Daily Reflections_____

Encouragement

But the Lord is faithful, and he will strengthen and protect you from the evil one. ❖ 2 Thessalonians 3:3 (NIV)

In the first five verses of Paul's second letter to the Thessalonians, we have a magnificent example of the interrelatedness of all Christians—how we strengthen and support one another. Paul begins by asking that his friends in Thessalonica pray for Silvanus, for Timothy, and for him that the word of the Lord may triumph. This is his need of them. They are not to forget about the work of the Lord that he is doing. They are not to feel that because he is out of their sight they can no longer help and sustain him. He needs their prayers, their interest, their spiritual support; for the church is one body, and the arms can't get very far if the legs are sitting down. When the church moves, it all moves.

Then Paul assures his friends of his continued love for and interest in them. He send them words of comfort, cheer, and Christian encouragement. They need him, and his prayers, counsel, and pastoral care.

TERRENCE Y. MULLINS

Almighty and most loving God, you have remained faithful throughout all ages even though humanity has turned away from you to seek its own destruction. Be merciful, Lord, and turn us away from everlasting sin and death to everlasting life with you. Amen

Prayer concern: Christians in Turkey

Daily Reflections

Rekindled Love

> There she shall respond as in the days of her
> youth, as at the time when she came out of the
> land of Egypt. ❖ Hosea 2:15b (NRSV)

Against a background of political turmoil, the musical *Fiddler on the Roof* explores the emotional upheaval in a traditional Russian Jewish family caused when the daughters insist on marrying men they love, instead of men the matchmaker recommends. In the musical, the father, never heard of such a thing. He challenges his wife with the question, "Do you love me?" After listing all the ways she has taken care of him over the years, she gives in and finally admits that she loves him.

The book of Hosea uses marriage to describe the relationship between God and the people of Israel. Hosea reminds the people of the love they once felt for God, who rescued them from slavery in Egypt. The prophet describes all God will do to rekindle their love. But he also identifies the qualities necessary for the relationship to endure beyond the stage of honeymoon euphoria. God's people live out their faithfulness to God by living in righteousness, justice, and mercy. God woos us with these same gifts, inviting us to grow old in a love that truly will last forever and ever.

MARSHA GILPIN EHLERS

Gracious God, help us receive your unending love with faithfulness toward you, and justice and mercy toward others. Amen

Prayer concern: Stronger marriages

Daily Reflections

Already Filled

The afflicted shall eat and be satisfied; those who seek him shall praise the LORD. May your hearts live forever! ❖ Psalm 22:26 (NRSV)

Some people are perpetually hungry, as they never get enough to eat and they never feel satisfied. Hunger is a sad commentary on a world where so many people have so much. Yet it is equally sad to be filled and still not feel *fulfilled*—to have everything except satisfaction.

Those who hoard are never able to put away enough so they feel secure. Craving demands more and more. It becomes an idolatry—covetousness—separating us, cutting us off from each other and from God.

Still, there is hope for the afflicted of whom the psalmist speaks. Whenever anyone seeks the Lord, praise is a natural response. When we get outside ourselves and seek things that are above, we find a Lord worth praising forever. And look what happens. He turns the afflicted one's plight to praise.

JOHN SPEERSTRA

Lord, you have given us hearts that can live forever. There can be no more fulfilling gift. Amen

Prayer concern: Those tempted by materialism

Daily Reflections

The One-Minute Prayer Manager

I hated all my toil in which I had toiled under the
sun, seeing that I must leave it to those who come
after me. ❖ Ecclesiastes 2:18 (NRSV)

Job distress must go back a long way, and it is still prevalent
today. We start a new job full of enthusiasm but are soon
overwhelmed by negative supervision, silly rules, work that
never gets caught up, and an uneasy feeling that we could be
laid off at any time. If we do our work for the paycheck, we
might not find much joy in it. By the time the bills are paid,
we can still be behind. If we do our work for the pleasure,
that too can disappoint us. Any job can produce stress and
frustration on a daily basis. The people who seem happiest in
their work are those who take pleasure in doing the task, in
grateful response to God's many gifts to us.

A woman in our office says one-minute prayers, both for
herself as she approaches her tasks, and for the people—
known and unknown—who will reap the benefits of her hard
work. And when she has prayed for the beneficiary of her
work, she never feels useless, spiteful, or burned out by her
job. One-minute prayers can turn the burden of work into a
blessing of gratitude.

MARY NIXON

*Help us to do our work with a willing and cheerful
heart, dear God, ever caring for those who receive the
benefit. Amen*

Prayer concern: People who are unemployed

Daily Reflections

The Almighty

"I am the Alpha and the Omega," says the Lord
God, "who is, and who was, and who is to come,
the Almighty." ❖ Revelation 1:8 (NIV)

The abuse of the book of Revelation by various cults and
sects causes many of us to avoid it, but others should not
scare us from this treasure in the Bible.

Revelation is full of many basic Christian truths. Basic in
its message is the power of our almighty and eternal God. No
matter how confused and troubled this present life may be,
God is in ultimate control of the universe. Destiny is in God's
hands.

While imprisoned in a Nazi concentration camp, Lutheran
Bishop Hans Lilje drew much strength from Revelation, and
wrote a commentary on this book: the last book in the Bible.
God spoke to Bishop Lilje, and God will speak to us if we
steep ourselves in the message in Revelation. It is gospel—
fear not, I bring you good news—Jesus Christ, the faithful
witness, loves us and has freed us by his blood from our sins.

ROBERT R. STROHL

*Almighty God, you are the beginning and the ending of
everything. Unveil before us the truth of life that we
might walk in your way throughout the year. To you be
glory and dominion forever. Amen*

Prayer concern: Those who feel confused or troubled

Daily Reflections_____

_____

_____

_____

Strength in Storms

God is our refuge and strength, an ever-present
help in trouble. ❖ Psalm 46:1 (NIV)

In the courtyard behind Robinson School in Santurce, Puerto
Rico, stood a lovely tree. It was sheltered by the three walls of
the school and had been watered and cared for since it was
first planted. It had done well despite the fact that it grew in
sandy soil.

One night a storm struck. The wind came from the open
side of the courtyard and uprooted the tree. To the surprise
of all who saw it, the roots were very shallow. Because of all
its protection and care, the tree hadn't needed to put down
many roots.

Outside the school, other large trees that had no
protection had stood up against the storm with little damage.
They had withstood storms before, and their roots went down
deep into the ground and held the trees strong and sturdy.

We see that this is true in our lives. Storms make us
strong. They cause us to put our roots down deep in God's
word, and in faith hold to him. Thus we become stronger by
each hard thing we conquer.

LOIS E. ELLINGSON

*O Lord, let me stay rooted in you through all of life's
storms. Amen*

Prayer concern: Those suffering as a result of natural
disasters

Daily Reflections_____

_____
_____
_____

When the Accounts Are Audited

For everyone who has will be given more.
❖ Matthew 25:29 (NIV)

How can one describe events at the end of this world and age? Jesus used a parable to give us a picture of God's final accounting practices. The books of a wealthy man were audited after his return from a journey. He had turned over custody of his possession to trusted employees during his long absence.

The parable tells us that he expected good stewardship of his resources. His employees were to be rewarded. So God holds us accountable for all that has been entrusted to us: health, various capabilities, time, material possessions, and influence on others.

There is also a warning here to the careless—to those who think their lives may be lived, their talents used, their money spent only as they see fit, with no accounting to anyone. And there is a promise of recognition and reward to those who act responsibly in use of time, health, talents, material possessions. It is very serious—so much is at stake!

HAROLD L. YOCHUM

Lord God, we ask the Spirit's guidance that we may make the most of this life. Amen

Prayer concern: Better use of our time and talents

Daily Reflections_____

_____

_____

_____

Piety or Charade

Be careful not to do your "acts of righteousness" before men, to be seen by them. If you do, you will have no reward from your Father in heaven.
❖ Matthew 6:1 (NIV)

Pride in religious accomplishments is a natural pitfall. Jesus tells us to test the sincerity of our actions. Are the things we do in his name genuine or fake? Are they done to the glory of God or to impress our friends and neighbors?

Our text is not a command against acts of piety. Reverence and devotion to God breed charity, prayer, love. These things are expected from everyone.

What is condemned is the practicing of good works before others in order to be seen by them. It is the motivation of an act that is called into question.

The test of a pious act is motivation. Is it done because we love God and his love compels us? That is piety. Is it done because we love ourselves and seek the admiration of others? That is a lie, a fraud, a religious charade.

PATRICK FLYNN

O Lord, show us each day what is expected of us and what is compelled by your love. Help us to do the same, and afterward to say, "We are unworthy servants. We have only done what was your duty." Amen

Prayer concern: True piety

Daily Reflections____

God's Glory

Arise, shine, for your light has come, and the glory
of the Lord rises upon you. ❖ Isaiah 60:1 (NIV)

Watching the coming of dawn from the floor of the Grand
Canyon is an unforgettable experience. First we see only the
vague outline of the rim and the darkness of the lower
canyon. Then as the day slowly dawns, we have fleeting
glimpses of peaks and valleys. Vague outlines materialize.
Shapes and forms appear, and light slowly filters down to us.
Long shadows move lower and lower. Finally the sun bursts
over the rim, flooding the canyon with light. We are amazed
at the color, symmetry, and breathtaking beauty of our
surroundings—where all was darkness only a short time
earlier.

Isaiah speaks of a glory even greater than this. It was like
the dazzling glory the shepherds experienced at Bethlehem.
It is the glory of the Lord. Such a sense of awe and wonder of
God in Christ needs a revival in our civilization. We see so
many marvelous sights that our appreciation is blunted.
Surely thoughts of the glory of the Lord in our midst will
renew our enjoyment and pleasure in worship. Let us take
time to meditate upon the glory of the Lord for the
enrichment of our lives.

ALFRED O. FRANK

Lord, grant us a child-like imaginations of your glory.
Amen

Prayer concern: Nature's wonders

Daily Reflections_____

Modern Betrayals

While they were reclining at the table eating, he said, "I tell you the truth, one of you will betray me—one who is eating with me." ❖ Mark 14:18 (NIV)

Who would have thought that one of them would do such a thing! Had they not all been faithful to him throughout his life? They were even willing to go with him to Jerusalem, though it could have meant death. But now they were told that one of them would betray him. How unbelievable!

Do not be too ready to judge. Even today there are many people who eat at the table with Jesus and yet betray him. There are those who bear the mark of Christian, but whose lives belie that mark. The church member who squeezes the last penny from a poverty stricken family as a slumlord; who spreads gossip and rumor; who cheats on his income tax—all these illustrate modern-day Judases who fail to understand what it means to be a follower of Christ. They are the ones who will betray him.

RUSSELL M. LONG

Dear Lord Jesus Christ, we dare to eat with you because we know that you have the only food that can save us. Forgive us when we, while eating, betray you and by our actions show to the world that you have no meaning for us. In your name we pray. Amen

Prayer concern: Those who mourn

Daily Reflections_____

_____

_____

_____

Day 357 ❖ 1 John 1:1-4

Song of Life and Joy

We write this to make our joy complete.
❖ 1 John 1:4 (NIV)

If you want to know how your joy may be complete, read the entire First Epistle of John. It is one of the most intimate of all the inspired writings. John leads us into the Father's house. This epistle makes us at home there. believers are "little children." When they sin it is against the Father, and the sin is primarily a family matter.

Have you ever been homesick? Then you know how dark and unhappy life can be in a "far country." And you know, too, the joy and newness of life that coming home can bring you. It is that way with our souls. God has made us for himself, and we can never find rest, joy, and life till we are back in the Father's house.

This fellowship is possible through the coming of Jesus. It is part of the "Tidings of great joy." God is not far away. God lives among us as a loving Father. So we will not fear, no matter what changes may come over our earth.

Russell F. Auman

O God, you are the hope of hearts and the home of our souls forever, you are our dwelling place from one generation to another. We praise you for the coming of Jesus and for the glorious fellowship we have in you around him. Amen

Prayer concern: Fathers

Daily Reflections_____
_____
_____
_____

When Praying Is Difficult

We do not know what we ought to pray for, but the
Spirit himself intercedes for us with groans that
words cannot express. ❖ Romans 8:26b (NIV)

How often you and I know that we can't pray satisfactorily.
Thoughts and memories crowd into our minds when we
would pray. They seem to stop us in our tracks. The very line
of communication seems to be cut off. We rise from prayer as
if nothing took place, or, even worse, as if we were moving
further from God.

For such situations, this verse comes as comfort. There is
one who pleads for us. He takes our unexpressed thoughts
and words, our sighs and groanings, and brings them before
God's throne. The Holy Spirit is God's gracious gift to the
troubled soul. This Spirit is a helper and strengthener in our
prayer life. God does not ever let us walk alone. The Holy
Spirit is constantly with us. Let this truth strengthen you.
Even when we don't seem able to pray ourselves, there is one
who knows us, and takes the deep longings of our hearts and
presents them for us in prayer.

OSWALD ELBERT

*Grant to your servants, O Lord, the power to pray. But
even more, O Lord, when prayer does not come easily,
grant your servants the knowledge that your Holy Spirit
is praying for us. Amen*

Prayer concern: Those who struggle in prayer

Daily Reflections_____
_____
_____
_____

An Empty House

[Christ sent me] to proclaim the gospel, and not
with eloquent wisdom. ❖ 1 Corinthians 1:17 (NRSV)

During the late 1800s, a family residing on the North
American prairie summoned stone masons from Europe to
build a new house. An impressive residence soon rose in a
region where some families still lived in log houses.

The house is now abandoned and all its windows are
broken. Cattle roam freely in and out the door where the family
once welcomed guests. The family used all its resources to
build the house and had nothing left to maintain it.

The apostle Paul knew that impressing others was the
problem at Corinth, so he refused to make the gospel
impressive.

It is expensive to maintain an image. It is costly not being
honest with God and with those who love us. When images
are important to us, we easily judge and envy others.

Jesus is God's promise and guarantee that God is not in
the image business. God doesn't set the cross and tomb
above our messy turmoil and doesn't place it out of reach of
those whose spirits are low.

DONNA HACKER SMITH

Loving God, open my eyes to see myself as you see me.
Amen

Prayer concern: Churches in conflict

Daily Reflections_____

_____
_____
_____

Hear and Be Strong

The LORD God has opened my ear, and I was not rebellious, I did not turn backward. ❖ Isaiah 50:5 (NRSV)

After years of service, a friend of mine lost her job recently when her company faced an economic crisis. Suddenly she joined the ranks of the unemployed. Some of her coworkers complained that the company had no compassion: *She was such a good worker. Others could have been dismissed. Why her?* There is a tinge of bitterness in their complaining. But not in my friend. "I'll listen to God, who will keep me strong," she said.

There was a tinge of bitterness in the voices that complained to the prophet Isaiah. Why has God forsaken us? When will his promises be fulfilled? Almost daily the prophet heard the people complain. But today the prophet heard another voice and, as he listened, he was reminded of God's goodness from the day of creation to the present. Isaiah did not join the rebellious ones, and he remained strong.

There are many voices to hear. Learn to open your ears. Listen, and let God speak to you to keep you strong.

ALBERT LORCH

Heavenly Father, we give thanks to you that through the noisy complaints of our friends you have reached our ears and spoken to us. Amen

Prayer concern: People who are unemployed

Daily Reflections_____

_____

_____

Fools of Faith

So the word of the Lord has brought me insult and reproach all day long. ❖ Jeremiah 20:8b (NIV)

Jeremiah feels sorry for himself. He has spoken the word of the Lord to his generation, and they mock him, holding him in derision. For millions of people in our day, the same thing has happened. In many nations, not only have believers been rejected as fools, but they have suffered outright persecution.

On a milder scale, anyone who follows the Lord in paths of purity and integrity may be regarded by others as "square," not quite "with it." To be utterly faithful in marriage, to be absolutely honest with one's tax reports, to be scrupulously fair with expense accounts, to never cheat in examinations, to help someone who has snubbed you or lied about you—this often is regarded as being "too good." The person who lives this way may get some "flack" from people who don't.

But we are not to be conformed to this world, said Paul. We are to be transforming agents, conformed to the kingdom of our Lord.

ALVIN ROGNESS

Give us courage, O God, to seek your approval, and not the approval of the world. Amen

Prayer concern: The persecuted

Daily Reflections_____

_____

_____

_____

He's Been There, Too

Because he himself suffered when he was tempted, he is able to help those who are being tempted. ❖ Hebrews 2:18 (NIV)

How do you choose your friends? Are they people you grew up with? Are they people who share a common interest? In most cases we choose friends who are like us, people we feel comfortable with, or people with whom we have shared a common experience that helps us understand each other.

When we are in need of help it is natural to turn to a friend whose common experience yields understanding for our problem. Sometimes we forget that Jesus is a friend who can understand. Because he came to earth and lived as a human, he has experienced the same joy and fears and temptations that we have. He knows that it is not always easy to face what life has to offer. He can help us over the rocky places because he has been there, too. As the hymn "What a Friends We Have in Jesus" tells us, we can take everything to the Lord in prayer.

DONNA MORGAN BERKEBILE

Lord, thank you for understanding. Amen

Prayer concern: The ministry of healing

Daily Reflections_____

Who's in Charge?

Therefore my heart is glad and my tongue rejoices;
my body also will rest secure. ❖ Psalm 16:9 (NIV)

"I think Peter is confused about who is the adult and who is the child," said that teacher to Peter's mother.

Children often act as if they would like to have a great deal of control over their own lives. We know, however, that it can actually frighten a child to sense that he or she is "in charge." No matter what is done or said on the surface, the child wants and needs to know that the adults are in charge.

I remember one time when my daughter woke up crying. I went into her room, hugged her a little, and said a few reassuring words about bad dreams and about daddy being here. Very quickly she was sound asleep again, secure and satisfied.

To be able to take charge someday, children must first have the experience of knowing that someone else is in charge. Parents who thus give security to their children are reflecting a similar gift first received from a caring God.

CARL JECH

Lord, make us secure and strong through your loving lordship. Amen

Prayer concern: An end to terror

Daily Reflections_____

_____

_____

_____

God's Continuing Creation

Behold, I will create new heavens and a
new earth. The former things will not be
remembered, nor will they come to mind.
❖ Isaiah 65:17 (NIV)

I haven't thought about my last toothache since I had it.
That's a good thing. If we had to remember constantly all the
painful or unpleasant things of life, we'd be completely
immobilized. The mind has a way of blotting them out.

God's creativity helps, too. God never quits making new
and good and wonderful things to take our minds off the
pains and problems of the past. A new challenge, a new
situation, new people, a new way of looking at things—
all gifts of God to captivate our minds.

So vast is this continuing creation of God that the prophet
describes it as "new heavens and a new earth." But more
than just thinking on them, we can give our very selves
to these "new things" of God in this day. And we can be
changed, too!

J. DEAN GEVIK

*Dear God, we thank you for your powerful and creative
Spirit. As you renew the world, transform us also by the
renewal of our minds, that we may prove what is your
will; what is good and acceptable and perfect. Amen*

Prayer concern: Daily renewal in Christ

Daily Reflections_____
_____
_____
_____

Joy in Heaven

> I tell you that in the same way there will be more rejoicing in heaven over one sinner who repents than over ninety-nine righteous persons who do not need to repent. ❖ Luke 15:7 (NRSV)

By passing a law, a legislative body can collect our money in taxes, grant us a privilege not previously enjoyed, or establish a program that will affect us all. The government may respect us as individuals, but by its very nature must act over against us as a whole citizenry. So it is with so much of life. We get absorbed in clubs and business organizations and in all sorts of impersonal groups.

The polls tell us what we think and how we plan to vote and the advertisers aim at what they think is the mood of most of us. But amid all this there are people like you and me.

God has a wonderful way of reminding us that no matter how we may get lost in the crowds of our society, we never escape his concern for each of us. God and the angels of heaven rejoice over every person who believes. There is no life that escapes that heavenly love, the divine search for souls. And when a life is "found" through faith in God, God is the one who rejoices most.

SIDNEY A. RAND

We thank you, Father in heaven, for your loving concern for each of us. Amen

Prayer concern: The church, the body of Christ

Daily Reflections _____
_____
_____
_____

Just Passing By?

Those who passed by hurled insults at him, shaking their heads and saying, ". . . save yourself! Come down from the cross, if you are the Son of God!" ❖ Matthew 27:39-40 (NIV)

Those who just passed by the cross wanted a Savior, but without a cross. Perhaps the same is true of many people today who want Christ but not his cross. They do not realize that without Christ's death on the cross there would be no forgiveness of sin, life now, and life to come. They want God but on their own terms. They may even want the teachings of Jesus for their children as long as it doesn't mean getting involved. They never understand the meaning of the cross because they just pass by and never linger long enough to find out what it is all about.

Don't just pass by the cross of Christ. Linger often and long enough at the foot of the cross to realize that it was for all of us that Jesus suffered and died. We are involved in his death whether we realize it or not. It was for us! He calls us today as the risen Lord and Savior to walk with him and to follow him, not just to pass by him. He calls us to take up our cross and follow him.

JAMES E. VOELKER

Lord Jesus, help me to become involved in the world around me and to share with others what you have done for me and want to do for all people. Amen

Prayer concern: People suffering for their faith

Daily Reflections_____

_____

_____

_____

Easter ❖ Luke 24:1-11

The Lord of Life

> Why do you look for the living among the dead?
> Remember how he told you . . . "The Son of Man
> must be delivered into the hands of sinful men, be
> crucified and on the third day be raised again."
> ❖ Luke 24:5-7 (NIV)

Easter—what a happy day! All because Jesus lives. Jesus had often talked about not only his suffering and death, but also about his resurrection. But when the women came out to the tomb on Easter morning and found it empty, they did not understand. They did not remember Jesus saying that he would rise again until the angel told them what had happened. When they brought the good news to the disciples, they would not believe either. The idea of Jesus being raised from the dead was too difficult to believe. We can understand from this why so many people today do not believe that Jesus was raised up and still lives.

But Jesus is not dead. He is the Lord of life. We are his. We have been baptized into his name. Now we have the promise of eternal life. He said, "Because I live, you will live also." Let us share this good news with everyone. Some may not believe, even as the disciples did not believe on that first Easter morning. But it is true and must be told. Christ is Lord of life!

CLARENCE H. HINKHOUSE

*We know that our redeemer lives. He is the Lord of life
and Lord of our lives. Amen*

Prayer concern: Those who proclaim the good news

Daily Reflections

Pentecost

All of them were filled with the Holy Spirit and
began to speak in other tongues as the Spirit
enabled them. ❖ Acts 2:4 (NIV)

There was nothing cozy about the first Pentecost. In fact, the
report of the occasion in the New Testament gives a picture
of a state of confusion and misunderstanding. It was,
however, a confusion in which the single-minded purpose of
the Christian church was being developed. Out of it came the
intense evangelism and missionary work of the early church.

Neither is the situation in the church cozy today. The
degree of confusion within the church is great—about its
purpose, its witness, its forms of worship, and its attitude to
the world. The image it presents to a puzzled world is
possibly an even more confused one. All this, nevertheless, is
the confusion in which the Holy Spirit is at work in strange
ways. Out of it the church ready for the great encounters of
today and tomorrow will be born.

Pentecost is one of the three major festivals of the church
year. Unfortunately many people see nothing significant in
this festival; many people who wouldn't think of missing
Christmas or Easter services don't even go to church on
Pentecost. But Pentecost is "believing of the church."

O. K. STORAASLI

*Pour out your Holy Spirit upon us, O Lord, so that we
many receive new power. Amen*

Prayer concern: The body of Christ

Daily Reflections_____

_____

_____

_____

Thanksgiving ❖ Psalm 118:1

O Give Thanks

Give thanks to the LORD, for he is good; his love
endures forever. ❖ Psalm 118:1 (NIV)

The Christian life is one of thanksgiving. On this day of the
year we remember this especially. Throughout the Bible, the
reminder is found that the person who belongs to God is a
thankful person.

We are thankful for many reasons: for God's gracious
action in creating and sustaining the world. Without God
there would be chaos again, but with him there is order and
plan. He make his rain to fall on all the earth, he is graciously
present restoring and sustaining.

We are thankful for his redeeming work. He has not left
us, cast off and lost in rebellion, but has acted in our Lord
Christ to redeem us, to call us back, to make us once again
the children of the royal house.

We are thankful for God's continued presence among us
in the church, where the Holy Spirit moves in word and
sacraments, shapes, and sustains the life of faith. O give,
thanks to the Lord, for he is indeed good, his love endures
forever.

CHARLES S. ANDERSON

*Lord, your mercies are renewed to us each day. We give
thanks to you and praise your holy name. Amen*

Prayer concern: People suffering from famine

Daily Reflections_____

_____

_____

_____

Christmas Eve ❖ Luke 1:26-38

Expecting the Impossible

For nothing is impossible with God. ❖ Luke 1:37 (NIV)

"Is it possible?" That seems to be an ultimate question in today's society. We pride ourselves on being realistic and practical, with down-to-earth expectations of what can or cannot be accomplished. We demand the facts. We believe that we can function more effectively if someone will just tell us, "Is it possible?"

In truth, however, our spirits cry out for the impossible dream. We long to reach past the borders of the "possible." We instinctively strive to set new records to build, and dream. This no-nonsense society is also a people intrigued with the occult, unidentified flying objects, the subliminal. Such fads and fascinations are signs of our desire to break through what is predictable and expected.

Mary's first reaction to the angel's announcement of her pregnancy was an understandable "Is it possible?" The messenger's reply is a premonition of the gospel. It is a prelude to the *Gloria in Excelsis* sung by the angels. The angel said, "For with God, nothing shall be impossible."

WALTER HUFFMAN

We magnify you, O Lord. Our spirits rejoice in you, Savior of the world. Amen

Prayer concern: Peace on earth

Daily Reflections_____

The Nativity of Our Lord

To you is born this day in the city of David a Savior,
who is the Messiah, the Lord. ❖ Luke 2:11 (NRSV)

It was just a few minutes before closing time. I rushed through the store, trying to find one last gift as others scurried by me on similar frantic missions. As I rounded a corner, I almost ran over a preschool child standing in the middle of the aisle joyously singing "Silent Night, Holy Night!" Oblivious to the function of taped Christmas music in encouraging last-minute splurges, he created within the commercial din a moment that was truly "calm and bright." As others stopped to listen to him, he announced for us a time and space in which he could glimpse the true holiness of the season.

The gospel also announces that within our own cities of busyness and activity a Savior has been born for us—a Savior who is Christ our Lord.

MARSHA GILPIN EHLERS

Lord, help us to give birth to a true sense of wonder and holiness as we worship our Savior, "born this day in the city of David." Amen

Prayer concern: The holy Christian church

Daily Reflections

Prayers for Every Day
of the Week

Sunday

We give thanks to you, Lord God, through Jesus Christ our Lord, for this day of rest and refreshment. Bend our hearts and spirits to hear your Word, to celebrate your promises, and to be united with your special family, the church. Be present in us and give us energy to do your will. Help us present our bodies and our lives as living sacrifices before you. For the sake of your Spirit we pray. Amen

Monday

Holy Spirit, guide us and keep us in our daily tasks. While this week is still fresh and young, strengthen our resolve not to waste the time you have given, but rather to answer the call that you lay before us. Turn us to see the hurts and needs of the rest of our family, wherever in the world we may meet them. Let our caring be to your glory. In Jesus' name we pray. Amen

Tuesday

O God, help me this day to listen before I speak, to seek your will before I act, and to forgive others as I have been forgiven. It is so easy to forget that my life is a gift from you. Remind me of this gift, that I may live with thankfulness and humility. In Jesus' name. Amen

Wednesday

Lord Jesus, when I think of all you endured for my sins and the sins of the whole world, I am overwhelmed by the mercy of God and the power of your love and care. Strengthen me by the remembrance of your sacrifice and the glory of your victory that I may live a godly and useful life. Amen

Thursday

Spirit of God, lighten my darkness of vision, enliven my weakness of purpose, and quicken my strength of conscience that I may live this day in nobler accomplishment and greater service. May it be evident that Christ lives in me, no matter what I say and do. Amen

Friday

Gracious Redeemer, help me to live each moment with the prospect of eternity before me. Help me to build for things eternal rather than to seek what is only temporary. Forgive my sins, ennoble my character, and purify my thoughts through Jesus Christ, my Lord. Amen

Saturday

Joy and hope come from you, O God, in many ways, but chiefly through the message of the gospel. This week, I felt your blessing in friendships shared, relationships renewed, and work accomplished. May I, in both labor and leisure, experience your goodness, through Jesus Christ, my Lord. Amen

Lord, Hear My Prayers ...

Use the following space to write down prayer requests and
the names of people you wish to remember in prayer.